A Muddy Trench:
A Sniper's Bullet

'Poetry, more than any other platform, can capture a moment and preserve it forever. Centuries on, poems allow us to understand what people in the past were feeling and let us feel it for ourselves, which is why the work of the literary generation who fought at the Battle of the Somme is so precious and remarkable.'
(War of Words, BBC 2 TV documentary, 2014)

Dedication

This book is dedicated to the memory of one such poet, Hamish Mann, and to all those who fell: 'the men who slumber in the Sleep that knows no dream.'*

* A line from Hamish's own poem *One by One*, reproduced in full in Chapter 4.

A Muddy Trench:
A Sniper's Bullet

Jacquie Buttriss

Pen & Sword
MILITARY

First published in Great Britain in 2018 by
Pen & Sword Military
An imprint of
Pen & Sword Books Ltd
Yorkshire – Philadelphia

ISBN 978 1 52674 509 5

A CIP catalogue record for this book is
available from the British Library.

Printed and bound in the UK by TJ International Ltd,
Padstow, Cornwall.

Pen & Sword Books Limited incorporates the imprints of Atlas,
Archaeology, Aviation, Discovery, Family History, Fiction, History,
Maritime, Military, Military Classics, Politics, Select, Transport,
True Crime, Air World, Frontline Publishing, Leo Cooper, Remember
When, Seaforth Publishing, The Praetorian Press, Wharncliffe
Local History, Wharncliffe Transport, Wharncliffe True Crime
and White Owl.

For a complete list of Pen & Sword titles please contact

PEN & SWORD BOOKS LIMITED
47 Church Street, Barnsley, South Yorkshire, S70 2AS, England
E-mail: enquiries@pen-and-sword.co.uk
Website: www.pen-and-sword.co.uk

Or
PEN AND SWORD BOOKS
1950 Lawrence Rd, Havertown, PA 19083, USA
E-mail: Uspen-and-sword@casematepublishers.com
Website: www.penandswordbooks.com

Contents

Foreword

As an officer who did his soldiering in the late twentieth and early twenty-first centuries in Northern Ireland, Germany, Iraq and Afghanistan, it is sometimes difficult to imagine the conditions that our forebears endured as they fought in the mud of France and Flanders. I enjoyed the benefits of high-technology clothing, satellite communications, helicopters and a plethora of aids to make life easier for all soldiers in this modern era but, as we all know, soldiers of the Great War did not.

It is also difficult for many people to understand what motivated the soldiers of 1914 and how they kept going among the mayhem that was the Western Front. What was it that drove the thousands of young men like Hamish Mann to volunteer for King and Country?

In this book, Jacquie Buttriss has crafted a very personal reflection of Hamish's life in Edinburgh before he was commissioned, his time training as a young officer, preparing for the challenges of commanding soldiers and then his actual war service in the trenches. It is an illuminating and very personal story.

The book is based on quotes from his notebooks, his musings and poetry and answers some of those questions. His pride in his men of the 'Fighting 14 Platoon' is evident, as were his efforts to look after them as best he could. The book conveys the feeling of friendship that existed between the ranks of the 8th Battalion of Scotland's senior Highland Regiment. It was a team and it was a family.

During the Great War, the Black Watch (Royal Highlanders) had a number of talented artists and poets who served in its ranks; the 'fighter writers' of the 4th (City of Dundee) Battalion were well-known but while Hamish Mann was a recognized poet, no lasting record of his work was available to the wider public.

Just over 100 years after the death of Second Lieutenant Alexander James 'Hamish' Mann on 10 April 1917, Jacquie Buttriss and Hamish Mann's family have produced a highly-readable and personal epitaph that is long overdue. I salute their hard work in bringing the works of this officer-poet to a wider audience.

Major General J.M. Cowan CBE, DSO
Chairman
The Black Watch (Royal Highland Regiment) Association

Introduction

Robert Stewart's account of how he and his sister Rosie found their Great-Uncle Hamish's wooden chest in a Scottish family attic, unopened for 100 years, packed full of his trench-diaries, writings and memorabilia … and rescued it all from the house-clearance men, just in the nick of time!

Our 98-year-old mother was admitted to a nursing home and we were forced to sell her house, after forty-two years as our family home. The sale went through and the target date for exit was imminent.

At around the time they had moved into this house, Mum and Dad (Hamish's nephew) had inherited a substantial amount of furniture and belongings accumulated by Dad's parents and untouched for many decades. My mother could never throw anything away, so it all went into the cavernous loft, where it had remained untouched ever since.

After Mum went into the nursing home, by far the greatest burden of all the necessary sorting out fell to my older sister, Rosie. With Marjorie in South Africa and me in the south of England, Rosie was the only one of the family who lived remotely near, so she had been our mother's mainstay for years. However, she was still working part-time as a piano-teacher and had a busy life of her own, so she needed help. Rosie called and asked me to come and spend a few days with her in Edinburgh so that we could try to go through everything at the house together, a mammoth task.

As soon as the sale of the house was agreed, we were pressured by house-clearance firms, antique dealers and auctioneers, beseeching us to part with things blindly. They wanted to take all the contents away untouched and relieve us of the hassle, they said. It was just as we had told Mum it would happen. The carrion crows gathered around the house and, it seemed, roosted on the rooftop overnight, but we held out as best we could. It was a daunting prospect, but we couldn't let them just take everything away without checking it all first, so Rosie and I set to work.

We had to concentrate on the main areas of the house initially, but did have a cursory look in the chests in the attic, just the top layer of each. There were two camphor chests downstairs, and in the loft a couple of old blanket boxes, plus two or three school trunks, a huge wooden chest and perhaps twenty elderly suitcases, missing either their straps, handles or buckles. Each and every one was a Pandora's Box.

Rosie and I had laid out the family silver and special items on the large oval dining table and meticulously photographed each one in turn. When we had to go back to Rosie's at night, we thought we should hide it all, lest it should become apparent that the house was being emptied. So we took everything up to the attic, where we hid the smaller pieces in empty suitcases and wrapped teapots, trays and other large items in some of the copious amounts of linen we found stored in various trunks. In fact almost every container was stuffed full of old curtains, table-cloths, blankets and the like ... all except for one, as we were about to find out....

When we removed the top layer of linen in the largest wooden chest, we were astonished to find it filled almost to the brim with hundreds, if not thousands, of hand-written scraps of paper, plus battered old diaries, notebooks and assorted miscellanea. At this stage we had no idea that this particular Pandora's Box was in fact an Aladdin's cave.

I think we were offered £150 for the entire contents of the attic, chests and all. That would have been the easiest thing to do, but we held out. At the eleventh hour, we had to empty everything and simply discard as we saw fit. This left only the largest wooden chest with its papers unexplored.

On my last morning in Edinburgh, I woke up early and leaped out of bed, with the sudden realization that we hadn't checked through whatever the papers were in that final chest and the loft-clearance men were due to arrive at noon to take away everything that was too big for us to carry. We had only a few hours left to drive over there, search through the chest and make sure there was nothing valuable in it.

In fact, we arrived with so little time to spare that we didn't have the chance to go through any of it. We simply emptied the mountain of papers and notebooks and everything else out into all the carrier bags and cardboard boxes we could find. As we tipped it all out, we found some medals and other artefacts at the bottom of the chest. They went into the carrier bags too. Rosie took everything from the chest back to her house and I returned to Sussex.

A few days later, Rosie rang. I could tell by her voice that she was excited about something…. She explained that since I left, she had started to look through some of the papers we had found in the chest. Immersed in my own family and everything at home, I'd almost forgotten about that, but now I was intrigued to hear what she had discovered. All these papers seemed to belong to someone called Hamish Mann.

The only thing we had ever known about our great-uncle Hamish was that he had died at a young age in the First World War (like so many others). There had always been a photograph of him in his Black Watch Highlanders uniform on display on the bookcase in the hallway, but nobody had ever told us the details of his tragic death, nor of his immense charisma and talent. However, I do remember feeling a sense of pride when I was told as a child that both my father and I had been named after him, in my case as my middle name.

Over the following weeks, Rosie spent all her spare time going through our great-uncle Hamish's trench-diaries, notebooks, poems, plays, articles, letters and other ephemera, trying to marry up the loose pages and work out what they all were. The more we read of his writings, the more we liked his quirky sense of humour, his compassionate nature, his utter loyalty to the men in his beloved platoon and theirs to him, his amusement at the idiosyncrasies of higher command and his refusal to give in to anything that tried to stop him doing what he felt was right. He gave up his dreams to fight for his country and, ultimately, he gave up his life. His writings show that, although inwardly fearful, he was not only willing but also proud to do so.

It was at this point that we both realized we had something very special here and it was our responsibility to do the right thing with it. This really was a treasure-trove and we felt we couldn't just keep it to ourselves. We wanted to honour Hamish Mann's memory by sharing his treasure with a wider audience. We were just wondering how, when a writer friend suggested it would make a great book. It seemed like a good idea, so we asked her to write it.

This book is the culmination of our discovery and rescue of Hamish's oeuvre. It spans just two and a half years, from the outbreak of the Great War to Hamish's premature death on the bloodstained battlefield of Arras. It tells of his short but talented life, much of it through his own eloquent writings, arranged within the context of the paraphernalia of war, the events he experienced, the places he passed through and the people he met along the way. We think it is a fascinating story. We hope you do too.

Robert Stewart

Notes:

Alexander James 'Hamish' Mann
Rank: Second Lieutenant (commanding 14 Platoon)
D Coy (Company)
8th Battalion Black Watch
Regiment: The Black Watch (Royal Highlanders) Infantry

Part of:
26th Brigade
9th Division
III Corps
3rd Army

Hamish's full birth name was Alexander James Mann, but he was Hamish to everyone who knew him. A second lieutenant in The Black Watch, Hamish was killed while leading his men 'over the top' and across no man's land at the Battle of Arras on 9 April 1917, five days after his 21st birthday.

Arrangement of Hamish's writings

Hamish's own writings – his eloquent prose and poetry – speak volumes just as they are, so they form the key components of most of the chapters in this book. To help the reader to readily distinguish his contributions, direct from the trenches, his content appears in italics in text boxes throughout the book, between the writer's contextual contributions in roman text.

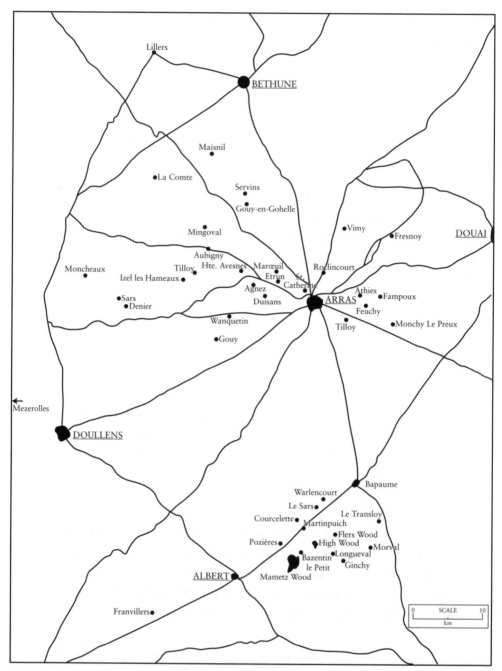

Map showing locations of Hamish Mann's actions and billets in Northern France 1916–17.

Chapter One

The *Craigleith Chronicles*

'With the utmost reluctance and with infinite regret, His Majesty's Government have been compelled to put this country in a state of war.'
(Herbert Asquith to Parliament, 6 August 1914)

For 18-year-old Hamish Mann, with his career mapped out as a writer and actor, the declaration of war came as both an obstacle to fulfilling his dreams and a patriotic call to serve his country. 'A fearful anticipation,' he wrote in his notebook, next to details of the first of his friends to enlist: his long-time school friend C.S. Nimmo.

Inspired by the wave of patriotism that enveloped the nation, Hamish picked up his pen, as he always did at important moments of his life, and the words tumbled out onto paper. It wasn't his best poem, but it certainly expresses the fervour he felt for the ideals of war against injustice.

BRITAIN IS AWAKE!

Sound the trumpet, beat the drum!
Throngs of khaki warriors come;
Belgium's burning at the stake –
Britain is awake, awake!

Sound the pilbroch, blow the fife!
Honour's dearer far than life.
Mark, O Germans, your mistake –
Britain is awake, awake!

Look! The guns go rumbling by,
Out to know the reason why;
Rattling wagons jolt and shake –
Britain is awake, awake!

Wave on high the Union Jack,
Send the foemen hurtling back!
Shout until Earth's bowels quake –
BRITAIN IS AWAKE, AWAKE!

Later, Hamish wrote the first three pages of what he intended to be his personal memoir. The first paragraph looked back to this momentous sequence of events:

> *When the war broke out and overwhelmed the world in a veritable tornado of martial fury, I found myself of no use to the Army on account of a temporary weakness of the heart. It was not the little god who had caused this weakness, but something much more prosaic and matter-of-fact, namely too much physical exercise on a 'push-bike'!*

The youngest of a family of five, Alexander James Mann, known to all as Hamish, attended George Watson's College, Edinburgh for most of his schooldays, where he took part in the Literary Club's challenging debates, gave talks on natural sciences at the Field Club, enjoyed sports and joined the school's Officer Training Corps (OTC) as a cadet.

A bright and popular boy with a talent for words, Hamish did well at school ... until he fell seriously ill, aged 16, with an enlarged heart (now known as cardiomyopathy and potentially of much greater consequence than what he referred to as his 'temporary weakness of heart'). Private tutoring at home occupied some of his obligatory quiet hours during his year-long illness and convalescence. His prolific output of seventy-three poems, plus articles, plays and other writings during this period, twenty-nine of them published in newspapers and periodicals, attest to his making the best use he could of his enforced bed-rest to polish his literary skills.

At the age of 17, while recovering some of his old impishness, Hamish fired off a variety of ironic and provocative letters to the editors of Scottish newspapers, all signed by a twist on his name, Jamie d'Homme. His first, on the opening of Edinburgh's new Zoological Gardens, dared to suggest that wild animals might fare better in captivity than in the wild, thereby drawing, as he knew it would, much high dudgeon in the resulting letters of protest.

In response to Hamish's next topic of clothing, his tongue-in-cheek criticisms of 'women's undress fashions' and his suggestion that men too should be permitted to wear brightly-coloured clothes for all occasions brought a short but very clear put-down from an active group of 1913 feminists:

How dare he suggest that our sober (sometimes) and respectable males should convert themselves into circus funny men? If he thinks he'd look nice in pale blue satin knee-breeches, yellow stockings and

a tartan coat, let him by all means don these elements of lunacy. ...
We are afraid 'Jamie' is a frivolous boy, and now that we have a zoo
in Edinburgh we would advise him not to stray too far from home.
'The Suffragettes'

(*Edinburgh Evening Dispatch*, 24 July 1913)

Known to have a keen sense of humour, 'Jamie' (or Hamish) must have
enjoyed this repartee, which he carried on for the next six months, alongside
his more serious writings.

Being a prolific writer in various genres, Hamish wrote plays, some of
which were performed on the Edinburgh stage, as well as in smaller venues.
Indeed, Hamish himself, once he was well enough, regularly acted on the
stage of the Lyceum Theatre as a member of a repertory company.

Hamish kept a scrapbook of programmes and newspaper cuttings of some
of his published plays and performances on various stages in Edinburgh and
beyond. These include reviews (all of them complimentary) taken from the
Edinburgh Evening News and the *Edinburgh Dispatch*, including this example
from *The Gentlewoman* magazine of 9 January 1915:

On Saturday evening there was a really delightful entertainment, the
principal feature being the production of a farcical ridiculosity by
Hamish Mann, entitled *My Eye! A Spy!* arranged for two players,
the author himself sustaining one part and Miss Rudland, a well-
known Edinburgh actress, the other. This sketch found great favour
with the audience, the crisp wit and droll situations provoking
much mirth. Both players are to be congratulated on their clever
representations.

A cutting from *The Stage Year Book* of 1915 lists Hamish among its 'Authors
of the Year' for his play *For £1,000*, written when he was 18 and clearly
making a name for himself on the national scene.

However, Hamish loved writing for local charities too. Indeed, he relished
every challenge, as he demonstrated by writing a one-act play *The King's
Enemy* especially for the Boy Scouts, in which two clever young scouts track
down some secret documents stolen by a German spy and repatriate them
to the authorities.

Hamish subsequently received an enthusiastic letter from the scoutmaster:

Dear Sir,

I have your esteemed letter to hand. I am so glad to hear that you were satisfied with the characters in your play. I can assure you it was the hit of the evening, and thoroughly deserved the success it attained. You have placed me under your indebtedness for all time. I cannot express in mere words our gratitude to you …

Wishing you every success in your future career,

Yours most respectfully,

J. Robertson

A magazine review in the *Catholic Herald* recorded 'high praise' for both the acting and the play itself: 'The play is well written and the characters well-defined. There are situations that completely carried the audience away. The play is thoroughly patriotic. Congratulations to Mr Mann!'

It was this very patriotism that evoked painful regrets for Hamish. Always lurking in the background of his daily life was the knowledge of his friends fighting the foe, 'doing their bit' for the war effort. As Hamish's writings attest, hidden deep in his daily thoughts was his sense of disappointment and even despair that he could not pass the stringent medical necessary to join the army. This prompted him to write a short story: a 'fiction' that in fact mirrored almost exactly his own experience:

THE CHANCE

Lyndsay Macdonald was downcast and sick at heart. All his life, Fate had dogged his footsteps with misfortune. Changes often began to materialise, and then, just as he was about to take advantage of them, they would vanish in some mysterious fashion before his very eyes.

It had been the way all along; but, unlike many another similarly placed, he had not become cynical or indifferent. On the contrary, he was always good-hearted, expectant and ambitious. Each time bad luck knocked him down, he was on his feet again in a moment, hoping to be treated more generously next time. All his days seemed to have been spent in getting bowled over and then getting up again with s smile on his face.

But he had never been struck as hard as now – never.

The Great War had suddenly crashed about the ears of Europe. Thousands upon thousands of men would be required to crush the devilish militarism of

Germany. Every mother's son who was ready and willing was needed to grind overbearing Prussianism into ignominious pulp. Lindsay Macdonald was both ready and willing. It was a privilege and an honour to him to be able to wield arms in such a glorious case. He loved the hedges and fields and rivers of his homeland, and the idea of the professors of 'Kultur' devastating the fair, sweet countryside made his blood boil. His imagination — which was neither sentimental nor morbid — brought before him the bloody scenes of Belgium. He thought of his mother and his sisters ... and he went to the nearest recruiting depot.

Here was a chance indeed! His blood was racing through his veins as he walked briskly down the street.... Already, in his mind's eye, he was on the field of war, fighting his country's battles. The prospect was inspiring.... But his dreams were interrupted by a display of posters, and the words: 'RECRUITING OFFICE'.

He walked in ... and then the blow fell.

Fate had chosen the Examining Medical Officer as her agent: Lindsay Macdonald was told that he was 'unfit for military service'!

Ill-luck had knocked him down again and, on this occasion, it took him some time to get up on his feet. The splendid future he had been picturing crashed in shatters about him ... he was unfit ...

And then, Hope came to him, as it always did. He would try another recruiting depot and another Medical Officer.

He tried dozens, but he was always told the same thing: two years must elapse before he would be fit enough for military training.... Two years!

Lindsay Macdonald cursed the excess of zeal which had caused him to indulge in athletics to such a degree that he had strained himself. For the time being, he was sick of the world, sick of life, sick of everything. Never before had he felt quite as he felt now. What was the use of it all? It was always the same.... His ideals, his aspirations were always beyond realisation ...

He walked dejectedly along the streets, silently envying each man that passed in khaki, and imagining that every eye was fixed scornfully upon him. His tweed suit became as hateful to him as the arrowed garments are to a convict.

Suddenly, in the distance, came the sound of a military band. Everyone looked about and strained eager ears. Gradually came the steady and regular tramp of feet; then the battalion came into sight. Instantly there was a surge towards the curb to watch the troops go by. Lindsay Macdonald felt a lump rise in his throat, and what looked suspiciously like tears blurred his vision. But no one appeared to notice him: he was in plain clothes, merely an onlooker.

The soldiers swung past, while he who was unfit watched, wishing devoutly that he could change places with any man of them. But, even had this been possible, not one member of those stalwart ranks would have changed places with the civilian on the pavement. Cheer upon cheer rose into the air ... and each outburst of enthusiasm pierced him to the very soul.

He could stand it no longer. He turned up a side-street, his heart like a lump of lead within him. Certainly never before had fate struck him quite so hard.

Lindsay Macdonald had been unable to bear his life at home: everyone kept asking him why he wasn't in khaki. It hurt him. He had therefore gone abroad, so that he might escape from his unknowing tormentors and try to recover his strength in the stilly waste of solitude.

After six months of resting, however, he found that he was still worrying and wishing; angry with his own idleness.

Unlike his alter ego, Hamish had stayed in Edinburgh. Now, in mid–August 1914 and more or less well again, though not well enough, he had to make a decision. Maybe one day they would let him join the army, but for now he must do something purposeful. He could have looked for a job, leading to a career in journalism or in the theatre; no doubt he would have relished either of those, but this was not the time for fulfilling his personal ambitions. His upbringing had instilled in him a sense of public duty, so surely there was something he could do for the war effort, but what?

It was during a routine visit to his doctor that the perfect opportunity arose:

My own civil doctor, who happened to be a Territorial Major in the Royal Army Medical Corps, took pity on me and offered to employ me as a voluntary worker in the military hospital where he was stationed. As can be readily understood, I took advantage of this chance to 'do my bit', and before long was installed in the Scottish General Hospital.

So, as the first wounded soldiers were transported back from the battlefields, Hamish started work as a volunteer at what came to be known as the Craigleith Military Hospital. He was put to work in various capacities, starting with clerical duties in the Quartermaster's Stores. With the vast quantities of deliveries and supplies for such a large hospital, there was plenty of work to be done.

After a few weeks, Hamish and three other staff members gave additional time to setting up a hospital magazine, with the joint aims of raising the morale of the troops, informing the local community about the hospital's work and raising funds to provide treats for the patients.

Thus the *Craigleith Chronicle* was born, with its first edition published at Christmas 1914; professional-looking and entertaining from the outset. Its pages featured popular poems, a letter from the front, army notes, anecdotes, hospital news, drawings, photos and reviews, some of which were written by Hamish himself under various pseudonyms. There were also persuasive adverts for such items as portmanteaux, confectionery, surgical instruments, tobacco, a fearsome 'knife cleaner' contraption, hosiery, 'Christmas Comforts' and a beautiful cabriolet – 'New Overland Car' – for £198. (That same model now, as a restored veteran car, commands tens of thousands of pounds.)

One short ditty, published in that first edition of the *Craigleith Chronicle* above one of Hamish's pen names, gives a cheery impression of the sounds wafting from the busy wards of Craigleith Military Hospital:

A PATIENT PATIENT

Tell me not in mournful numbers
Life in dressing-gowns is bad,
While the gramophones that holler
Make my heart and soul feel glad.

Hark! The pianola's music,
Like a sylvan choir in spring!
List! The merry chorus ditties
That the joyful patients sing!

'Alexander's Ragtime Band' is
Better far than drugs to me;
'Tipperary's' tuneful music
Makes all gloom and sadness flee.

Tell me not that life is rotten
While the 'motor drives' are there;
And the bugle's call to luncheon
Echoes forth its grand fanfare!

Hamish always kept a notebook in which he wrote his impressions of everything that happened. When a large group of wounded Belgian soldiers were due to be admitted at Craigleith one afternoon, Hamish wrote what he saw and felt:

The arrival of the first batch of Belgian wounded creates a deep impression at the Military Hospital. Silence replaces the usual busy afternoon activities, but it is not the silence of rest; it is the tense quiet of expectancy.... The first motor ambulance draws up at the foot of the steps; the doors are quickly opened, the stretcher bearing the wounded man is firstly and carefully withdrawn, and, preceded by an orderly, is borne to the ward and bed consigned for its occupant. Car after car glides in and, with respect and dispatch, all patients are conveyed to their well-earned repose.

It is a touching sight to see these sixty-five wounded warriors of our valiant little ally arrive to find a haven of peace within our hospital walls. Scenes like this make one think deeply, and sometimes painfully.

Hamish's notebooks show that he didn't stay at his desk any longer than necessary. He often walked round the 600-bed hospital, through various wards, talking with the wounded men and, above all, listening to their experiences and anecdotes. The following example was clearly one that stuck in his memory:

They are an interesting lot, these patients – ever ready to relate their experiences. One man had been lying on the ground in France, sniping at the enemy 200 yards away, when a 'Jack Johnson' (a heavy artillery shell) burst right above him. Before he could get to cover, a tapering splinter of shrapnel pinned him through the foot to the ground, where he lay helpless. As can well be imagined, he suffered excruciating agony; and when at last he was taken to an ambulance station, his boot had to be cut away. In due time he was sent to Scotland, where he became seriously ill with tetanus, but eventually recovered and regained the use of his foot. The battered boot, with the piece of shrapnel in it, has become his most treasured possession: it is an heirloom of which to be deservedly proud.

It wasn't only the patients who made Hamish laugh. It was often the unconscious humour that can occur in any hospital, with the use of unfamiliar terminology:

One of the R.A.M.C. recruits had been put on the job of 'telephone orderly', his duty being to attend to all 'phone messages sent to the hospital'. One morning he came into the orderly room and said: 'A major has just telephoned to say he is sending in a man suffering from an <u>electric leg</u>!' This being a complaint that no one there had ever heard of, an officer went to confirm the message and found that the patient's trouble was a <u>septic leg</u>!

On another occasion, a mother came to see her soldier-son who was undergoing treatment at Craigleith Hospital. On enquiring his ailment, she was told it was major epilepsy. Can you imagine the consternation she caused when she returned the next day and said at the door: 'I've come to speak with Major Epilepsy.'

Throughout his productive months at the hospital, during which Hamish became joint editor of the *Chronicle*, he maintained his contacts with the local press and repertory companies. In the evenings, he acted various parts in repertory and wrote a number of humorous one-act plays, in which he performed in theatres and halls around Edinburgh to considerable acclaim: 'Hamish Mann has all the necessary qualities for a successful stage career,' wrote Graeme Goring, a Shakespearian actor.

At the Craigleith Military Hospital, regular concerts were held for the walking wounded in the hospital's large concert hall. These included various entertainments, such as music and songs, comedy turns, plays and skits. Hamish's contacts and friends in the theatre helped ensure that some of the top actors and singers of the day turned out to put on a good show for the patients. These concerts were reviewed in the *Craigleith Chronicle*. One such review includes a glowing report of one of Hamish's comedic one-act plays, in which he also acted a part:

The first performance on any stage of Mr Hamish Mann's sketch, *Caught Napping!* had aroused in all of us expectations which were more than realised. The idea is ingenious, the dialogue crisp and witty, and the presentation given by the Author and Miss Gertrude

Ayton displayed most convincingly the histrionic talent of those two artistes. The O.C., in proposing a vote of thanks, took occasion to recognise publicly the voluntary services rendered to the Hospital by Mr Mann.[1]

Indeed, Hamish was making quite a name for himself, or rather four or five names. His birth name was Alexander James Mann, but everyone called him Hamish, except in official circles, and he signed most of his published articles as Hamish Mann. His play-scripts were sometimes credited to H.D. Mann, or Hamish Derek Mann. Jamie d'Homme was a play on his name that he had used on his humorous letters to the press. However, for much of his more serious poetry, he took the pseudonym Lucas Cappe. He gave no reason why. Yet although the use of alternative names may have seemed pretentious, it was perhaps more likely to have been for the prosaic reason that he needed a ruse to allow him to have more than one submission accepted for any given publication, as occasionally happened.

As part of his hospital work, Hamish was charged with the task of collecting and collating statistics. He listed each day's deliveries of food, in vast quantities, the daily number of operations, the number of sheets being laundered; everything, in fact, right down to a note that in the first three months of the war, there had been 1,300 extractions of teeth in the hospital. The most encouraging statistic of all, he comments, is 'the astonishingly low mortality rate' despite the grave injuries of many of the patients. Hamish puts this down to the doctors' and nurses' excellent care and, especially, the 'spirit of optimism and inextinguishable cheerfulness' of the soldiers themselves, as in this example of overheard conversation:

A patient who arrived at Craigleith from General HQ (somewhere in France), was commiserated with for missing the King's visit to the Front. With a quiet smile and twinkling eye, the patient said: 'But sister, the King just went across to see that everything was all right because he heard I'd gone sick!'

Throughout his time at Craigleith Military Hospital, Hamish continued to write poetry, of friendship, love and war, alongside his more philosophical

---

1. *Craigleith Chronicle*, June 1915, p.50.

poems. Several of his poems were published in the *Chronicle*, including this short but poignant verse:

THE DIGGER

He was digging, digging, digging with his little pick and spade,
And when the Dawn was rising it was trenches that he made;
But when the day was over and the sun was sinking red,
He was digging little Homes of Rest for comrades who were dead.

Hamish also read a lot of poetry, including that of fellow Scot, Private Alastair Shannon of the 9th Royal Scots. Hamish was astonished that it was possible to write so coherently in the trenches: 'It is almost beyond comprehension for a soldier to write philosophic lines in such a "study" as a trench!' In his keenness to join the war himself, Hamish did not seem to consider that he may one day follow Shannon's example.

It was not only in the hospital or from his friends at the front that Hamish collected stories. He always listened to people speaking in theatre foyers, hotel restaurants, walking the streets of Edinburgh, or among his family. One of these tales made a particular impression on him, feeling, as he did, so wretched that he couldn't yet go to war. So he wrote the story down (with the names changed and no doubt a modicum of imaginative embellishment):

Watson Wilberforce had three sons serving with the colours and one of them had been wounded. It was a source of great pride and self-satisfaction to know that his sons had turned out <u>men</u>, and not merely 'human beings in trousers', as he scornfully termed the slackers. The sight of a healthy young man in mufti was to Mr Wilberforce what a red rag is to a bull; the only difference being that it inspired loathing instead of rage.

On one occasion a shirker tried to defend his position, bringing forward all the time-honoured excuses and futile arguments beloved of cowards.

Watson Wilberforce contemplated him cynically for a moment, and then said drily: 'Of course, the country doesn't need you.'

'I know it doesn't,' responded the young unmilitary knut, rather pleased with his remark. 'Besides …'

'No,' interrupted the elder man in the same quiet, terse voice. 'It only needs <u>men</u>.' With these cutting words, he turned on his heel and walked off.

> *One evening he was out at dinner, where he revelled in the joy of speaking of the sacrifice his three soldier sons had made, how one was wounded … and so on.*
>
> *An immaculately dressed youth sat next to him, shewed great sympathy and asked innumerable questions.*
>
> *At last Watson Wilberforce could stand it no longer.*
>
> *'You seem very interested in my sons' doings,' he said. 'Why don't you get into khaki and go to help them?'*
>
> *The youth was silent for a little, and then, pointing to his snowy-white cuffs, said: 'You see these cuff-links?'*
>
> *'I do,' was the bewildered response.*
>
> *'Well, these were made of shrapnel, taken out of my lungs at Mons.'*

Working within a military hospital, Hamish often heard first-hand accounts of the war direct from the front told by incoming patients, and the Edinburgh newspapers kept him informed of the wider picture. In early 1915, the new German submarines known as U-boats started to ply the waters around Britain. This was the talk everywhere in Edinburgh. In the first months of the war supplies had not been much of a problem, but with the German U-boat blockade, supplies into the Quartermaster's Stores at the hospital began to be hampered, which was the first time Hamish had been personally impacted by the increasing wartime shortages.

In April 1915 there was shocking news from the Battle of Ypres, where the enemy had used their newest weapon to devastating effect. There had been an earlier report that the Hun had developed poisonous gas and had tried it out against the Russians, but now the headlines bewailed the terrible losses these gas canisters had caused on the Western Front. The effects of this chlorine gas were terrifying for the soldiers, causing more than 7,000 casualties, and horrifying for the families, like Hamish's, who had sons fighting overseas. This development caused a renewed patriotic fervour across our islands. Hamish was no exception.

The next big shock was in May with the sinking of the *Lusitania*, a large American passenger liner, hit by a torpedo from a German U-boat. She sank within twenty minutes, with the loss of 1,200 lives. This tragedy dominated the front pages for several days, with various theories about how and why the vessel sank so quickly and damning the Germans for killing so many civilians from a neutral country. There was even a rumour that the ship's passengers were a 'cover' for the transport of armaments to Britain for the war. Hamish and his friends at the hospital speculated that this might bring the United States into the war, but President Woodrow Wilson seemed reluctant.

The lure of joining his contemporaries at war preoccupied Hamish every day, as he attempted to enlist and gain a commission. The more he read, both in the press and in sporadic letters from his friends already in the thick of the fighting, the more frustrated he became that he had passed his 19th birthday and still had no right to a uniform. It was not that he wanted to put himself in danger, but rather that he was desperate to serve his country at war, to play the most important part of his life, this time for real, in the prevailing blaze of patriotism and glory.

He wrote letters to various regiments from April to July 1915, seeking a way in. Though the evidence is sparse, it seems that Hamish may have had some difficulty getting through his medical, presumably due to his heart condition, which might have left him with detectable after-effects such as an irregular heartbeat and impaired lung capacity. This must have been very demoralizing to a young man, now in relatively good health, who was full of zeal to do his duty.

All those applying to enlist had to fill in a form declaring their past medical record, as well as undergoing a medical inspection. While it was important for all ranks to be passed as fit to serve, it was especially important for would-be officers since they might be leading their platoon into battle, responsible for the welfare and safety of their men.

With a doctor in the family – one of his older brothers – it is possible that Hamish may have been able to try and try again to be passed fit, from September 1914 onwards. If he did, he wasn't successful. It seems that Hamish never reached the form-filling stage of the proceedings during those early months of the war.

Fortunately (or unfortunately), by the summer of 1915, the high numbers of casualties on the battlefields prompted the War Office to amend the medical requirements for new enlistments. Instead of the previously thorough medical examination, a man's vital statistics were noted, followed by a cursory health check and a declaration form that the would-be recruit was required to fill in, thereby putting more of the responsibility for his medical suitability on him.

Thus on 2 June 1915, Hamish, a fresh-faced, fair-haired young man of 19, attended yet another recruiting office for his medical, no doubt with the fervent hope that this would be the one. There are three documents in his service records[2] about this medical. There is a report that lists his age, height of 5ft 7¾in, and notes his chest girth, weight, hearing, teeth and vision, all of which passed muster. In the column for 'remarks' is the one word: 'Fit'. Next came the candidate's 'declaration', in which Hamish was required to delete what didn't apply to him. The first sentence on this form was: 'I declare upon my honour that I have never suffered from any serious illness or injury, except as listed below.' Hamish crossed out the last four words. We don't know whether he hesitated for a moment, or just deleted them with alacrity. Knowing his situation and his desperation to be one of the boys, fighting for their country, who can blame him?

The most important of these records is the certificate signed by the medical officer that states Hamish was 'Fit for Military Service'. How Hamish must have cheered inwardly as he walked out of that recruitment office. As he wrote later that day in his notebook: 'Much to my gratification, I was passed by the military authorities as fit for service.'

Now at last he was on his way. All he had to do was to find a regiment that would take him. The first draft of a letter in Hamish's notebook, written in early July 1915 and addressed to the commissioning officer of a regiment betrays, through its two crossed-out words, the difficulty he had experienced but had finally surmounted:

Sir,

I have the honour to write to ask if you are prepared to consider applications for commissions, and, if so, whether I may offer myself as a candidate.

About six weeks ago I ~~managed to~~ was passed fit for service and applied direct to the War Office for a commission in the New Armies. As I have not yet been gazetted, I am feeling rather impatient.

---

2. The National Archives, WO 339 35102.

> *I am in my twentieth year and I was for two and a half years in the George Watson's College O.T.C.* *
>
> *I should be very glad to hear from you on this matter at your earliest convenience.*
>
>

I have the honour to be,

Sir,

Your obedient servant
>
>
> ---
>
> * O.T.C., Officer Training Corps.

Thus, at last, Hamish was accepted and offered a commission as a second lieutenant in a reserve battalion of the Royal Highlanders, Black Watch, and he had His Majesty's commission certificate to prove it. This document carried the promise of his appointment being published in the *London Gazette*, hence he proudly headed a fresh notebook page with the single word: 'Gazetted!'

He left the Craigleith Hospital with mixed feelings. He had enjoyed his ten months as a volunteer there and as joint editor of the *Craigleith Chronicle*, whose new editor recorded his thanks: 'Mr H. Mann has resigned his position as Joint-Editor on receiving a commission in the Black Watch. While much regretting that we shall no longer have his help as a member of the Editorial Staff, we offer him our hearty congratulations on his appointment.'[3]

Yet this was only the beginning…. It would be some time before he could fight on the front. First he had to do his officer's training.

---

3. *Craigleith Chronicle*, August 1915, p.108.

Chapter Two

The Art of Soldiery

'To our trusty and well beloved Alexander James Mann, Greeting: We, reposing special Trust and Confidence in your Loyalty, Courage and Conduct, … Appoint you to be an Officer in the Territorial Force from the twenty-eighth day of July 1915. You are therefore carefully and dutifully to discharge your duty as such in the rank of Second Lieutenant …'

(His Majesty King George V[1])

Hamish's euphoria on finally having gained his commission spilt over into his writings and letters. 'I'm in the army now!' begins a short story he wrote that week. He was clearly elated to be included at last in the nation's great venture to vanquish the Hun. Of course, he had been in uniform before as a cadet for three years in his school's officer training corps when he learned to march and drill, which would stand him in good stead, as he wrote:

As I had done some years of military work previously, my appearance in khaki was as an officer, and my regiment was the Royal Highlanders, more commonly known perhaps as the Black Watch. As was usual with 'recruit officers', I did not at once join my battalion, but was delegated to attend a School of Instruction, where I duly reported myself for duty, and so began my work as a Subaltern in His Majesty's Forces.

It was indeed a proud day for me when first I donned my uniform and sallied forth in all the glory of a Highland kilt! Probably Kitchener himself was not more swelled up with pride than I was. Do not infer from this that I am inordinately conceited: I'm not. But a soldier's garb does make one feel so big, so important, and (in some cases at least) so conspicuous – at first in any case.

---

1   Extract from Hamish's First World War Officer's Commission, 28 July 1915.

> *The press described this School of Instruction as a 'school for young officers'. From the point of view of age, this description tended to be misleading, as one at least of my fellow subalterns was – well, nearer fifty than forty, I should think. His hair showed steel-grey beneath his Glengarry bonnet, and his voice was so deep that it reminded one of distant thunder, or the roar of a cataract! Another has been through the Boer War as a sergeant – one of the straightest fellows I have ever had the pleasure of meeting, whilst yet another was a middle-aged farmer, more accustomed to agriculture than soldiering, but nonetheless full of limitless enthusiasm.*

Sadly, there ends Hamish's putative memoir, but fortunately he left behind a wealth of other writings that tell his tale. As he put on hold his literary ambitions and embarked on his new life in the army, he temporarily adopted a more light-hearted style to mark his attitude to the changes he was about to take on:

A SONG

Sing me a song of the Army,
Of khaki and rifles and drums,
Sing me a ballad of heroes,
Taking each day as it comes.
Sing of the Colonel who bellows,
Sing of the Major who swears,
Sing of the slackers who don't care a jot,
And the Second Lieutenant who cares.
Sing of the raptures of marching
(I may interrupt, but don't grieve!);
But above all come tell me, come tell me
The glorious myth about leave!

Perhaps Hamish hadn't grasped the full realization yet that, from now on, his life would be controlled by the army, and the War Office. Hamish had never been fond of rules and regulations, even at school, but now, as a second lieutenant, he would need not only to obey but also to be obeyed, not only to be cared for, but to care for others:

> *In a country defined by class, only 'gentlemen' from the upper-and middle-classes were expected to become new officers ... the new leaders needed en masse to manage the hundreds of thousands of new soldiers in the ranks. Young officers were taught how to control and care for men and how to command their respect. The most junior infantry officers, second lieutenants, were often only teenagers. Each had to lead a platoon of around 30 men, many older and from much tougher backgrounds than themselves. The time spent in training created a spirit of comradeship as soldiers became familiar with each other's habits and lives, and men learned to operate as a cohesive unit.**

---

* Civilian to WW1 Soldier, [web-page], Imperial War Museum (accessed 2017) at www.iwm.org.uk/history/from-civilian-to-first-world-war-soldier-in-8-steps

Hamish had never been one for ideas of 'class'. Despite coming through a public school education, many of his writings before and even more during the war show that he was more inclined to 'socialism' and egalitarianism, often stressing his view that to be a decent human being, caring for and about others, was his main aim in life. As his later writings show, he carried this into his role, not only leading but also loving and respecting the men of his platoon.

When he opened the letter that told him the starting date for his training, Hamish could at last be certain that this was real. His immediate reaction was one of exhilaration, followed by apprehension. Yes, he was excited to take that first step of his army career, but what would training involve? Who would he be with? Where would he sleep? All sorts of mundane questions he had never thought to ask before. He had been told to report to Bedford Camp in a few days' time, so he had a lot to do if he was going to be ready to leave his civilian life behind.

As he journeyed down through England by train in early August 1915, Hamish must have mulled it all over in his mind. He wasn't too worried about the military side of things. After all, his three years of officer cadet training at his school had accustomed him to marching, drilling and setting up tents. This early experience had given him the understanding that different people react or respond in their own individual ways to army life and he felt sure that, mentally, he would be able to adapt to whatever was demanded of him.

He must have had the occasional twinge of anxiety when thinking about the immense physical challenges his body had to face to get as fit as everyone else only eighteen months after completing his recuperation, and especially that his heart itself must stand up to the pressure of all that exercise. However, he soon put that out of his mind.

Most of his old school friends had already completed their training and gone out to the front. As his writings show, Hamish couldn't wait to join them. He wasn't going to let the small matter of officer instruction stand in the way, so he determined to pace himself as best he could and make the most of learning so many new skills.

When Hamish began his training in Bedford Camp as a member of a reserve battalion – the 11th Royal Highlanders (Black Watch) – the first thing he and his fellow officer recruits did was to copy down a list, in their neatest handwriting, of the timetable of what they would be expected to learn in their first few weeks:

Recruit Programme

1st Week

Drill (Close order)	[30 hours]
Lectures on: (The Soldierly Spirit	
Discipline	[6 hours]
History of the Regiment)	

2nd Week

Drill (Close order)	
Drill (Extended order)	[20 hours]
Lectures on: (Field Work	
Musketry)	[3 hours]
Marching	[3 hours]

This programme continued for eight weeks, with variations including lectures on a range of other warfare topics and the learning of more basic skills, which Hamish and all the officer recruits had to practise and perfect for many hours, week by week. One of these was bayonet fighting. As Hamish wrote in one of his notebooks:

Bayonet fighting is a curious pastime and as fickle as a twentieth-century flapper. It can be compared – in civil life – only with the fashions of the fair sex, because it changes so frequently. Hardly a week elapses but a new 'on-guard' is invented, or some improved method of delivering the point finds its way into the curriculum of bayonet work.

The teaching of bayonet fighting is, in all good sooth, a strange and uncanny practice. It is a weird spectacle to see a meek-looking little man being initiated into the secrets of how best to insert several inches of cold steel into various parts of the Teuton's corporation, and the callous relish with which the instructors impart their gruesome knowledge is both interesting and awe-inspiring.

One of the professors of the science in our battalion (Sergeant Jett) is a real enthusiast, the way he gets worked up being quite prodigious. His subject seems absolutely to carry him away, like an actor who is 'living' his part. Even when thrusting his gleaming bayonet into a perfectly harmless sack, his face becomes contorted with a look of hostility; horrible to behold.

'Jam yer bay'net well 'ome!', he counsels. 'An' if it sticks, press the trigger and blow the ******* to Kingdom Come! Unless you kill 'im, 'e'll kill you. You can choose for yerself!'

I often think that if the Kaiser could see us carrying out the sergeant's genial instructions, he would give up his campaign in utter horror...

Sergeant Jett had a grim sense of humour, which was not altogether untouched by sarcasm. He frequently made use of this when addressing his class of recruits.

'Class – point! Nah then, Corporal Fillet, it's a German you're supposed to be a-sticking of, not a bloomin' piece o' blotting paper! Thrust it well 'ome, as if ye meant it. Try it again!'

But we need the real thing. We need a German in front of us, who is also armed with a bayonet. An inoffensive sack of shavings does not succeed in inspiring our men with the appropriate spirit; they cannot see red as Sergeant Jett appears to do. ...But the sergeant is an artist in a way – a consummate artist!

Basic training was a must for everyone joining the army, though the officers didn't do so much of the repetitive physical and obedience training as the men because they had to learn a lot about leadership, strategy and tactics as well. The main objective of basic training was to build up each soldier's physical fitness, confidence, discipline and obedience, as well as to learn all the military skills and teamwork they would need on the battlefield.

Every day was planned out to the minute, starting with reveille, sounded by a bugler, at about 5.30 or 6.00 am. The men had an hour to get up, wash and shave, dress, tidy and clean their quarters, then have a brew of strong tea to start their day. At 6.30 or 7.00 am the recruits had to parade for an hour and a half to improve their discipline and fitness, before finally having breakfast. After this, they spent the rest of the morning drilling on the parade ground, and learning different marching formations. They had a good long lunchtime before returning for more drill or skills training sessions till tea-time. The average working day of a trainee soldier or officer was longer than in civilian life and, with extra fatigues and work parties, it often lasted round the clock. After an evening meal, their time was usually their own, although a lot of that went on shining boots, darning socks and cleaning their kit. There being no leisure facilities at the camp, whatever time they had left was when they could write letters home and sit round the stove, if they had one, sharing stories and jokes.

Although Hamish mostly spent any leisure time he had either writing or occasionally socializing in the officers' mess, it was with the men that he truly felt alive. In particular, he clearly loved the Tommies' humour, and the way they tended to see the funny side of everything:

The life of Tommy in training is a hard one, but it does not prevent him cracking a joke. In every battalion, in every platoon as a rule, there is a comedian, and he is usually very popular indeed. He is the man who, on a twenty-mile route-march, will keep telling funny stories and making comical remarks the whole time; he is the fellow of infinite jest, who causes the miles to slip past unnoticed while his comrades listen eagerly to his ludicrous sayings and witty popular songs. The man in the street will doubtless think that a soldier after marching twenty miles with a pack on his back and a rifle slung across his shoulder can have little to laugh at, but the Tommy is not an ordinary man, and his ways are not the ways of the civilian. The average fellow would probably be a limp lump of perspiring adipose tissues, while the soldier still wears a smile on his face and a light heart in his breast.

When the company is on the march and the order comes: 'On the left form line', the leading man marks time while the remainder double round in a semi-circle into line with him. When the column is lengthy, it will readily be seen that the rear man has quite a big run to make. The other day, our brigade was on the road (and it should be remembered that a whole brigade covers miles), when our mischievous Tommy, in the extreme rear of the column, was heard to remark:

'I wonder what would happen now if we got: "On the left, form line"!'

'Why,' replied his friend. 'The leading man would be marking time till tomorrow morning!'

On another day, when the Battalion was on tedious manoeuvres, our comic turned to the man next to him and said, with a perfectly solemn expression:

'It's the worst thing you can do.'

'What is?' queried his companion.

'Blow your nose on a broken bottle!'

This retort may appear silly in cold print, but the reader cannot realise how comical it sounded in those circumstances.

As well as learning and practising new skills such as trench-digging, attacking, defending, route-marching, marksmanship and night operations, there was always more of the same endless 'square-bashing' on the unforgiving parade ground. No doubt Hamish and his companions were sick of marching and all the other drills by this time, and none too keen on practising hypothetical war in a patch of ground next to a peaceful Bedfordshire field, with only the sheep to bleat their inscrutable comments. However, the trainee officers all knew that they had to concentrate for long hours, to listen, do and learn everything well, as they might soon be expected to deliver some of this training and these lectures to their own platoons behind the lines.

Not long after he arrived at Bedford Camp, Hamish had an idea for a new 'war sketch', so he found a quiet half-hour one evening and wrote it for the *Craigleith Chronicle*:

THEN AND NOW
A War Sketch in Three Strokes

I

'War with Germany? Nonsense!' The speaker was Randolf Ross. It was the summer of 1913, and he was lying by a burn-side in the Scottish Highlands, whither he and his friend, Captain Walter Watson of a Highlanders Regiment had gone for a week's fishing.

'You army men,' he went on: 'seem to have developed a disease called Germanitis. You're always prophesying hostilities with our Teutonic cousins, but your forecasts never come true – nor never shall, as Shakespeare would say!'

'All right, old man,' responded Watson. 'I don't want to argue with you. I merely say that, in my very humble opinion, Germany wants war with us, and that, sooner or later, she'll invent an excuse for having it.'

'Fiddlesticks,' yawned Ross. 'I'm very fond of the Germans: their beer is quite excellent!' Saying which, he rose to his feet and resumed his task of catching trout.

Captain Walter Watson smiled to himself.

II

A shell screamed overhead and a perfect hail of bullets whizzed over the men in the trench. Second Lieutenant Randolf Ross of Kitchener's Army spoke words of encouragement to his men.

A 'Jack Johnson' exploded up above … three men in the trench laid down their rifles for the last time…. Another fusillade of bullets hissed past. An enemy aeroplane floated like a hawk in the heavens … again a shower of bullets whistled over the parapet … a man fell back and lay motionless in the trench.

Hell had settled upon the fields of Flanders.

Then the order came to advance and take the Germans' position.

Second Lieutenant Randolf Ross jumped from the trench, and, with a shout of exhortation, led his platoon forward…

III

The telephone bell rang in the officers' mess of the No. 2 Scottish General Hospital.

Lieutenant Lunn, R.A.M.C., raised the receiver and put it to his ear. A minute later, he turned round and said: 'Callan, you're orderly officer today, aren't you?'

'I am, yes,' was the response.

'Well, an officer's just been admitted suffering from bullet wounds. Better go and have a look at him.'

'Right!' Lieutenant Callan put on his hat, adjusted his belt and left the mess.

Shortly afterwards, Second Lieutenant Randolf Ross was in bed in the officers' ward. The medical officer stood beside him. 'I suppose you've seen enough of the firing line for the present?' he asked.

'Not I!' cheerily responded the wounded officer. 'You see, when I was lying wounded a swine of a German came up and kicked me and spat in my face.!' Then he added: 'I want to have another word with that German!'

They both smiled – a little grimly.

'Good night,' said the medical officer.

'Good night,' returned Second Lieutenant Randolf Ross. 'And see you have me fit again as soon as ever you like!'

Lieutenant Callan waved his hand and softly closed the ward door. *

---

* *Craigleith Chronicle*, September 1915, p.181.

Although the beginning of his memoir petered out after just two and a half pages, Hamish continued to write in his notebooks, which formed a sort of diary and included some of his poems.

Hamish and his cohort of Black Watch officers were the only Scots in the camp among the English and Welsh battalions. Indeed, Hamish himself was 'honoured' with the offer of an opportunity to transfer to a Welsh regiment – a variation of 'head-hunting' as we might call it today, but he clearly didn't consider it an honour – far from it, as he expressed in this poem:

A SCOTSMAN'S REPLY TO AN OFFER TO TRANSFER TO THE ROYAL WELSH FUSILIERS

The Royal Welsh is a regiment with record grand and true,
And they've fought like noble Britishers in France and elsewhere too,
But the lads who wear the kilt can teach the Welshmen what to do –
The 42nd Highlanders (Black Watch)!

Let Welshmen keep their Regiment, and fight with pride and will;
Let Highlanders retain their plaid and wield the claymore still:
So I'll keep my kilt until the Germans find that they can kill
All the 42nd Highlanders (Black Watch).

O, I'm dreaming of a mountain-side where the torrents leap and roar,
And the skirling of the pipes upon a barren, rocky shore,
Where the sad-faced Scottish lassies pray for lads they'll see no more
In the 42nd Highlanders (Black Watch).

Yes, I'm longing for the heather moor, the murmur of the Tilt,
The wild and rugged places where red Highland blood's been spilt,
So, if I must die fighting, I'll die fighting in the kilt
Of the 42nd Highlanders (Black Watch).

Chapter Three

Army Types

'*It is not true, as some critics of the First War British high command have suggested that Kitchener's army consisted of brave but half-trained amateurs, so much pitiful cannon-fodder ... the troops had months and months of severe intensive training. Our average programme was ten hours a day, and nobody grumbled more than the old regulars who had never been compelled before to do so much and for so long.*'

(J.B. Priestley,[1] describing his training)

Once Hamish was settled into his billet nearby and getting used to all the routines of army life in the camp at Bedford, he began writing about his day-to-day routines, experiences and thoughts in letters home to his parents. Thus we learn in a letter Hamish wrote in late autumn 1915 about his frustration at not yet being able to go and fight in the war itself:

> *Orkney House,*
> *Clapham Road,*
> *Bedford.*
>
> *My dear Mater and Pater,*
> *It's a horrible afternoon, wet and miserable, and as I don't have to be on parade until 3.30, I'm writing this letter to you.*
> *I got the old man's note this morning. Dai* is lucky, getting over the water so soon! I only wish I was going with him. Alas, there seems to be little hope of my getting abroad for some months yet at any rate. It's all very well in its*
>
> ─────────
> * Dai was Hamish's eldest brother, the first-born of the family (thirteen years older than Hamish).

─────────
1. J.B. Priestley, *Margin Released*, p.73.

way, training at home and hearing people say that you're doing your duty and all that sort of thing, but, dammit all. I'm getting awfully curious to see what it's like out there! I know quite well that, once I'm there, my enthusiasm to get home again will be much greater than my enthusiasm was to get out – but that's neither here nor there!

Dad asks about the horses I ride. The one I used to have has gone sick, so I'm riding another one now. I only manage to go riding about once or twice a week. ...

Please tell Sue Gray that I'm eagerly awaiting the pair of sox that she started knitting for me some years ago. She <u>must</u> be a slow knitter!

I heard from the Lightfoots a day or two ago. They asked me to tea, but I couldn't go. In fact, I don't like 'going out' much – as you know!

What news of Alan?** He owes me a letter now. Is he still at Boulogne, or has he gone to the trenches now?...

** Alan was Hamish's older brother (six years his senior and the nearest sibling in age).

Hamish had recently heard that his great friend C. Stuart Nimmo had been wounded while attacking the Hun, badly enough to be taken out of the battle zones to a proper military hospital for treatment. Hamish must have told his parents, who knew Stuart well and who were evidently worried on his behalf, and no doubt on theirs too, with all three of their sons now in uniform and far away from home. However, it seems that Hamish had had word of him, as he continues his letter:

I'm glad Dad saw Mr Nimmo. There is really nothing to worry about Stuart for: he's very comfortable and comparatively well in hospital in Boulogne for eight days, but could find no one who knew anything of Alan. Of course, in such a place as Boulogne, Alan is very small fry indeed.

I wish I could get up to see all the people in Edinburgh and Dundee, but I'm afraid I can't manage it – unless Alan comes home or something like that happens.

Yours ever, with much love,

Prof.

P.S. I want a haggis sent to me at Christmas, you know!

The only other of Hamish's letters to his parents that survives from his time at Bedford Training Camp was written just before Christmas 1915, with some presentiment of what might be to come.

Clapham Road,
Bedford,
Sunday

Dear Mater and Pater,
   Thanks ever so much for the goodies and letters, all of which gladdened my military soul! I'm sure you must be sorry that none of your khaki boys will be home for Christmas, but it can't be helped, you know.
   A most interesting ceremony took place here this morning when the General commanding our Division (General Sandbach) presented one of our sergeants with a medal of St George, awarded him by the Czar of Russia for Gallantry at Givenchy last January. It was an impressive sight – which, needless to say, I am embodying in my 'book'! The same sergeant has already been decorated with the D.C.M.* …
   The Watsonian** was sent to me with the best wishes of the Old School, as it contains my name on the roll of honour. I see that some of my friends have been killed. You might buy another copy in Edinburgh and send it to Alan. I know he'd like to have it. You might please get Alastair's address from Mr Shannon, as I'd like to write to him.
   I see from this week's Stage that Esmé Percy*** has joined the London Scottish as a private. I think this is splendid of him. You must admit he's given up a lot, hasn't he? Fancy Esmé in a kilt!!!
   'Armlets' are fairly common here. Are they wearing many in Scotland?
   The weather here is bitterly cold, and Dad tells me it is the same with you in Edinburgh. Tell Dad not to get cold smoking in the garden!!

---

*   Distinguished Conduct Medal.
** The *Watsonian* was and still is the school magazine of George Watson's College, Edinburgh.
*** Esmé Percy, trained by Sarah Bernhardt, was a rising stage actor who later starred in forty films.

Here's a poem which you may like:

MAY I HAVE STRENGTH

When the supremest Hour of Test is nigh,
*   And all the sky reflects a field of red,*
When stern-faced Death extends its bony hand
*   And mocking, gloats upon the Glorious Dead –*
May I have strength, Great One, may I have strength.

And if it be that dread Hand of Bone
*   Will seize my heart and tear it from my breast,*
Then throw my corpse among the myriad slain –
*   May I have strength enough to stand the Test,*
May I have strength, Great One, may I have strength.

Write soon, please!
Yours ever, with much Love,
Prof.

It is not difficult to imagine how Hamish's parents must have felt, reading that poem at Christmas-time with all three of their sons in the army, two in the line of fire and one about to be. Hamish himself must have wondered how he would spend the following Christmas, if he should live that long.

The New Year 1916 began, still based at Bedford camp, where Hamish's cheque book stubs show that he was paying £1 per week to a Mrs Pipe for his 'billet'. The weather was bitingly cold and living in huts meant having to put on several layers in an effort to stop shivering. However, being an officer offered some benefits in that Hamish and the others in his hut shared officers' servants, who would light the fire and do any other jobs the officers required. Hamish was clearly impressed by one servant's ingenuity:

'HERCULES' O.S.

There's no doubt about it, 'Hercules' ought to go down to posterity as one of the noblest personages of this great war. His sense of initiative is as highly developed as his waistline, and his outlook on life is as rosy as his countenance.

We have three servants in our hut, but Hercules (who ministers to my personal wants) is easily the best of them. Make no mistake about it: he is no ordinary orderly, no mere button-cleaner and boot-brusher, no mere military menial of the usual calibre:- he is IT.

Of course, his real name is not Hercules, nor does he know that we call him that. We do not tell him, for fear of offending his dignity, and that would never do. For instance, he might give up pressing my tartan slacks under my suitcase and blankets, or he might cease to warm my boots for me before parade… No; Hercules must not be offended.

When I open my eyes in the morning and turn over on my camp-bed, the first thing I see is a roaring stove, beside which Hercules O.S. is sitting, polishing one of my boots and imparting a gloss to it which would make a Prime Minister's valet yellow with envy. He appears to enjoy the process of Blacking, for he hums or whistles sentimental ditties as he brushes. But he does not look sentimental: he is wide of girth and he wears his sloppy Glengarry bonnet at such an extraordinary angle. Sometimes he makes one think that mayhap, many years ago, he was a Cabinet Minister, and that someone must have left him standing in the rain for a considerable length of time…

This, of course, is all mere supposition. I have never informed him of my conjecture – he is, I imagine, easily offended….

My tunic too basks in the sunshine of his favour. I really believe he takes a personal pride in my appearance, although I myself never do. Were I to go on parade with a dirty belt, I fancy it would cause Hercules much remorse. When I exhibit a disinclination to 'show a leg' in the mornings, he reminds me, in his own words of course, that 'Time, Tide and the Early Parade wait for no man.' Or, he may even coax me by rhapsodising over the lusciousness of breakfast delicacies. Hercules is so fatherly…

But he does not speak very much, or very often. He usually converses by means of facial contortions, or a series of monosyllabic grunts, which are very expressive, and quite comprehensible by the initiated. I am privileged to be one of these.

Now and again, I admit, Hercules is a trifle tardy in paying us his first visit. (This frequently happens on Sunday mornings.) But then he is so incomparable in a myriad other ways, that we overlook these things. Indeed, I have found that if I let him do as he likes, he does what I like. It is a sort of mutual understanding, and it works very well.

His rubicund physiognomy positively thrills with wisdom; and in addition to this, it reminds one of one's early childhood visits to Pantomime. Probably, he could make a fortune as a knock-about comedian...

One day he informed me that he had six blankets on his bed, down in his hut.

'Where did you get them?' I asked enviously.

'Och,' was the nonchalant response. 'Walkin' in my sleep, Sir!' He smiled wisely, for he is very wise. He is an old soldier! I may be as wise when the war is over: pessimists tell me I shall be a very old soldier by then. (Mr Bottomley* thinks otherwise, so that's all right!)

At one time, when the snow lay six or eight inches deep outside the hut, we were short of coal. Our stove was black out, and we huddled round it, calling down imprecations on the authorities. (This is strictly forbidden in the army, so don't tell anyone!) I don't know whether the Reader has ever lived in a hut, but if he has, he will realise our predicament.

One of the other O.S. (Officers' Servants) came in and we sent him out to look for fuel. We sat there waiting, full of hope and eager anticipation.

Ten minutes passed: the orderly came back.

'There's no coal in the camp, Sir,' he said.

'Damn!' came from all of us in unison.

Then Hercules came in, and I told him our grouse. He scratched his head and went out. Ten minutes passed, quarter of an hour, twenty minutes, half an hour.... I was beginning to think it was all up.

Shortly afterwards, the door opened and IT entered, a huge sack of coal on his back.

'Where did you get all that?' we shouted, after our enthusiasm had subsided.

---

* Horatio Bottomley, newspaper proprietor and editor of the *John Bull* magazine.

> *Hercules put the sack down quietly on the floor and, with a twinkle in his eye, remarked: 'Och, Sir, walkin' in my sleep; walkin' in my sleep!'*
>
> *Next day I discovered, about half a mile from our hut, on the railway, a truck full of coal … Hercules had wandered far afield in his slumbers!*

One of the things that irked Hamish most, as he made clear in his notebook, was the range of what seemed to him unnecessary layers of petty officialdom, such as the chain of command required for the completion of one simple task:

> **If you want something done in the army, this is how it happens:**
> *The Colonel says to the Second-in-Command: 'Major, I want this done.'*
>
> *'Yes sir,' says the Major, who turns to his Captain and says 'I want this done.'*
>
> *'Very good sir,' is the reply. The Captain instructs his Lieutenant to carry on.*
>
> *The Lieutenant passes it on to the Second Lieutenant.*
> *The Second Lieutenant orders his Sergeant to get busy.*
> *The Sergeant tells his Corporal to get a move on.*
> *The Corporal tells the Lance-Corporal to see that it is done.*
> *The Lance-Corporal commands the Private to do it.*
> *It can go no further than this. (We have no Lance-Privates in the Army.)*
> *The Private accordingly does the job.*
> *He reports to the Lance-Corporal that the job is done.*
> *The Lance-Corporal tells the Corporal that the work has been completed.*
> *The Corporal advises the Sergeant it has been attended to.*
> *The Sergeant assures the Second Lieutenant it is accomplished.*
> *The Second Lieutenant passes this on to the Lieutenant.*
> *The Lieutenant so informs his Captain.*
> *The Captain lets the Major know.*
> *The Major tells the Colonel: 'I've seen that thing through for you all right sir.'*
>
> *This may all seem very strange to the uninitiated reader, but it's a way we have in the army and one soon becomes accustomed to it. Even the private soldiers get accustomed to it.*

Also, talking of rules and regulations, Hamish says the sergeant major is always the man most feared among the ranks:

THE SERGEANT-MAJOR

There is only one thing on the face of the Earth the private soldier does <u>not</u> get accustomed to … and that's the Sergeant-Major.

Now, the Sergeant-Major is quite in a class by himself: he knows everything. One is not made Sergeant-Major unless one can recite at least fifteen handbooks, word for word, as well as being able to give advice on all military topics, from squad drill to – well, subjects far beyond my ken. If one has had the misfortune to tie one's platoon in knots on parade, all one has to say is: 'Carry on, Sergeant-Major,' and he does carry on. The men tremble before his august personage and do his bidding without murmur.

'The motto of this regiment,' he says, 'is clean chins and clean rifles. If any of you come on parade with a face like a stubble-field, or a rifle like a rubbish-heap, take care <u>I</u> don't see you, that's all.' He takes a breath before launching on. 'Some of you wear your hair too long. I don't know whether you were poets or artists before you enlisted, but you're supposed to be soldiers now. You're supposed to be, I said. Now, in <u>my</u> old regiment, we had to shave before every parade, and anyone who didn't had to shave the whole company before breakfast next morning!'

The Sergeant-Major is, so to speak, the Colonel of the non-commissioned and warrant-officers, and he rules his command with a rod of iron.

Hamish later wrote a 'light verse' about the sergeant major at Bedford Camp.

THE S-M

List to the Sergeant-Major,
  Hark at his manly voice,
Like streams that leap in the spring-time,
  Like angels that rejoice!

List, he is giving orders:
  His tones are soft and rare,
Like a father crooning his children,
  His locks grow grey with care!

Look at his kindly features;
  Look at his dear blue eyes,
As he says, with a sob of sadness,
  'Size, Battalion, size!'

You see! His face is clouded –
  Now hear what he has to tell:
'In the name of God, you bloody sod,
  Wake up, or go to hell!'

Hamish was, by now, known among his friends for his impatience with unnecessary bureaucracy and petty rules. He was particularly amused therefore to hear the story of a young recruit who acted on his own disdain of such situations:

> *In a certain regiment, an officer had played havoc with a man for not having folded his bedding according to regulations. Going his rounds again the following day, the same officer was thunderstruck to find that the delinquent had tied his blankets up very neatly with pink ribbon.*
>
> *'What's this?' demanded the astounded subaltern.*
>
> *'Red tape, Sir,' replied the man as he brought his hand smartly to the salute.*

It was at about this time that Hamish must have come across an amusing circular, or perhaps, more likely, he may have written this one himself. There have been more recent versions based on this idea, but with many differences. Here is the one that Hamish wrote out and kept among his papers:

THE ARMY'S TEN COMMANDMENTS
The following 'Ten Commandments' have been received from an officer at the Front:

1. *The Colonel is thy only Boss; thou shalt have no other Colonels but him.*
2. *But thou shalt make unto thyself many graven images of officers who fly in the heavens above, or staff officers who own the Earth beneath, and or submarine officers who are in the waters below. Thou shalt stand up and salute them, for the C.O., thy Boss will visit Field Punishment onto the first and second degree on those that salute not, and shower stripes on those that salute and obey his commandments.*
3. *Thou shalt not take the Adjutant's name in vain, for the C.O. thy Boss will not hold him guiltless who taketh the Adjutant's name in vain.*
4. *Remember thou shalt not rest on the Sabbath Day. Six days shalt thou labour, and the seventh day is the one of the C.R.F. On it thou shalt do all manner of work, thou and thy officers, thy non-commissioned officers, thy sanitary men, and the Kitchener Army who are within thy trench.*

5. *Honour thy Army Staff that thy days may be long in Corps Reserve, where one day they may send thee.*
6. *Thou shalt kill only Huns, slugs, lice, rats, and other vermin which frequent dug-outs.*
7. *Thou shalt not adulterate thy section's rum ration.*
8. *Thou shalt not steal, or at any rate be found out.*
9. *Thou shalt not bear false witness in the Orderly Room.*
10. *Thou shalt not covet the A.S.C.'s job; thou shalt not covet the A.S.C.'s pay, nor his motors, nor his wagons, nor his tents, nor his billets, nor his horses, nor his assess, or any other 'cushy' thing which is his.*

On 27 January 1916, news spread fast around Bedford Camp of the British government's announcement that, due to falling numbers in the fighting ranks following heavy losses on the Western Front, reinforcements were needed. Therefore conscription was to be introduced for all single men and widowers between the ages of 18 and 41, unless they were unfit or employed in jobs of vital importance, in which case they would be exempt from army service.

That was certainly a talking-point in all the huts around the camp that evening. All the men who had volunteered since the beginning of the war constituted the 'New Armies', or what was more commonly known as 'Kitchener's Army'. Now there would be a new and perhaps unwilling 'mob' to train: how would they integrate into the existing ranks? What were these exempt jobs? Would there be a sudden rise in those claiming to be 'unfit'? (No doubt Hamish kept quiet on that question, although, in fact, his situation was the reverse, having 'omitted' to declare his previous serious illness.)

Two days later, Hamish and his fellow trainee officers and men of the Black Watch were sent off to spend a few weeks on a bombing course at Lochend Camp, Dunfermline, the official home of the Reserve Black Watch … and even colder than Bedford.

This was where Hamish described an inadvertent scare:

THE BOMB-SCARE

Hasting and Bennett, the bombing officers, were holding the class in a large marquee, utilised as a messing room. Three piles of tin dishes were neatly stacked around the canvas walls, and a large collection of them rested on the table in front of the door.

Bennett was explaining to an N.C.O. the mechanism and method of firing of the No. 5 Mills Grenade. Needless to say, it had been thoroughly examined beforehand, as the utmost care is required in such a subject as bombing.

When the pupil withdrew the safety pin, however, the bomb started to fizzle. This interesting occurrence had no sooner happened, than the entire class stampeded. Tin dishes flew in every direction and Jamison, who happened to be standing in the doorway, was swept off his feet by the pupils in their panic to get some distance away!

In reality, there was no danger, as the grenade had been disabled. The incident was distinctly amusing, however. I can't think I have ever seen men scatter so quickly before!

As always, Hamish made very detailed notes and drawings of a wide range of bombs, shells and other aspects of artillery, complete with names, measurements and main features. For a literary man, Hamish took pride in becoming quite an expert on the mathematical and scientific aspects of the paraphernalia of war.

While at Lochend Camp, Dunfermline, a stray dog – a scruffy and very hairy Airedale – tagged along behind Hamish one day as he hurried towards an afternoon training session. He reached for the biscuit in his pocket and threw it to the mutt, leaving him to devour it.

To Hamish's great surprise, sitting patiently outside the door when the session had finished, was the stray. Feeling sorry for him, Hamish procured some leftovers from the kitchens and from that day on, he was Hamish's dog, following him everywhere he could, albeit at a distance to avoid the noisy bombs. However, Hamish would soon have to leave him behind.

Chapter Four

Apprehension

'*Conditions in training camps were often basic and supplies of equipment were limited.*'

(Clouting, IWM)

From Dunfermline, in early March, the trainees were moved on to Catterick Camp, then simply an outpost of the main barracks 3 miles away at Richmond, Yorkshire. Here they received a somewhat ignominious welcome for officers and men alike, as Hamish described:

A huge encampment of huts, planted in a sea of mud … a heavy snowfall … and no camp hut allocated. Thus was I greeted at Richmond. After the luxury of private billets, my heart sank within me and I could have wept for bitterness of soul.

No one knew anything about me, or where I was to go. No one cared a jot what became of me. No one did anything save, to <u>my</u> mind, stare at me with curiosity and amusement. I was senior to the majority of them and I had commanded men for about seven months. Now I was but a lance private, so to speak, in the company of officers, many of whom were ridiculous, mentally, physically and morally.

At length, night came and I retired to a hut where, along with the other newcomers (quite junior subalterns), I curled up in my three army blankets on the deal floor and slept, as best I could, in the agony of coldness.

Lights out at 10.15., <u>and an officer, forsooth!</u> Truly, the army is a curious place, and the habits of the War Office are beyond human explanation…

Hamish and the other newcomers appear to have made the best of what they had, and obtained some coal for their stove the next day. Here they settled in for the final stages of their training. The timetable was packed, so there was barely any free time. Hamish's meticulous table of the features and subtle differences between various sizes of grenades demonstrates the depth of knowledge and complexity of detail the trainees had to learn. His pages of accomplished drawings and diagrams of everything from shells and rifles to trench designs and battle formations show the thoroughness of instruction at Richmond and the importance of this new expertise to his future role, leading his platoon on the front line.

Despite all these demands on his time, Hamish managed to find a few moments to write a letter home to his parents, giving them a taste of what camp life was like at Richmond:

> *Richmond*
> *9/3/16*
>
> *My dear Mater and Pater,*
> *I am writing this on my knee beside our hut stove, so excuse the wobbly writing. The other fellows are playing cards, reading, mending sox, or doing other soldierly duties!*
> *This sort of life is becoming second nature to me now, in spite of the fact that there's about 18 inches of snow outside and a strong blizzard is in full force. The huts are wonderfully comfortable when one gets used to them, and already I look upon it as my home. Of course, it must be more pleasant during the summer, for I am told that Richmond is exceptionally pretty then.*
> *You should see me in my new gum boots! Some treat, I can assure you. This sort of thing you know [a drawing of a gumboot here with an arrow]. Made of rubber and coming up to the knees. They're really necessary here, for the slush, snow and wind are awful.*
> *I can't understand why my article hasn't appeared in the* Herald. *The* Dispatch *also has one of mine. I've sent an article on Hut Life to the* Weekly*, *so look out for it. We don't have very much time for writing, but I do as much as I can.*
> *Thanks for paying for my sweater, but I really didn't mean you to buy a new one. Thanks all the same – and thanks for the poster. It now adorns one of the walls of the hut.*
>
> ---
>
> * This refers to the *Weekly Scotsman* (the two others are Edinburgh newspapers).

> *I wrote some poetry yesterday. I don't think you'd like it, so I'm not sending it on.*
>
> *Give my love to Daisy and ask her to write soon.*
>
> *Yours ever with much love.*
> *Prof.*

Hamish's used cheque stubs for early 1916 include one for 'gumboots' at 25 shillings, two-thirds of his weekly pay.

It was at Richmond camp that Hamish and his fellow officers became aware that they and their Black Watch platoons were the only Scots among all the English and Welsh regiments. Indeed, Hamish was surprised to find how the other British nations reacted to the sight of men wearing kilts; not just the soldiers in the camp but, when he went into the town, either alone or with his men, he seemed to cause something of a stir. He wrote about this one evening:

> *A SCOTSMAN AMONG THE SASSENACHS*
> *Since I joined the Regiment, I took the kilt and all the other paraphernalia of the Highland Officer pretty much as a matter of course. Now, however, I have gradually come to look on them as phenomenal curiosities, spectacular accoutrements, and even glorious relics of a noble barbarism. When I walked along Auld Reekie's* streets in my uniform, no one appeared to take any particular notice of me; I was merely one among many. But when I sally forth in the thoroughfares of Richmond, I am regarded as a curio, a strange personality, an object singled out for special attention and (may I whisper it?) admiration! People nudge one another and remark in mysterious awe: 'Scotch Officer!' or 'There goes a 'Jock!' We are all Jocks in England, you know. In the corner of my eye I can see them looking after me in the streets. I can hear them chatting about my uniform (although they do not know it by that, or indeed any name); and I have heard the snatches of conversation about my dirk, and the uses thereof.*

* 'Auld Reekie' is the colloquial name for Edinburgh.

When I march in solitary state at the rear of B Company, curious street types follow me, dazing dumbstruck at my unaccustomed garb, or express further wonderment that I do not catch cold or die of rheumatism. On more than one occasion, their interest and their remarks have become so personal that Captain Salmon has advised me to drop a rear guard!

But I believe it is the same almost everywhere: a Scotsman draws a crowd, provided he is in his national costume.

I fancy some of my English fellow officers are just a trifle jealous of me…. You have no idea of how the fair Sassenach damsels dote on 'Jocks'. Lieutenant Larrop, for instance, is an extremely handsome youth, and he presents with an alluring appearance in his heavy-cut breeches and perfectly adjusted putties, not to mention his monocle! But when he and I go out for a stroll together, I am the centre of attention; all eyes are fixed on my dirk, my Glengarry and my spats. It is really very unfortunate for Larrop. Meseems I have taken the wind out of his sails somewhat. Not even his gold-rimmed monocle can regain for him the prestige which he has lost.

But, to be frank, my popularity is not so enviable as might appear at first blush. More than once I have felt like a lion escaped from the zoo, like the Wild Man of Borneo, or like some other freakish thing out for exhibition purposes.

For example, the other day I went out down town to buy some odds and ends. Suddenly I became aware that I was being followed by a little girl and a little boy, aged respectively about five and six. In their faces shone the look that gleams in the eyes of a child during their first visit to the pantomime – a kind of bewildered astonishment. They continued to dog my footsteps for about three hundred yards, when one of them could stand it no longer. Turning to his companion, he said 'I say, Dolly, that is a woman!' The titters of the passers-by did not embarrass me at all – it was altogether too amusing!

Winter turned to spring at last and Hamish now became more imaginative in some of his correspondence. In this letter below, always perceptive, he clearly enjoyed writing tongue-in-cheek cameos for his parents of some of the different character-types among both the officers and the men at Richmond Camp.

Richmond, Tuesday evening

My dear Mater and Pater,

The army is a wonderful place after all. There are so many different types to study, so many different temperaments to analyse, so many human beings in such a small space.

For instance, there is the young subaltern who has been indifferently brought up, and whose home-comforts and food haven't been of the best. Now that he is an officer, he thinks he ought to show his superiority to other mortals by going to the other extreme:- it is, after all, only the force of reaction. He wears a gold watch-chain, though strictly against regulations. He complains about quite edible food; he shouts loudly for waiters, and passes caustic remarks about the flavour of the soup, etc. He is quite noticeable and quite contemptible ... maybe I am a trifle harsh; probably he is to be pitied...

Then there is the country bumpkin who is quite dazzled by the wonder of holding the King's Commission. He feels awkward, looks awkward and is awkward. He drops bread in his soup, snivels, and seems composed mainly of hands and feet. His features are usually large and ruddy, and his speech does not always conform with the rules of Grammar. He is sincere, lovable and – above all – natural. A good fellow as a rule, he will probably make a splendid officer. In the regular army, of course, in peace time, he would not be tolerated. Yokels do not grace a mess-room of the Guards. But of course nowadays it is <u>manhood</u> that is wanted, and a power of leadership. Occasionally this life makes one blunt, but that is all.

We also have a <u>Snob</u>. He is the most abominable of all. At the present time the army is a huge, happy family, and the man who stands apart from his fellows because his father owns a grouse-shooting estate in Perthshire is a pest. We cannot even leave him to himself (much as we would like to), we must come in contact with him; we must eat with him, go on parade with him, have quarrels with him. In some cases he is fond of his men; in some cases he treats them as dirt. In the latter case he does not live long when he goes on service.... All around, he is not a favourite – except with his own select (?) coterie.

There is also a Good Sort. <u>He</u> is the ideal officer and companion. He knows human nature, he values camaraderie, and his temperament is of the hail-fellow well-met variety. Probably you will recognise the type. Loyally *well set up, he looks upon his men with pride, he <u>leads</u> them – not <u>drives</u> them. He is not finicky and he ignores snobs and other vermin. A great smoker, he is not tee-total, nor does he hold any narrow and out-of-date ideas on Religion. Do not run away with the idea that he has no religion. He has, but it is a religion of his own. Clergymen probably would not understand it; they very seldom understand anything important…*

There are scores of other types – the officer who knows all in <u>theory</u>, but nothing in <u>practice</u>; the one who knows both, but can't handle men; the one who knows very little, but 'has a way with him'; and many others.

The men also have their types, and they are as many and as varied as the officer … yes, the army is of great psychological interest.

We have so many officers in the Battalion that we don't know what to do with them all. I always think of us as being fattened for the slaughter, but doubtless I am pessimistic!

My camp kit arrived yesterday; it had been lost on the railway. I had been sleeping on the floor, so a canvas bed seems luxurious now! We are no longer chocolate soldiers, you see; I shall probably be sleeping on one of the garden seats (or in the bath!) when I come home on leave!

Love to Daisy.* Why doesn't she write?

Yours as ever,

Prof.

---

* Daisy was the nickname of Isobel, Hamish's eldest sister.

In between the training and drilling were the long, countryside route-marches. These were always a chore, especially for new recruits who weren't fit enough to sustain the pace without frequent stops or diversions, but the typical 'Tommy Atkins' humour often helped to ease the strain.

When leading my platoon, I have often had the tedium of a long march whiled away, listening to the clever banter of the men behind me, and I have often experienced difficulty in restraining loud laughter.

I remember one day on the march, our battalion passed a little, old-fashioned thatched cottage.

'Ullo!' exclaimed one. 'It ain't often as yer sees the likes o' them nahdays, is it?'

> *'No, Bill,' was the response. 'An' I dessay it needs a shave and a 'air-cut nah and again!'*
>
> *Another day, as we were marching through a little hamlet, an oldish and rather disagreeable-looking woman was watching us from the door of the rural post-office. One of the men caught her eye as he went past and he called out: 'Are you the <u>only</u> girl in the village?'*
>
> *A little after that, there was a small stream to be crossed. Over it had been placed a hurdle, but this was so unsteady and the banks so muddy that the first dozen or so floundered clumsily into the water, much to the amusement of those behind. At last, however, one man got dry-shod almost to the other side, whereupon he turned round and said, very solemnly and almost pathetically: 'Don't cheer, chaps. Don't cheer!' Everyone laughed and the witty one fell incontinently into the stream!*
>
> *Later, one of our subalterns was telling of his adventures in France, when he had been one of a listening post, between the British and the German trenches. Captain Best listened attentively to his hair-raising narrative for some time, then quietly said: 'Yes, Millar, most exciting. But what I really want to know is – how does one keep one's ears from flapping in the wind?'*

Throughout his time in officers' training at Richmond Camp, Hamish continued to write for the newspapers and for his old friends at the Craigleith Military Hospital. For example, in the April 1916 edition of the *Chronicle*, there are two of Hamish's writings. One is a story for children about a soldier stricken down by his enemies in the second year of the Great War and left 'in the woods of Craigleith', where a fairy ministered to his wounds and gave him her heart. The other piece is an adventure of his favourite (fictional) character, Private Crumplethorne. However, it is another short story of Crumplethorne's, from the following edition, that is included here: the tale of when he first joined up as a raw recruit, and, like many new recruits, quickly regretted it:

PRIVATE CRUMPLETHORNE, RECRUIT

'I wish I was dead!' said Private Crumplethorne.

'We all do,' replied the Sergeant-Major. 'Only we're too tired to die.'

Crumplethorne smiled, but the S.M.'s face did not betray the fact that he accomplished his object, namely, to show the recruit that he was rather a fool. A sergeant-major seldom smiles in the presence of a recruit, for he is a very dignified gentleman with a carefully concealed, but nevertheless very human heart.

Private Crumplethorne lit a cigarette and, thrusting his hands into his trouser pockets, leant against a tree in the parade ground, his unbuttoned coat flapping in the wind, and a look of infinite boredom on his suspiciously-stubbly face.

'I'm sick of the army,' he said to himself. 'It's beastly!'

This summing up may reasonably be considered a trifle premature when one reads that he had experienced the military life for only two days. But then he had never been accustomed to work, and discipline (spelt with a very large D) was a thing of which he was as witless as a newborn babe.

'Shaving and marking time every bloomin' hour of the day fairly flummoxes me,' he continued to ruminate, ending with a very malicious rendering of a now popular expression: 'Damn the Kaiser!'

Pushing his cap on the back of his bullet head, he vigorously scratched his bristling hair and spat vehemently on the ground.

And thus it was that the Colonel suddenly coming round the corner discovered 8888 Private Christopher Crumplethorne.

'Why don't you salute, man?' demanded the Colonel.

'I forgot all about it,' was the response, delivered in an attitude of extreme repose, which gave the irate C.O. great difficulty in restraining himself.

'Stand to attention, can't you!' came the thunderous injunction. 'Button up your coat, put your hat on straight, take that cigarette out of your mouth and try to look like a soldier!'

'I don't feel like one,' said Crumplethorne, humbly obeying the demands about his apparel.

'You never will feel like one, unless you try and look like one,' remarked the Colonel. 'When did you join up?'

'The day before yesterday.'

'Say "sir" when you address me. D'ye know who I am?'

'No sir.'

'I'm the C.O.'

'The what, sir?'

'The C.O. – Commanding Officer – Colonel!'

'Yes sir,' said the recruit, saluting again.

'What are you doing?'

'Saluting, sir.'

'I thought you were trying to wrench your arm out of its socket. Ask the Sergeant-Major to give you a few more lessons.'

'Yes, sir.'

The Colonel walked away, smiling.

'Funny bloke, that,' mused Private Crumplethorne. 'I wonder if the Sergeant-Major often tells him off.'

Feeling thirsty, the recruit went off to oil himself. But, on arrival at the door of the hostelry, finding that he was absolutely devoid of cash and remembering that treating was obsolete, he felt wondrously sad and extraordinarily thirsty.

'Are you coming on parade, Crump?' shouted Lance-Corporal Blokesby, who happened to be passing (or was it coming out of?) the establishment.

'Parade?' reiterated Christopher in a tone of dazed bewilderment. 'Another parade?'

'Yes my lad, but you'll enjoy this one; it's for pay!'

8888 Private Christopher Crumplethorne brightened up instantly and set off at a brisk pace for the parade ground. He looked quite smart when he eventually, in his turn, came up to the table, saluted, received the shining shekels from Captain Gorren, saluted again and marched off.

Half an hour later, seated in 'The Blooming Fuschia', with a pot of ale at his elbow, Crumplethorne came to the momentous decision that His Majesty's Army isn't such a bad place after all!

The time was passing and every so often a draft of men or officers or both would parade and be sent off in glory on their journey to France to join the war. On 27 May 2016, Hamish wrote in his notebook:

> *Today a draught of 100 men left camp for France. They looked absolutely splendid in their khaki aprons* and Balmorals, and my heart swelled with pride as I watched them.*
>
> ---
>
> * The plain khaki 'apron' was part of the Black Watch uniform in wartime, taking the place of the sporran, worn over the kilt to protect and conceal it.

It could not be long now before Hamish and his cohort would follow, but first they would be given leave, his first visit back home for a year, and he was greatly looking forward to it. He couldn't wait to return to his writings full-time, and maybe a stage performance too, and a visit to his friends at Craigleith to visit the wards again.

Looking ahead, in hopes that the war would not last long, Hamish drafted a letter as a kind of insurance for the future, however near or far off that might be; something to look forward to in these difficult times:

> *Dear Mr Percy,*
>
> *As it is my intention to take the stage up as a profession after the war is over, I ask if you could see your way to make use of my services in your company on the conclusion of hostilities. You may recall that I played various small parts for you during your recent visit to this city.*
>
> *I have had a good deal of amateur experience, being a member of the Carlton Dramatic Club, and having appeared in various productions, including – this season – three of my own plays in Edinburgh and district. (I may mention that one of these plays reached its 15th performance.) I have filled straight, character and comedy parts.*
>
> *A pupil of Mr Graeme Goring,* I was informed by that gentleman that I had 'all the necessary qualifications for a successful stage career.'*
>
> *I fully appreciate the usefulness of a repertory company, and realise the splendid experience a young artist would secure under your management.*
>
> *In the event of my still being in the land of the living when the present campaign is over, I should be very glad if you would find a place for me in your repertory.*
>
>
>
> *Hoping to hear,*
> *I am,*
> *Yours most sincerely,*
>
>
>
> ---
>
> * Graeme Goring was a well-known Shakespearian actor.

Summer arrived late in 1916. Consistently low temperatures made it the coldest June for forty years and the weather was poor, with strong winds, rain and leaden skies. This lack of sunshine and warmth lowered the mood of Hamish and all the other trainees, still living in draughty huts, still drilling daily on the parade ground, buffeted by the gales.

SOMETIMES

Sometimes I'd rid me of this khaki yoke,
  And wander far afield and o'er the hills,
List'ning enraptured to the skylark's song,
  Gazing enchanted at the leaping rills.

Sometimes I long to leave the dusty square
  And seek the buttercup and daisy fair,
Dreaming beneath some hoary rev'rend oak,
  Breathing the myst'ry of the fragrant air.

Sometimes I would forget the deep red blood
  That sprinkles all; the wonder of the Land,
And watch the rolling billows of the Sea,
  Sitting contented on is golden sand.

These thoughts are sweet, but sweeter, sweeter far
  The noble pledging of our Country's word. ...
Therefore the Poet now must arm his Muse,
  And, with a shout of pride, take up the Sword!

The officers and men were by now in a state of high anticipation, as they neared the completion of their training. For many, despite their patriotic bravado, the mood in the camp turned to apprehension and, for Hamish at least, a sense of foreboding when the news came of the massacre on 1 July, the first day of the Battle of the Somme.

The press described it as the worst day in British military history, with nearly 20,000 men killed in action and another 40,000 wounded, not to mention so many others who were unaccounted for in the confusion and chaos. One of these, as Hamish discovered a couple of weeks later, was Alexander Robertson, who had been his English teacher for a year at George Watson's College and who had inspired Hamish to write poetry. It seems they must have kept in contact as Hamish had in his personal possession a small inscribed volume of his former teacher's poems. Robertson was reported missing and must still lie under the ground that was no man's land. Other Watsonian old boys he knew were also among the dead of that day, which prompted Hamish to write of their loss in a sombre frame of mind, almost on the eve of his own departure to the Somme:

ONE BY ONE

Seldom a day goes by, it seems, without
A name by me held richly in esteem
Appearing in the lists that mark the men
Who slumber in the Sleep that knows no dream.

My friends are slipping past me one by one,
And leaving me to justify their death…
So may my strength be equal to the task,
O may I carry on while I have breath.

I know I am not what I might have been,
That I have oft proved wanting in the test…
Yet may I be a worthy friend to them
Ere I – like them – sink grimly into rest!

In early August 1916, Hamish was at last back home in Edinburgh, spending his few days' leave with his parents and friends before his embarkation for France and all the turmoil of war. On the eve of his return to the next stage of his officer training, Hamish wrote in his notebook: 'This is the last day of my "final" leave.' Then a few lines further on, apprehensive about what was to come, he wrote:

I may see sights that make my blood run cold – or not. Then of course, I may not return at all. I may do what thousands of other men have done before – die for my Country. I may not see my home again. I may never kiss Cathie again. But I'm not grousing – it's all in the day's work.

The King has paid me seven shillings and sixpence a month … to get killed. One doesn't get paid this princely sum simply to drill and do bayonet fighting, day by day. Nor is this remuneration because one has to take part in The Great Gamble, in which Death is one's opponent. It seems a peculiar way of putting it, but it's the truth. My only hope is that when it comes to the push, I shall have enough strength to bear it well.

Most officers have the same feeling, I think. We are not afraid of the enemy; we are afraid of fear, which is much worse. …Few men know how much their nerves can stand until actually up against reality…. It is a very strange thought.

I have <u>lived</u> during these few days of leave – final leave, because I knew I had to give each hour, to make the most of every minute. Each hour that passed made my holiday shorter. I knew that all too soon the day would come (as it is now) for me to go back to duty and leave all the comforts and the pleasures of home behind me.

In a few hours, I shall have left Edinburgh, and the train will be rushing me through space to a regiment I have never even seen; I shall have to make new friends; I shall have to command new men. Then, when the time comes, we shall go abroad, and the possibilities – the possibilities are great. Everything rests with myself. Above all, I must bear in mind the undying honour and fame of my regiment, and I must realise that any deed I do reflects not only on myself and my family, but also on the fair name of a very noble regiment. <u>This</u> is <u>esprit-de-corps</u>, and it is this that has carried many a man through tight places, inspired him with courage; reminded him that he was a <u>man</u> and a Briton. I am both. Pray God I may never forget it!

As Hamish said his goodbyes, not knowing for how long … if ever, he handed his mother a poem he had written specially for her to keep and to cheer her on lonely days, that he was about to do what he wanted, for his people's pride … and his own.

ENVOI

Be calm. I follow where my friends have gone.
  Have nought of fear.
I go to herald in the Glorious Dawn
  Which breaks not here.

Be brave. A myriad mothers' sons before
  Have trod this path...
Think of my comrades, stifled to their gore –
  War's aftermath.

Be proud. Thank God I go o'erwhelmed with pride:
  My hackled bonnet
Bids me be proud. Pray on the Other Side
  No stain be on it.

Be calm! Be brave! Be proud! No conscript base
  Is this thy son.
I go light-hearted, tired of peaceful days,
  To strafe the Hun!

Edinburgh, 9th August 1916

Chapter Five

Journey into War

'The poets who arrived at the Somme were soldiers first ... and poets second. But nothing had prepared them for the sights they saw when they got here.'

(*War of Words*, a BBC documentary)

Finally the great day arrived, the day on which Hamish's cohort of Highlanders would leave their native shores to join the 8th Battalion of the Black Watch and plunge themselves straight into the Battle of the Somme. Wearing their Black Watch uniforms and kilts with pride, they formed up on the parade ground for a patriotic send-off by the commanding officer. As Hamish wrote later:

There was great excitement on the Battalion Parade Ground. A throng of eager soldiers swarmed round the hundred men who were about to leave Camp for service overseas. My heart swelled with pride as our comrades surged up to wish us goodbye and Godspeed. There was much talking, hand-shaking, laughter and well-wishing, for the men, with their khaki aprons, Balmoral bonnets,* red hackles** and full packs, were going to take part in the 'Great Adventure'; the time for which they all longed had at last come.

'Goodbye Sandy; the best of luck tae ye and a safe and speedy return,' said one doughty trooper.

'Gi'e ma compliments to Kaiser Bill, Jock, an' tell him ah'll be oot tae see him in the next draft,' added another.

A burst of laughter followed; everyone was in the best of spirits. It is not in a Scotsman's nature to show sadness at such a parting as this; soldiers are not at

---

* A Balmoral is a soft woollen flat-topped hat (bonnet) like a large beret, worn by Scottish soldiers.

** A hackle is a thick feather plume attached to Scots military headwear, red for the Black Watch.

all sentimental about going out to face Death. The spice of adventure appeals to us; we were now to achieve the goal for which we had been trained...

The pipe band was waiting on the right flank to play the draft to the station. It was a proud and pleasant duty, which does not stale with repetition.

The officers came out from the Mess, for everyone turned out to see the draft off. Although they didn't throw their bonnets in the air, as did the men, they were just as interested and as moved by the scene as the others. A fellow officer, not yet ready to be drafted, went up to one of the men in his platoon who was going, and clasped him warmly by the hand. 'Godspeed on your way,' he wished the brawny soldier. 'I only wish I was coming with you,' he added, with great sincerity. 'So do we, sir,' was the man's hearty response as he nervously fidgeted with his rifle.

As the time for departure approached, the Sergeant-Major cleared the well-wishers away to the sides. We who were going were brimful of eagerness and energy. As I looked round, our red hackles on our bonnets set off our uniforms to a nicety – like crimson poppies in a field of corn, and our equipment presented a workmanlike aspect that suited the occasion admirably.

The Conducting Officer took his place in front of the draft and called the parade to attention, while the Colonel rode out onto the parade ground. He was a grand figure of a man, the Commanding Officer, and he looked every inch a soldier as he sat astride his big black horse...

After the C.O. had inspected us, he remounted his horse and made a short speech: 'You all belong to a noble Regiment and you must always uphold its great name. If each man of you looks after himself, as I'm sure you will, the Regiment will look after itself.' He paused. Then the absolute good-heartedness of the Colonel showed itself as he exalted the men: 'And remember to write home on every possible occasion. Don't forget, your folks will be wanting to hear all about you. Scratch a few lines on a postcard as often as you can. And now, good luck and Godspeed to every one of you.' How many C.O.s would have thought of that?

'Three cheers for the Colonel,' called the Sergeant-Major. Three lusty cheers rang out.

'Draft, 'shun! Move to the right in fours! Right! By the left, quick march!'

The band crashed forth and, amidst wild enthusiasm, with the cheers ringing in our ears, we Hundred Soldiers – officers and men, marched out of the Parade Ground, down the road and out of sight of the camp.

Their first destination was the railway station, where they began the long journey to the front line. First they went by train to the south coast of England, from where they crossed the choppy Channel to Boulogne. From here they had transport laid on to travel the 55 miles south-east to La Comté, near Béthune.

On 25 August 1916, a warm day with heavy showers, Hamish (whose name was officially recorded as A.J. Mann) and eleven other second lieutenants arrived at La Comté to join the 8th Battalion of The Black Watch at the 4th Corps rest area, where, next day, they took over their new platoons – the 14th Platoon for Hamish – and joined the battalion in training and practising for an ambitious attack. This was due to take place on or soon after 30 August, involving 120,000 British and French troops. The skies opened and the rain continued all week so that, by the end of the month, the ground was saturated. After all the build-up and anticipation, the planned attack was cancelled due to 'the scarcity of shells'.[1]

In those days following his arrival on the Somme, Hamish keenly felt the differences between the ordered army training on the parade ground at Richmond and this busy, noisy and confusing melee of men in active war mode. No matter how well-prepared he thought he was, the contrast took Hamish by surprise and he recorded his responses to these new challenges through verse:

THE ARMED MUSE

Now comes the time when I must lay aside
The rosy rhymes of am'rous sonnets sweet,
And make my harmony a martial air,
Breathing the melody of marching feet.

Each line must tremble with a warlike clash,
Or cast a mellow glow of beauty rare
Upon the deeds of heroes lying dead,
Their very heart's blood matted in their hair.

---

1   Wauchope, p.27.

Or I must sing a very dear sad song
About the ones at home who wait and weep,
Dreaming of those who fight in other lands,
Or keep a weary watch upon the deep.

Then I must sometimes let my Muse run mad,
And shout a ballad full of splendour wild,
Of those who, risking all, rush forth to shield,
Or to avenge, the mother and her child.

God! I must also sing in sterner strain
Denouncing those (defend them now who can!)
Who dare to symbolise with vile disdain
The honoured names of Soldier and of Man.

Then I must tune my Lyre for Victory,
And make Parnassus ring with grand delight,
Greeting the splendid dawn which puts to rout
The awful horror of a tragic night!

On 1 September, the 8th Black Watch moved to Gouy-Servins and on the following day they relieved the 2nd African troops in the trenches, opposite Vimy Ridge in the Berthonval sector. This was Hamish's first experience of real trench warfare. Almost immediately, the pace of hostilities accelerated as the Germans became more active in firing their mortars. Consequently, the Black Watch made good use of their Stokes guns and 60lb trench mortars, firing them all night and day in retaliation, so not much sleep for Hamish and his men. The sound and fury rose to a crescendo around dawn on 3 September with, in some nearby parts of the line, sniping at close range and fighting almost hand-to-hand.

Huddling in his dugout, scribbling away by the light of a 'guttering candle' that night, Hamish acknowledged in his army notebook that war was not as glorious as he thought it would be. Four soldiers (other ranks) of the 8th Black Watch were wounded, but fortunately nobody was killed, though the toll was higher in other battalions. However, the Germans fared worse on this occasion, losing ground as well as suffering more casualties.

The rain continued steadily for the whole first week of September, with overcast skies and little visibility, until the sun came out on the 7th and the air became another battleground, while planes from both sides carried out airborne surveillance in the lulls between and other planes sniped at each other, downing quite a few.

Once relieved from the trenches and out of the firing line again, Hamish was able to process and think about his experiences since his arrival. It was a sobering realization. Up till now, he had nobly thought that he would come to fight for freedom and, if necessary, die for his country, but now he realized that his principal duty was to kill for his country. Why had he not seen this before, during all those bayonet and rifle-shooting practices? He had previously thought of attacks in terms of defence, rather than all-out attack. This was an adjustment he would have to make and, though a poet, he was enough of a realist to do just that.

However, there were harder, crueller adjustments to come. In his third week on the Somme, he wrote to his parents from his active service British Expeditionary Force's address with what hyperbolic bravado he could muster, perhaps in response to his first shocking traumas of war:

> *8th Black Watch*
> *B.E.F.*
> *France*
> *10.9/16*
>
> *My dear Mater and Pater,*
> *The parcel and letters arrived last night. It was 'some' parcel and I cannot thank you enough for it. The cakes have not yet been eaten, but the shortbread is already a thing of the past. The contents are all splendid and just exactly what I want. It was a cheering mail distribution last night. I got five letters and two parcels, the other being some top-hole sweets from Toto [older sister]. The letters included a six-page one from Ruth. No one else in the dug-out got anything like so many! As you know, everyone out here looks forward to the post; it's one of the days' chief joys.*
> *I'm afraid that you take the war too seriously at home. Here we look upon it as a huge joke – as indeed it is. True there are tragic portions in the play too, but then one can appreciate the humour of it more when there is The Other Side as well. Our good friend Mr Boche – naturally enough, I suppose – can see no element of fun in the affair at all, and that is precisely where he fails.*

This morning, as there was an Autumn mist, I paid a visit to 'No Man's Land'. It was a strange sight ... here and there about, dead (or unexploded) shells lay half-buried in the earth, their compressed death never having got loose. In other places, pieces of equipment – all shattered and torn – were strewn about, and a Hun boot, with a skeleton leg protruding from it, rested beside a tangled heap of barbed-wire. In a fairly large shell hole, I found the chaotic remains of what was once a German soldier. His skull was face-down, but I turned it round with my foot, and gloated over the ghastly smile it gave me. From his pocket book I ascertained that he was 25 years old and between the pages there was a 5 mark note. His watch reduced to a pulp lay near and a letter was also at hand. The envelope of his letter I enclose as a souvenir – a most ghastly one I admit, but nevertheless of interest I think. His erstwhile uniform was represented by long, clammy threads of sopping cloth, through which bones showed. I am ashamed to say that the spectacle amused me. I smiled and then laughed: dead bodies are so engrossing ... and yet, <u>somewhere</u>, someone is weeping for him, for this mayhap husband of hers who was killed a year ago. ...But they are human like us.

I am looking forward to the arrival of Common Sense and the War, and I shall of course let you have my opinion of it after I've read it.

I hope you, Mother, have got rid of your cough by now. You mustn't develop these things, you know, as soon as ever I go away!

I can't tell you how much I am enjoying life out here. It's grand! The only fly in the ointment is the knowledge that people at home are becoming prematurely and unbecomingly sick with worry! There is no need whatever for anyone (even <u>you</u>) to grow thin over us out here. <u>We</u> are growing fat, and every day fatter! It's quite amazing you know. We have a continuous pantomime from the Huns and in some degree our loud laughter aids our corporeal extension!!!

Cheer-O! And a thousand thank yous,

Yours,

Prof.

P.S. I may not be able to write so often now, as a vast amount of pioneer work is coming our way, I'm told.

Hamish dwelled on the haunting memory of that skeleton, and the letter; the only remnant of the man he had been. As he turned over the gory scene in his mind, the initial, self-protective bravado left him and he did the only thing he knew to help him deal with this first traumatic meeting, at close hand, with death. He poured it out in a poem:

THE SHELL HOLE

In the shell hole he lies, this German soldier of a year ago;
But he is not as then, accoutred, well, and eager for the foe
He hoped so soon, so utterly, to crush. His muddy skull
Lies near the mangled remnants of his corpse — war's furies thus annul
The pomp and pageantry that were its own. White rigid bones
Gape through the nauseous chaos of his clothes; the cruel stones
Hold fast the letter he was wont to clasp to his am'rous breast.
Here, 'neath the stark, keen stars, where is no peace, no joy, nor any rest,
He lies. There to the right, his boot, gashed by the great shell's fiendish whim,
Retains — O horrid spectacle! — the fleshless stump that was his limb!
Vile rats and mice, and flies and lice and ghastly things that carrion know
Have made a travesty of Death of him who lived a year ago.

On 14 September 1916, in preparation for the major attack planned for the following day, the 8th Battalion of the Black Watch took part in a combined Scottish raid. Sixty men of Hamish's battalion with sixty Cameron Highlanders were sent out on the surprise raid. It was to be a quick, fifteen-minute strike, starting at 10.15 pm, with the objective of securing German prisoners and identifications. As the plans, reports and telegraphs attached to the regimental diaries show, there had been meticulous planning for this raid. This night was chosen for its forecast level of cloud, enough to obscure the moonlight and give the men as long as possible undetected. All positions and timings had been worked out for optimum cover and efficacy.

Earlier in the evening, after dark, a work party had laid out a line of tape, stretching halfway across no man's land. Another group cut paths through the barbed wire. Now all watches were synchronized with their Battalion HQ and the raiding parties crawled out into no man's land and got into their positions, twelve paces apart in front of the allies' line. At 10.07 pm, with barely any moonlight, they started to crawl forward towards the enemy lines, as far as the agreed position.

At 10.13 pm the Scots fired off a Stokes barrage and the men crawled closer, unseen under the barrage, to within 30 yards of the German line. The ground at that point was very broken up, pitted with large shell craters and, now they had been alerted that something was going on, more shells and gunfire rained down randomly. The Scots had no artillery support for this raid, but twenty-four Stokes mortars created a barrage to make it easier for them to cross no man's land under cover. At 10.15, the raiding parties stormed the enemy lines and found that, due to the panic the raid had provoked, many of the German soldiers had run at once into dugouts and piled up so tightly in their rush that they could not escape the Mills grenades that bombed them out. Others were scattered in all directions in the trenches and had died where they were, out in the open, killed by the allies' Stokes mortars, of which 4,500 rounds were fired in the fifteen minutes of the raid, accurately hitting their marks. Only one Hun was found alive and he was taken prisoner. As reported in the regimental diaries: 'One prisoner was brought in. He was caught in No-Man's-Land in a bewildered state, apparently not knowing what he was doing.'

At 10.25 pm, it was time to recall the raiding parties. As an experiment, the military planners wanted to see which would be the best way to signal to the troops across a noisy battlefield. French horns were blown by the officers. Bugles were blown in pairs by three parties of men. From the firing-line, several bunches of green rockets were also fired. Of these three methods, the Black Watch regimental diaries tell us, the bugles were found to be 'quite useless and only heard by a few'; the French horns were 'most distinct and heard by all, and the green flares also proved of the greatest value.' It is not known whether all bugles were withdrawn from then on in favour of French horns, but it can't be denied that the latter would make a vivid image to raise a smile.

The element of surprise had been effective and the raid of 14 September was successful. Despite a great many enemy deaths, only five allied soldiers were wounded, by German 'whizz-bangs'. Hamish described these small-calibre shells in a letter to his parents:

Whizz-bangs are strange contrivances. They're there before you know where you are, and frequently you don't know where you are for a considerable time after! They travel faster than their own sound – and sound travels fast enough, in spite of the fact that the sound of guns doesn't seem to have reached America yet.

He wrote in his notebook about the solitary captured Hun:

ON CAPTURING A GERMAN PRISONER
There's something uncannily engrossing in the sight of a man who's been doing his best to kill you since 1914. Some of them are so docile and inoffensive – after they've been caught. Others look sneaky and vicious, like captive bears, or more aptly, clipped eagles. Why did Germany adopt an eagle as her insignia? Mayhap because she is so flighty.

At the end of the day, the Scots had gained the German front line and some ground south-east of Thiepval. The mood was positive among both officers and men in the battalion that the balance might be on the turn towards the allies at last.

This hope was strengthened on the following day, 15 September, when a combined allied attack made advances of 6 miles into what had been enemy-held land, including the strategic gain of High Wood. This was helped, if only due to the shock effect on the Germans, by the first appearance on the battlefield of tanks; no doubt a great worry to the enemy but a point of considerable interest and some degree of pride to the allies, despite the fact that several of them broke down. However, a third of them did break through.

A few days later, Hamish wrote his impressions of these metal beasts:

High Wood was important to me because it was the first view I got of the Tanks. Now the tanks were a great source of interest to me – before I saw them. However, despite a longing to see them, I was disappointed. I thought they would be huge land Dreadnoughts, about the size of a house; instead of which I found them comparatively small, though powerful. Tanks are, I think, insipient implements of war, so far as looks go, although I am told they are capable of accomplishing great deeds. The first one I saw was in the middle of High Wood. ...I fancy the best description I have yet heard is that they resemble a 'crouching toad'. They do look venomous and repulsive. But I am heartily sorry because I did not happen to be awake on the morning of the 20th (or was it the 19th?), when one of the Tanks actually rumbled about the Flers Line. Rae tells me that he saw it and it was a sight he is not likely to forget. They are strange containers, though I am not looking forward to meeting the German ones!

As the first tanks in action, they represented the very latest technology in British warfare, to the potential detriment of the enemy. They were, as yet, relatively untested in battle and at this stage somewhat unreliable, not to mention the extreme heat and thick fumes causing great discomfort inside the tanks and, even worse, the danger to their crews when enemy bullets hit the fuselage and caused shards of metal from the inner shell to ricochet around the enclosed space, often wounding the crews.

However, these lumbering beasts could break through barbed wire, surmount fallen trees, cross muddy terrain, trenches and small shell-holes in no man's land, though they did tend to get stuck in larger bomb craters. Despite the number of breakdowns in that first front-line trial, our tanks were pronounced a success and there were some good lessons learned to improve them before their next outing.

The French had at the same time been developing their own tanks, with similar teething troubles, but soon both British and French tanks were considerably improved and became a great boon to the allies in every future battle.

No doubt Hamish was highly relieved when no German tanks came a-threatening any of the actions in which he was involved. In fact they built only twenty, which did not make their first appearance on the battlegrounds until March 1918.

On 16 September 1916, the heavy rain drenched everyone and everything, filling Hamish's trench and turning the clay earth to oozing mud. The parapets collapsed into the trench and it was an almost impossible task repairing them. As soon as one part was patched up, another fell in, and another, all down the front line. Conditions were awful. Those last three days holding the line were the most miserable of Hamish's life, up to that point.

In an effort to cheer himself with the thought that at least he was still alive when others were not, he wrote a few lines:

LIFE

At least I live. Emotion's fiercest winds
 Sweep through my soul.
Sometimes my heartstrings play the brightest chimes —
 Sometimes a toll.

I am not stagnant. All my Being thrills.
 A raptured song
Resounds throughout my Self with varied tones
 The whole day long.

At least I live: I am not stagnant. Though
 My joy or pain
O'erwhelms me with the terror of despair —
 'Tis not in vain.
 So, when oppress'd with fervour let me say:
'Tomorrow I shall sing a richer lay!'

Hamish and his men were desperately weary, wet and miserable by the time they were relieved from front-line duty on the 19th and marched to the Berthonval sector, where they were given billets in Gouy-Servins. All they could think of was a hot bath and sleep. It's not certain that the first was possible; more likely a cold or tepid wash-down would have had to do, and the hope of a new, clean, lice-free set of clothing to change into, but they were so fatigued, they could have slept anywhere. While they were resting, Hamish looked around at the battle-scarred houses, deserted since the Hun invaded, and compared this place with what he'd left behind on that last home leave:

COMPARISONS

Here through the rotting window is a steading,
Deserted and tumble-down, with odours vile...
Way back at home (where She may now be treading)
Are fragrant woods and flow'rs and things worthwhile.

Out here the sky, convuls'd with martial thunder,
And valleys brimming full with awful dead...
Back there, there is the autumn's golden wonder,
The mellow beauty when the sun is sped.

Out here there is the ghastly devastation,
The cry of pain, the wail of dull despair...
At home there's love and laughter, fascination,
There's joy and life and glowing embers there!

Out here there is the strain that knows no telling,
The all-night vigil fighting heavy sleep,
At home I often find my thoughts are swelling –
And that is why I sometimes dream ... and weep!

While 'resting' for three days at Gouy-Servins, in-between work parties, Hamish read some of his favourite poetry to relax. On the 22nd he marched his platoon to new billets in Mingoval, where they learned that their top brass had switched around and Major Sir George Abercrombie was now in command of the 8th Black Watch. Hamish had to leave his men there to rest, in his sergeant's charge, while he went on a short course. On the first evening, he found time to pen another letter to his parents:

8th Black Watch
B.E.F.
France, 23/9/16

My dear Mater & Pater,

  At the moment, I am detached from the Battalion and at one of the many Army Schools. The course is only a week, however, after which I'll be glad to rejoin the 8th boys. I fear I shan't receive any letters until then, so I'll get all yours at once. My address, of course, is still as of yore, and in any case I'll be back with the Battalion (wherever it is by then!) when you get this letter.

  It is a glorious afternoon; away in the distance is the din of a tremendous bombardment; and I have just been reading the refreshing peacefulness of John Masefield. He is a wonderful man: he seems to set the fragrance of the country into his poems every time. He can be tragic too, but his tragedy is not the tragedy of Grand Opera. One turns to Shakespeare for that sort of thing – the conflict of former passions, the gamut of human emotions. In John Masefield one finds the tranquillity of a sylvan pool at eventide, or the cry of 'a white gull ... along the desolate sands ...'

  Probably you will wonder how I can read poetry out here. I read it everywhere – in the firing line too. It is like bathing one's forehead by the roadside on a dusty Summer's morn. And it is astonishing how many prosaic-leaning people one meets who yet love to lose themselves and their troubles in the pale lanes of the meditative muse. Sometimes also one finds overwhelmingly practical persons who snatch hours wherein to wander in the company of Keats, Browning, Shelley or frequently Burns.

  I of course have long since been given up by the fellows here as a bad job, one of those hopeless poetical people! I enter the Dugout, and forthwith forget where I've put everything – my belt, my stick, my revolver, my tin helmet! Then, when I have to go on duty, I have to spend time looking for them! 'Mann's lost his helmet again! Why the devil can't you put things where you'll find them?' And so on. But I never do: it's not my way!! I'm so proud to be considered an artistic fanatic...

  It's beginning to get cold now. The sun will soon be out of sight but the observation balloon's still hanging up in the sky, and an aeroplane cruises above it, so high up that it appears like a mere mosquito! In any case, the mosquitoes are biting my legs, and I can't stand that! So Cheero!

With tons of love,
Thine,
Prof.

While on his course, Hamish's platoon was marched to the 3rd Army's training area of Denier, where his men stayed for a week and where he rejoined them. Wauchope, in his excellent account, describes Denier as 'a miserable little village with poor accommodation.' Nonetheless, it was better, and of course safer, than the trenches, so they put up with it and spent the next ten days training, hard: morning, afternoon and sometimes evening too, ready for the next phase in the Battle of the Somme, though they didn't yet know what that would be.

Chapter Six

High Wood

'The coming operation in which the Battalion was to take part was an attack on the Butte de Warlencourt and the trench system surrounding it.'
(Wauchope, p.28)

Since Hamish had arrived on the Somme six weeks before, when the 8th Battalion had shrunk considerably through the fierce period of fighting, they had been joined by several new officers and now there was a large draft of other ranks to swell their numbers closer to the desired complement. These men joined in the training as the whole battalion prepared and practised for the next big push, planned for the following week.

In-between the strenuous work schedules, Hamish found snatches of time to walk the nearby lanes and survey the area. Though he had lived most of his life in the city of Edinburgh, he was a country boy at heart, so he felt most at home in wide green spaces like the Highlands. However, the war had already stripped northern France of its beauty, as Hamish wrote in his next letter to his parents:

8th Black Watch
B.E.F.

My dear Mater and Pater,
Thank you – as usual – for all of your most excellent letters. I think you know how much the post is looked forward to out here, and it's most awfully good of you to write so often.
One of the patterns of life out here that strikes me very much is the state of the woods – their foliage all ripped off by shells, they stand out against the setting sun like gaunt skeletons, their poor stripped trunks, withered and lifeless, pointing to the skies like fingerposts of Death. Sometimes they remind me of innocent martyrs who have been burned at the stake. But the artistic

effect of the crimson sun behind them is beautiful. France (now how musical that sounds – 'La Belle France'!) after its war will be a wondrous and sorry sight. Many of her fairest pasturelands are now reduced to acres of shell-holes. Many of her hamlets tumbled down and reduced to heaps of scattered briars.

I often find myself wondering what the next life will be like. The present one is simply imagination run riot! H.G. Wells and his fictions are now proved to be no insane ravings of a sensational novelist. But above all there is the impression of the Bruce Bairnsfather* spirit, the marvellous mental state which enables a man to take his life in his hand and yet sing a popular ditty or crack a joke. Upon my soul, the men are inexpressibly wonderful; their esprit-de-corps is quite the most fantastic of all nations. The French are fanatically excited (I am told), the Germans are fairly hateful, but the Tommy is like the Scarlet Pimpernel – he jests while he scuffles with Doom! I don't think the people at home quite realise what a glorious fellow Thomas is. 'Hero' is too trite an expression to apply to him. He is more than a hero – he is a super-hero every moment of his life. He calls the German 'Jerry', and he passes witty remarks about the Hun all the time the said Boche is doing his best to make Tommy an angel!

I fancy I shall be a much greater artist after the war. War teaches one a great many artistic things, and probably more than anything else, SYMPATHY, FORGIVENESS, and an understanding of HUMAN NATURE. Do you know that I don't believe one person in fifty understands human nature?

A few days ago my Captain told me I had the power of leading men. I replied that I knew I had and that the reason is simply because I understand human nature. I don't pretend to be an <u>efficient</u> soldier. I could never make an efficient soldier – it's contrary to my temperament. I am not a SOLDIER. I am a PATRIOT. There is a vast difference between the two, I can assure you. But I fancy you will understand and appreciate the difference without my explaining it. In a word, Poetry and soldiering don't go together! But it's a Great Life – a great but ludicrous life!

The only thing that worries me is the fact that YOU worry, and worry needlessly. I know you must worry, and I also know that I must worry because I know <u>you</u> worry!! So don't let's worry any more!

---

* Bruce Bairnsfather was a popular cartoonist and humorist of the time.

> *I am writing this in a queer little 'funk-hole' and a guttering candle is my sole illumination. I am on duty and I shall have to go away out and see that the posts (or watches) are awake and doing their job.*
>
> *Isn't it a good thing the war didn't take place in Britain? It's bad enough seeing someone else's country being mangled out of recognition, but if it were one's own, it would be a thousand times worse.*
>
> *Give my love to everyone and write as soon as you can.*
>
> *Yours with tons of love,*
>
> *Prof.*

Early on the morning of 5 October 1916, Hamish and the other subalterns received orders to pack up and move on to Albert. They set off at 8 o'clock, leaving Denier behind, and marched through the dull, damp day in drizzle and wind by turns, to Mézerolles, where they were billeted overnight. At nine the next morning, they boarded a train to take them all on the next leg of their journey to the Talmas area. In temporary camp overnight, the following morning they boarded transport again, French buses this time, to Franvillers, with a last overnight stop before the final leg, marching up the line from Franvillers to their destination of Albert.

Here they saw the famed statue of the Virgin Mary, toppled from her stand and hanging on by her feet from the top of the church steeple. All the troops had heard the saying that when she falls the war will be over. She had hung like that for a while, but she looked quite steady. One of Hamish's bright sparks made the innocent suggestion: 'Well, let's pull her down and then we can all go home!'

In his notebooks and articles, Hamish often mentioned the marches and how the men sang as they went. Here he uses the generic name of 'Tommy Atkins' for a soldier:

> *Tommy is in many ways a perverse creature. He always sings and waxes joyful at a time least to be expected. For instance, when marching home after a heavy day's field-work in the rain, on rough ground and an empty stomach, he will chant all his favourite ditties with great relish and apparent mirth. But, on the other hand, when we march on a beautiful morning after a hearty*

breakfast, when all nature rejoices at the goodness of things, our revered friend Mr Atkins is strangely silent, marching along with a dogged expression.

Mayhap he sings only to cheer himself, raising his voice only when he is downcast and sick at heart and stomach. Mayhap his singing does not denote a light heart, but a heart requiring to be made light. When the soldier makes up his mind to sing – well, he <u>sings</u>! You should hear a homecoming battalion, with each company or platoon singing a song of its own! ...

It is not only the way that soldiers sing when they march that counts. It's what they sing. One favourite ditty includes the lines:

> *Good soldiers never die,*
> *But they bloody soon fa-ade away!*

Another is an old recruiting song:

> *You ought to join,*
> *You ought to join,*
> *You ought to join the 8th Battalion!*
> *One bob a day,**
> *Seven bob a week,*
> *Great big boots making blisters on your feet!*
> *You ought to join the 8th Battalion.*

All the popular pantomime songs are of course included in the repertoire, but the home-made ones are much more entertaining because of their originality and boldness of speech.... Another evinces an apparent dislike for the army (or a yearning to go on leave):

> *When I get my civvy clothes on,*
> *Oh! How happy I shall be!*
> *There will be no orderly sergeant*
> *Waiting at the door for me.*
> *Only one more little route march,*

---

* A bob was a familiar word for a shilling, 5p in today's money.

> *Only one more church parade,*
> *Only one more kit inspection,*
> *Then we're marching home again!*

Some marching songs are ruder still, which the men sing when they're out of earshot of the madding crowd, but whenever a village comes into sight, by unspoken mutual consent, they all strike up Onward Christian Soldiers! (Just in case there are any French civilians who might understand bawdy English.)

Such numbers as these, or favourites Keep the Home Fires Burning and It's a Long, Long Way to Tipperary, are wonderfully inspiring on a long march, and help to while away the time during which the Band stops playing to regain breath.

A band is a wonderful stimulant during foot-slogging; a body of men can keep on almost indefinitely when there is a band ahead of them. It is awkward, nevertheless, when one happens to be in the rear of a platoon or company, and the band of another battalion is just behind, for it is a human impossibility to keep in step with two bands at one and the same time.

After a night in billets in Albert, Hamish and his fellow officers had new orders. At 11.00 am on 9 October, they had to proceed with their men straight to the reserve trenches on the east side of High Wood, ready to take over from the front-line troops. Hamish scribbled a poem in his notebook to express his heightened sense of the potential significance of this day, and perhaps to hype himself up to face the challenge:

THE ZENITH

> *Today I reached the zenith of my life!*
> *No time more noble in my span of years*
> *Than this the glorious hour of splendid strife,*
> *Of War, of cataclysmal woe and tears.*
> *All petty are the greatest things of yore,*
> *All mean and sordid is my dearest lay;*
> *I have done nothing more worthwhile before …*
> *My hour, my chance, my crisis, are today!*
>
> *9th October 1916*

Here in High Wood Hamish and his platoon were bivouacked in what had previously been German trenches until the British took them three weeks before, on 15 September. It was an uncomfortable setting, right in front of a line of batteries, which repeatedly fired throughout the day and night and, to make it worse, this consequently drew intermittent fire from the enemy's heavy guns. It was eerie too, and quite a shock, when they realized that the white 'sticks' poking out from the trench walls were actually human bones. As they looked about them, along the battered, shell-holed trenches, they found various signs of human remains with fragments of both German and British uniforms, all left to rot.

The artillery fire was deafening, so there was little rest to be had. Indeed, all the main fighting that first day was within earshot of Hamish and his men. It was the attack from the British front-line trenches at Eaucourt l'Abbaye towards the Butte de Warlencourt. This was a strategic goal for the allies as it was a ridge that dominated its landscape, with excellent views across the flat lands surrounding it, making it the ideal vantage point for the enemy's surveillance of British positions. Once the Butte had been a lush green wooded hill, preceded many centuries before by an ancient burial mound, but now it was stripped bare down to its pale chalky ground with only the sticks of a few tree-trunks remaining.

In the early morning of 12 October, two Scottish Highlander battalions of the 9th Division, of which Hamish and his men were a part and held in reserve, attacked the barren Butte de Warlencourt and the trenches surrounding it.

Fighting was fierce and the combined efforts of the Seaforth Highlanders and the Argyll and Sutherland Highlanders could only gain 200 yards, at the cost of heavy casualties, before being severely repulsed by German machine-gun fire. Meanwhile, a South African division also made a degree of progress, halted by heavy shelling and gunfire. Yet, rather than retreat, these valiant warriors entrenched themselves halfway to the enemy's Snag Trench for a few hours, before being forced to withdraw to relative safety behind allied lines.

The stream of wounded soldiers being taken back to the dressing station must have demoralized Hamish's men, already weary from the constant sound of artillery, as they moved forward to take up second-line support on the Flers line of trenches that evening, at a section called 'Drop Alley'. Here, in amongst all the destruction and noise of battle, Hamish found enough time to scratch together a poem by candlelight:

A THOUGHT

Dare I regret to join the Splendid Dead
Who gave the fragrant blossom of their Youth
*   At Duty's call?*
*   My very all*
*   Is not enough*

Sing, O sad heart, the red blood opes the way;
Honour is found in all this bloody fray.
Although I did ... yet have I won the day!

Emblem of War, of rapine and distress,
Great forests stripped of all their leafiness...
Pointing above and solemn as a nun,
Or, like a copse when sets the crimson sun.
When all is o'er and fired the final shot,
The mem'ry of these times will leave me not.

Drop Alley, October 1916

Over the next few days, in the lulls between fighting and mainly under cover of darkness, Hamish and his platoon joined the rest of their battalion in the gruesome task of clearing the ground: the no man's land between the German and British front lines. They set about clearing the debris of battle, locating and retrieving bodies, some of them blown apart by shells, half-buried in the mud of no man's land. After a particularly traumatic day, Hamish penned his haunted reaction in the finding of one particular corpse, more of a clothed skeleton by now.

> ### THE SOLDIER
> #### (Drop Alley Trench)
>
> *'Tis strange to look on a man that is dead*
> *As he lies in the shell-swept hell,*
> *And to think that the poor black battered corpse*
> *Once lived like you and was well.*
>
> *'Tis stranger far when you come to think*
> *That you may soon be like him...*
> *And it's Fear that tugs at your trembling soul,*
> *A Fear that is weird and grim!*

There was little time for niceties as they buried these former brothers-in-arms nearby, with great respect and too little ceremony. Most of these bodies were Scots, soldiers they knew – some as friends – men of their own 8th Battalion. This was a terrible task and it took its toll on them all. Hamish's melancholic entry in his army notebook reflected the prevailing mood:

> ### THOUGHTS ON DEATH
> *We are a curious nation, the British. We sing songs about 'When the boys come home', but we evidently forget about the boys who will not come home, about the poor mangled bodies that are scattered across no-man's-land, the gashed and distorted limbs that are the ghastly contents of the shell-holes; the blackened hands and eyeless skulls that protrude from the earthworks, and all the other horrible things that make war hideous.*
>
> *I fancy it is not so much the fear of Death that is so overwhelming as the terrible idea of being oneself one of the fearful travesties of Death. I tremble when I think that one day I may lie there, under the cruel stars, my head blown from my body, my flesh black and stiff, my uniform rotted by the rain and torn to shreds ... no feeling of elation touches me when I come across a dead Boche. I do not behold a dead German. I only see a wizened human being, helpless and full of all the ugly stiffness of death.*
>
> *It is a dreadful thing to see a man killed and to witness his skin assuming the ivory whiteness of anonymity, to see the poor limbs become rigid in*

rigor mortis, to behold the red blood clot on the pale forehead. It is a weird thought that, shortly before, this man was alive and well, but now he has probed the greatest of all mysteries, that he is but part of the mud in which he is already partially submersed. It is pathos to think that somewhere in England a frail woman is sitting, waiting and hoping, witless of the Doom that has overshadowed her life. There is something very touching in the lines of Corporal Lee of the 4th Black Watch:

> *'Every bullet has its billet,*
> *Many bullets more than one:*
> *God! Perhaps I killed a mother*
> *When I killed a mother's son.'**

* Joseph Lee of Dundee, *The Bullet*.

In between all the horrors of war, the occasional light shone to provide a moment of cheer. Quite often, it might be in receiving a parcel or letter from home. Despite all the disruptions and movements across the battle zones, somehow the army transports managed to provide as reliable and swift a postal delivery service as possible to wherever the men happened to be or, if on the move, their next billet. Addressed only to 'B.E.F., France', it is astonishing to learn how often Hamish received his letters the day after they were posted; from Edinburgh to the Somme within twenty-four or forty-eight hours. The only exceptions, of course, were when he was in the front-line trenches, when his post would be kept for him to collect as soon as he was relieved from that duty.

In mid-October, Hamish received a very welcome letter from a member of his platoon, then recuperating in a military hospital back in 'Blighty':

Private J. Fast 10289
8th Black Watch
Ward A. Norfolk War Hosp.
Thorpe
Norwich
15 Oct. 1916

Sir,

I received your letter of the 2nd inst., and am very pleased to hear that I have been awarded the Military Medal, but I am more pleased to hear that there have been three awards to 14 platoon.

I am glad to say I am recovering from my wound and hope to be with my comrades again soon, who I am proud of ....

Sadly, the rest of this letter is missing, but even reading this short page, it is easy to imagine how touched Hamish must have been by Private Fast's pride in his 'comrades', and no doubt very happy to learn that this young man would soon be back in the platoon where he belonged. Hamish, like any good parent, loved to have his 'boys' back in the family, together again, and the rising tally of medals was a joy to them all.

By now, Hamish knew they would shortly be going into the front-line trenches again to take their part in the ongoing battle. He had his orders and studied the trench maps of both sides to ensure he learned them well. In the intermittent rain, together with the artillery smoke, visibility could be poor and complicated by the need to weave one's way around the deep shell-holes and wire, so a clear mental image of the battleground was essential. To help him learn, he drew copies in his notebook of the sections through which he would lead his men, showing the allies' trenches, strongpoints, defences and saps, as well as the main features of the enemy's firing lines.

For Hamish, the night before must once again have been one of great apprehension, for the welfare and safety of his 'boys' as much as for himself.

Chapter Seven

Snag Trench

'By the middle of October, conditions on and behind the battlefront were
so bad as to make mere existence a severe trial of body and spirit.'[1]
(Captain Wilfrid Miles)

Early on the morning of 17 October 1916, which dawned grey and misty
with persistent drizzle that continued through the day, Hamish and his
men, with their company, marched the 4 miles from Flers to the front line,
ready to take up positions in the reserve trenches. Allied surveillance planes
were sent up to reconnoitre the new German trenches and shell-holes, but
the observers could not see the ground through the haze, so it was decided
that plans would have to proceed without the desirable pinpoint accuracy of
enemy positions.

Later that day, the company was tasked to reconnoitre the ground between
the front lines to try to gain some necessary intelligence. Second Lieutenants
Balkwill and Hutchison led their men forward. They were both hit by heavy
artillery fire. Balkwill was killed and Hutchison was badly wounded. This
left the company short of officers, so B Company took over, remaining in the
trenches behind the 5th Camerons overnight.

Meanwhile, that afternoon, Hamish and his fellow officers received orders
for the battle which was to take place before dawn the following morning. It
was timed to catch the enemy by surprise and to benefit from the cover of
darkness. The 5th Camerons were to leave their front-line trench to attack
the German front line, including Snag Trench, which had eluded the allies a
few days before. They would be supported by B Company Black Watch, who
would take over the allies' front-line trenches as back-up. During all these
preparations, the rain continued relentlessly into the night and the clay mud
oozed everywhere, creating a quagmire that sapped the morale of the troops.

---

1. M. Gilbert, p.217, quoting Captain Wilfred Miles, IWM.

Hamish's D Company remained in the Flers trenches, on standby, to join the battle the following day.

At 3.40 in the morning of 18 October, in heavy rain, the 5th Camerons stole out of their trench and across no man's land, towards the enemy's front line, discharging both smoke bombs and tear bombs as they went, taking the sleeping enemy by surprise. Meanwhile, two companies of South Africans attacked the other end of the German line. This two-pronged attack caused such confusion that the Camerons were able to enter and capture their objective: the whole of Snag Trench. They consolidated their ground through the day, with Black Watch's A Company in support.

In the afternoon of the 18th, when the rain had stopped, a German counter-attack enabled the enemy to push back the Camerons and regain part of the trench, but the dogged Camerons managed to hold on to some of it and they pushed the Germans out again in the evening. This time the Camerons held their ground. They were joined by two companies of the 1st South Africans, who held Snag Trench and pushed on beyond it. However, the enemy's heavy machine-gun fire on the trench after dark took a heavy toll, reducing the Camerons to a small group. The Germans renewed their bombing at dawn on the 19th, with the addition of a flame-thrower. The Germans were now able to occupy a small section at each end of the line.

While all this was going on, D Company of the Black Watch, including Hamish and his loyal platoon, marched to the allies' old front line, took a short rest, then readied themselves to fulfil orders. These required Hamish and his platoon to keep up the ferrying of supplies to the forward troops. In particular, 14 Platoon was tasked to carry sacks of Mills bombs to the front line; a dangerous activity, since just one pin coming loose from one of the bombs would have blown them all away. Fortunately, that didn't happen and they kept going until it was time for another platoon to take over. Now they had to go behind the lines and take a rest, since they would be needed to relieve the Camerons later that evening.

After dark, at 8.30 pm, three companies of the Black Watch put the plan into action as they struggled to climb up the muddy parapets, between the streams of murky rainwater overflowing into the trench from the battlefield. The heavy rain had poured down all day and many of the men found it almost impossible to get footholds on the soft clay and slithered back down again into the mud. There were stories from other platoons that some fell so heavily they sank down into the thigh-high quagmire and, unable to pull themselves up through the cloying mud, they drowned unseen beneath its surface.

Fortunately that wasn't the case in Hamish's platoon, as he did all he could to raise their morale and encouraged them to keep trying. He led the way, scrambling up with great determination and valour, and they all managed to follow him out. Once over the top, Hamish led his men across the mire and round the rain-filled shell-holes and barbed wire of no man's land, through the sheets of rain, dodging enemy fire as they approached the right-hand end of Snag Trench to relieve the victorious but exhausted Camerons.

This was only the beginning of Hamish's worst nightmare, as he described in his notebook:

SNAG TRENCH

That newly-captured trench I shall never forget, nor the anguish I felt as we filed slowly in, through the clinging mud in the misty light of the moon. It was the most repellent sight I have ever seen, and the absolute horror of it was not in any way lessened by the splendid atmosphere of noble sacrifice that reigned everywhere.

It was almost impossible in many cases to distinguish between the dead and the living, so motionless did the latter lie in their exhaustion, after the terrible work of taking the trench. Some of the bodies were dreadful, seated on the floor of the trench in natural positions, their faces fallen back, upturned, ghostly-white, cheeks sunken, teeth gleaming through the grin of death that had parted their pale lips.

Others were face-downwards, clots of blood on their uniforms, gashed and bedraggled, half sunk in the mud – just as they had fallen in that last supreme moment. A few were terribly mangled. One had had his body from the waist upwards blown completely away, and the poor, pitiful legs were lying against the sloping parados of that unspeakable trench.

Wounded were littered everywhere, and it rent one's heart to hear them moan and rave in the delirium of their suffering, or cry aloud as someone stumbled against them in the dark. It was impossible not to do this, for many of these wretched men were almost smothered in the sucking slime that formed the bottom of the trench. Some were rapidly dying; some – alas! – had already 'gone berserk' from wounds, fatigue and exposure.

> *Still we filed along, all but sickened by the nauseating stench of decomposing human bodies, a distinctive smell which is even now in my nostrils.*
>
> *Dead Huns, too, were everywhere, the grey of their tunics assuming a weird aspect in the struggling light. The arm of one Boche was hanging by a mere thread, and the woeful expression on his face signified that not much longer would he have to endure his agonies. A tot of rum sent the blood tingling through his veins for a spell – like a flame that spurts up the chimney for a moment and then dies down for ever.*
>
> *Another was sitting in a scoop in the back wall of the trench, his legs protruding, one foot smashed to pieces, the blood showing through the bandages. Every time anyone came near, he braced himself for the kick which many had unwittingly inflicted upon him as they tripped over his sodden legs.*

Hamish and his men in D Company settled in as best they could manage for the night, but the rain accelerated to torrential proportions and conditions were atrocious, with very little shelter to be had. Worse still, those few maimed enemy soldiers with any vestige of consciousness started sniping at them in the dark. Though Hamish's writings make it clear that killing the enemy, even in self-defence, was abhorrent to him, his hard training and the prevailing conditions forced him to make a quick decision. It was either lose his own men or stop the enemy's sniping. He gave the order and the night air filled with rifle-fire as they dispatched those of the wounded Huns who had not been able to exit the trench when the Black Watch had arrived.

Hamish's account continues:

> *All these sights, and the indescribable horror of the whole scene, were accentuated as the dawn came stealing over the sky – reluctantly, as though unwillingly disclosing the terrors which the night had endeavoured to conceal.*
>
> *Before Day had shed its full light upon that ghastly scene, the men set about the grizzly task of digging half-buried men out of the trench and giving them as decent a burial as the battlefield permits. This, I think, is one of the most gruesome performances in a gruesome business. It is not pleasant to hack and plod away round a body which is not only of extraordinary weight (for dead men weigh like statues of lead), but which also exhales a smell that is overpoweringly repulsive.*

> *In the half-light, these burying parties were dimly outlined, tugging at the decomposing corpses, trying to pull them out of the earth, which appeared to consider them her rightful property. At last they were freed and heaved over the parados. A shallow hole was excavated, and the job eventually completed.*
>
> *In this and other ways was the trench rendered comparatively habitable, and the uncanny sensation of walking over a stiff corpse done away with. 'Dead men tell no tales,' people say. But they are wrong – terribly wrong. They speak to <u>me,</u> and I cannot help but listen to them. The tale they tell is too revolting to write here ... and there are those who could not understand...*

Lieutenant Colonel Abercrombie, Commanding Officer of the 8th Black Watch, wrote of the events that followed in his official report (attached to the regimental war diaries). His account demonstrates how chaotic the fighting was on the new front line and how difficult it was to find out what exactly was going on:

On the morning of the 19th, the Boches started a general counter attack by means of bombing about 5.30 a.m. On the right D Coy [Company] held its own easily, killing many Boches by rifle fire. The Boches tried to use a *Flammenwerfer* [flame-thrower] but this was knocked out before it could get into action, by a Mills bomb thrown by Private Tait.[2]

On the left, the Boches bombed out the South Africans, who retired in disorder to C Coy's trench, completely jambing it up and preventing measures being taken to block the trench or bring up bombs. The enemy bombed up the trench, inflicting very many casualties on C, and also drove in the two left platoons of A Coy up to the C.T. [Communications Trench], leading back to our support line. At this point, a rigorous counter attack by 2/Lt. Campsie and a battle section of A Coy held up the attack and drove back the enemy some 30 or 40 yards. The time was then about 6.15 a.m.

At this time Captain Taylor came up from the support line and found things more or less at a deadlock. He found C Coy was

---

2. Private Tait was a quick-thinking soldier in Hamish's platoon, who was later awarded the Military Cross for this act.

practically non-existent and had lost its Company Commander, Lt. Inglis and also 2/Lt. Anderson who had done excellent work before he was killed. Sergt. Major Findlay was wounded. In A Coy, 2/Lt. Campsie had been wounded and 2/Lt Craven killed and the Company had suffered about 40 casualties. 2/Lt. Young had formed a block to the left of the C.T. and the Boche attack was held up.

No definite news of what was going on at H.Q. and few facts of any value could be gathered from returning wounded. Capt. Taylor sent word that we still held part of our front line at about 6.30 a.m. Information was sent to O.C., 10th Argyll and Sutherland Highlanders about 8 a.m., asking for two companies to be sent down to support. One of these companies arrived; the other was cancelled.

About 7.30 a.m. 2/Lt. Campsie came down wounded and was able to give information that D and half of A Coy fronts were still held.

About 8 a.m. O.C. and 2/Lt. Ray went up to support line and located where our flank was. Capt. Taylor had organised bombing parties and in co-operation with a Stokes gun was pressing the Boche back towards the South African line. It had been raining hard for some hours and all trenches were in a terrible condition – all Lewis guns and rifles choked with mud. Vicars [Vickers] guns had failed and only one mortar was firing.

About 10 a.m. Capt. Taylor moved up part of A Coy to firing line and vigorous bomb attacks were carried out under Sergeants Murray, Barclay and McKinnon, all of whom greatly distinguished themselves.

By 12 noon, all our front line had been recaptured and bombing parties continued onwards, driving back the Boche out of the next sector. From 12 noon, no organised attacks were made against us, but our line was continually shelled, both by the Boche and our own guns. Capt. Rutherford of D Coy was unfortunately killed by our own guns.

Capt. Taylor organised the defence of firing line, moving the remainder of C Coy back to support line and B Coy to the left of our firing line. A Coy was in the centre and D Coy on the left.

Things remained fairly quiet during the afternoon, except for spasmodic shelling and bombing.

About 5 p.m., after a systematic bombardment, the South Africans re-occupied the line on our left and got into touch with B Coy.

The Battalion was relieved during the night by 12th Royal Scots under most trying conditions. Shelling was constant, and no C.T. could be used owing to the mud. Much equipment and many rifles were abandoned, as the men were barely in a condition to carry themselves, some taking 16 hours to get back to High Wood.

During the fighting, communications with Brigade were nearly impossible. A heavy barrage was on the road where Battalion H.Q. was situated and the lines were out every few minutes. There was no communication forward except by rumour.

Our casualties were:
5 Officers killed and 8 wounded.
18 men killed, 26 missing, 132 wounded, 2 wounded and at duty.

Lieut-Colonel Sir G. Abercrombie, Commander, 8th Black Watch.

Forty wounded men from this group and some officers too were retrieved and sent behind the British lines, including Second Lieutenants Campsie, wounded and Craven, killed. Both had journeyed across the sea and marched to the front with Hamish to join the battalion on the same day, just two months before. We can only imagine how that must have affected Hamish.

Thinking of the casualties he had seen among his friends and fellow men, and the bodies he had been required to clear from no man's land not long after he arrived on the Somme, Hamish wrote:

There are two ways of regarding the Nation's losses. There are the columns of closely-printed letterpress in The Times. *Words, mere words which convey nothing to the average reader. The smug business man props his paper up against the coffee-pot, rubs his podgy hands together, turns to his wife and says: 'A big casualty list today, my dear; It really is awful to think of the poor lads…' Then there is the other way – walking through the paths of desolation and despair, picking one's way among the mangled heroes of whom so many speak so glibly and with so little comprehension. I tell you, it is unspeakable, all but unthinkable!*

Now, on the morning of 20 October, relieved from front-line duty, the men of the 8th Battalion made their weary way back behind the lines, in desperate need of rest and reorganization. Hamish had to tell his men that there was no transport for them, so they would have to march back to their old bivouac on the east side of High Wood. They were cold, wet, very tired and hungry when they set off, and the mud was so thick on the ground that it was like marching through treacle. It took Hamish's men at least eight hours 'under the most trying conditions ... barely in a condition to carry themselves',[3] to march the 4 miles from the trenches to High Wood, pulling one foot after the other out of the oozing mire.

To sum up the enormity of the task and the atrocious circumstances in which the troops had to exist and in which the battle was fought, Edmunds in his *British Official History* provides the most appropriate analogy:

> Here in a wilderness of mud, holding water-logged trenches or shell-holes ... the infantry abode in conditions which might be likened to those of earthworms rather than of human kind. Our vocabulary is not adapted to describe such an existence, because it is outside experience for which words are normally required. Mud, for the men in the line, was no mere inorganic nuisance and obstacle. It took an aggressive, wolf-like guise, and like a wolf could put down and swallow the lonely wanderer in the darkness.[4]

Thanks principally to the 'much to be feared'[5] Scottish Highlanders – the Camerons and the 8th Black Watch – the attack had been a success and Hamish's battalion had been triumphant in fulfilling their orders by gaining enemy ground, holding the line and exerting full control in Snag Trench. Yet, as ever, it was an expensive victory in terms of the 191 Black Watch casualties during this one action, including 23 lives lost.

As Wauchope put it: '... success in recapturing the position speaks highly for the determination and fighting spirit of the (8th) Battalion.'[6]

---

3. General Abercrombie, report attached to the 8th Black Watch Regimental Diaries (October 1916).
4. Brigadier General Sir J. Edmunds.
5. Schofield, p.128.
6. Wauchope, p.29.

Wauchope records that Major J. Ewing MC, in his *History of the 9th Division*, added his own tribute: 'The whole of the defences were then reorganised, but the enemy did not venture again to tackle The Black Watch.'[7]

Now Hamish and his battle-weary men could at last look forward to a period of hard-earned rest and recovery. Finally, back in High Wood, sitting on a log under the stars with his notebook and pen at the ready, Hamish's thoughts turned back to the day he had first enlisted and how proud he had felt. That seemed so long ago and such an alien feeling now. With the echoes of battle still resounding in his head, he grappled with his thoughts.

His surroundings were about the worst they could be. 'High Wood' was not a misnomer: it was on a rising slope of land and there was some wood remaining but nothing green in sight. The tangled tree-trunks that remained were pockmarked with bullets and shrapnel, from both sides. The shell-holes were filled with muddy rainwater and battle debris. Used shells and weapons lay where they had been abandoned, strewn across the ground, along with the scattered bones of the bodies of men from both sides, killed in the long battles for High Wood. Finally, the allies had taken it from the Germans, but there was precious little of the woodland left, so there was hardly any cover from snooping by the enemy's reconnaissance planes and, even worse, their bombs from both the air and ground artillery.

Only eight weeks into his war service, Hamish had to acknowledge that his life, far from being precious, was dispensable on the battleground. In fact, of the eleven other subalterns (second lieutenants) who had arrived on the Somme with Hamish two months before, more than half had already become casualties of the war. Two had been killed in action and five others had been wounded and sent away from the front for treatment. That left only four plus Hamish so far unscathed, physically at least, but for how much longer?

In this poem Hamish expressed his thoughts on the fragility of life:

---

7. Wauchope, p.29.

MY LIFE

Once upon a time I thought that life was dear,
A thing to cherish and to lose the which
A tragedy appalling; but I see, through War,
  My life to me should not be great or rich.

My life is but a beauteous brittle cup
  Which may be dashed in fragments any day;
I should be pleased to hold it hour by hour
  And quaff its fruity sweetness while I may.

Just now 'tis mine! Tomorrow Death may come
  And snatch it from my fingers; well I know
That life lasts not forever – if it did
  'Twould be no prize – 'twould be a trial, I trow.

Chapter Eight

Battle Fatigue

'The division's role was to take part in a last attempt to gain ground before the winter. With German forces occupying the high ground above the Ancre river, Beaumont Hamel, a name which was to become a byword for the Highland Division's fortitude …'

(Victoria Schofield, p.113)

Hamish's High Wood bivouac, or 'bivvy' as it was called by the men, consisted of a tarpaulin stretched over a branch, if there was one, a length of wood or a pole if they were lucky, with another tarpaulin on the ground on which to sleep. With such little comfort, it was hard to sleep on the uneven ground, so they were all pleased to learn on the morning of 21 October 1916, with the temperature below freezing point and the mud turned to brown ice, that they could pack up and move to nearby Mametz Wood to the south-west, a little further back from the front, where life should be more restful.

It was indeed a great relief to return to some sort of bare comfort and a more normal life. At last, they had time to wash their socks and underwear, getting rid of any lice that nested in the seams of their vests. Here they stayed for four days, joined by two new subalterns to replace two of Hamish's joining cohort who had been killed: Campsie and Anderson. This took the pressure off Hamish to a certain extent, but many more officers and men were needed to bring the battalion up closer to full operating strength, following the loss of 200 casualties – killed in action, wounded or missing – over the past ten days.

The relentless rain continued every day, so Hamish and his platoon were relieved to move on with the 8th Battalion from Mametz Wood to the town of Albert on 25 October. Here they stayed for two nights, where they were joined by three more officers and four drafts of other ranks. The Quartermaster's Stores were constantly busy, re-equipping the men with new clothing, rifles and other items they had lost, damaged or had to leave behind on the battlefield when taking Snag Trench in the sea of mud, or on the long, arduous march through the quagmire to High Wood.

On 27 October, the battalion marched on through the drizzle to Franvillers, where they were joined by another new captain. On the morning of the 28th, the heavy rain was back again with a vengeance as they set off to march the 8 or 9 miles to Molliens-au-Bois. The heavy downpour continued all night, all the next miserable day and on to the 30th, when everyone was relieved to see the French buses that had been commandeered to drive them on the last leg of their journey to Arras.

While Hamish's 8th Battalion was resting and moving relatively peacefully from place to place, the war continued with the allies gaining ground, albeit at the expense of sustaining many more casualties, though generally losing fewer men than the Hun. The good news always got through to the troops away from the front to raise their morale, ready for their next spell in the trenches, but hopefully not too soon.

Most of the 9th Division were now billeted at the rear of Arras for rest and training, but the 8th Battalion had the good fortune to be the first to be billeted in the town itself in the Cavalry Barracks, with their HQ, officers' billets and company messes in nearby houses. This was because they were detailed to hold the line that ran close to the town and provide working parties.

Wauchope describes the conditions the 8th Black Watch found in Arras:

> At this time, Arras was unusually quiet and peaceful. Scarcely a shell was heard all day, billets were good, and after dark many shops opened, and luxuries, which the Battalion had not seen for months, could be purchased. Movement in the streets by day was forbidden, owing to the frequent visits by enemy aeroplanes. This precaution was very necessary as, although it appeared deserted, a large number of troops occupied the city – in fact, after dark the streets were nearly impassable owing to the crowd – and if the enemy had shelled Arras, casualties must have been very heavy.[1]

The troops had the best accommodation they'd experienced for months and even the rain had stopped for them! The rumour ran round that the army

---

1. Wauchope, p.31.

was planning a large-scale operation, a new battle that would start from Arras, a 'big push' to bring forward the end of the war. So the intention was to rest and retrain all the troops through the winter to bring them up to full strength and readiness for a new campaign.

This news pleased Hamish and his fellow officers. They knew that the fighting wasn't over elsewhere, with the last phase of the Somme still in progress following successes at Verdun and now pushing back the enemy at the Butte de Warlencourt and Transloy. They had also heard that there were preparations in hand for a battle at Ancre, including some Black Watch battalions, and they felt for all their compatriots still fighting at the front, but they were relieved that they and their platoons could now rebuild their numbers as well as their physical and mental wellbeing after such a hard run of duties through the previous two months, provided they could dodge the enemy's occasional daytime raids on Arras from the air.

The first thing everyone wanted to do was to stroll round this once-pleasant town (reminded by their officers that this was only officially permitted after dark), still operating a few shops and cafés and some elements of 'normality', despite the hostilities that occasionally affected them and the many battle-scarred or ruined buildings.

Hamish began a new notebook to record his experience of this place and his time there. So his first entry, on 2 November 1916, relates his first impressions of Arras and its people:

This is a city of the dead, a place of memories, a town of the past. The long, white streets resound their emptiness and – save for the drab clothes of an occasional civilian, who scurries along – khaki and the blatant blue, black and red of the French uniforms are the prominent colour notes. It must be a sad life for those few civilians to walk along the deserted pavements which once held the youth and beauty of the city, to pass through the many 'places' (squares), where once promenaded the well-to-do of the town, but where now weeds and long grasses hold sway.

Here and there one meets the Curé, the sombre black of his garments and picturesque hat standing boldly out against the white of the buildings. Everyone has a smile for him, and he a smile for all whom he meets. Old, bent widows bow gravely as he passes. The men lift their caps to him and he to them. He has a wonderful power over the people, this Curé, and he appears to be allowed a pretty free hand. It is not therefore to be wondered at that the Boche spies frequently don his flowing robes, behind which they hide the cunning hearts and treacherous souls that have made them abominated by all the clean nations of the world.

Some of the houses are completely ruined, not a single room remaining intact. Other buildings have the front wall torn away, leaving the interior in more or less perfect preservation – like huge dolls' houses. Others are pathetic sights. Beds and tables are cruelly mixed up with iron rafters, bricks and masonry. Richly papered walls are stained and bedraggled-looking with the rain which has poured through the gaping roofs, and piles of stones and dust and mangled iron lie in the middle of rooms which have once been the scene of family gatherings. This indeed is a city of memories, a garden of death!

But in the barracks, on the walls, there is the motto which inspires every Frenchman, which makes them suffer proudly and fight nobly:-

'HONNEUR ET PATRIE'

Poor France, a land of wrecked cities and devastated fields, of deserted farms and smoking ruins! La Belle France, over which has swept the self-devouring flame of war, is now in places merely a huge cemetery…. But it is worthwhile: 'Honneur et Patrie' is a noble cause. France will not forget, and Germany will be made to remember.

Hamish then goes on, the same evening, to give an ironic description of his billet:

COMPARISONS

Happiness and grief are most certainly merely matters of comparison. Everything in life is influenced in some way by comparison. I have come definitely to the conclusion, and I think that I could prove it and develop quite a philosophical theory, if I lived to take the trouble to do it.

Look at our billet here, for example. We consider ourselves to be living in the lap of luxury; but if we'd been put in a house like this during our training at home, we'd have made a fearful fuss about it. Out here, we've slept and lived in such dreadful places that our present abode seems like a palace. Let me describe it sketchily:

It is a fairly large house, but shells have made it rather too airy. Not a window retains its glass, and parts of the roof have failed signally to retard the progress of 8-inch shells. There are, of course, no carpets, except one very much frayed and worn on the staircase. Outside the room, where we feed, are the remains of a kind of verandah or conservatory, most of it lying at an angle of 45 degrees to the roof, and large pieces of glass and woodwork are continually falling to the ground. (The house adjacent is practically level with the street; several large and vulgar shells paid it a visit in August.) The curtains of this mess-room of ours have been torn off the windows to provide blankets for cold officers, lying on the floor next door, and the fireplace has suffered too badly to be able to maintain a fire! It's a good room all the same. The wallpaper is very rich, and not <u>too</u> damp!

The sitting-room (for we boast quite a suite of rooms you see!) is really and truly delightful. We keep the wind out by pulling the thick red curtain across the windows, and we close the shutters. There is a good fire in the grate, and half-a-dozen candles afford a great cheeriness. There is not only a table, but a writing desk as well. We must take care not to become soft and flabby in the midst of all this comfort!

My bedroom (or rather 'our' bedroom, for three of us sleep in it) is bare and cold. There are only two beds, one of which I won on the lucky toss of a coin. The third officer lies on the bare boards, in his valise and with a curtain to augment his blankets. (But, believe me, the floor makes quite an alluring bed, provided one's hip-bone has become accustomed to it. In any case, it's preferable to the damp ground, and all of us have slept there ere now.) We do not lack fresh air at nights, for the wind blows freely through the muslin, nailed to the empty window frames. There is a fireplace too, but we cannot procure fuel for it. (The coal we have in the sitting-room was stolen from a coal dump in the street!) But my bed has a spring mattress, and I am very snug with my flea-bag and army blankets. The walls have bulged rather with the damp, and in places the wallpaper is hanging down. But what of that? We have a bed! I have sat in the mud and gone to sleep ere now, and I have slumbered on my feet. I tell you, it is all a matter of comparison.

When I am eating bully beef and drinking ration-tea, I often recall how finicky I was at home; I sometimes smile when I think how much I would relish now the dishes I used to scorn in the good old days, in the good old country.

A strange world ... and full of comparisons.

Despite Hamish's serious illness as a teenager, which nearly barred him from joining the army, nowhere in any of his notebooks, which acted as his diaries, did he mention anything about his health. However, there was one army medical officer he clearly appreciated while at Arras: Major Jonathan Bates M.C., attached to the 8th Black Watch. Hamish recorded his admiration for him in what he described as 'Very Light Verse', shortly to be featured in *The Strafer*:

THE MEDICINE MAN

Who is it calms my frenzied brain?
Who is it soothes my every pain?
(Then quietly sends me 'up' again!)?
The Doctor!

Who is it gives us pills galore?
(The same for ailments, many a score!)?
Then for parade shows us the door?
The Doctor!

Yet who – when strafing's to be done
With mild contempt defies the Hun?
Yes, who for 'sang froid' takes the bun?
The Doctor!

In the first two weeks of November, fifteen new officers joined the 8th Battalion, together with several small drafts of other ranks. These new additions must no doubt have made a considerable difference to the capability of the battalion and to each platoon.

As well as training for the newcomers, Hamish's platoon was allotted a variety of tasks in and around Arras to keep them active and to provide work parties, but there was also a good amount of free time, giving them the chance to fully recuperate from their battle fatigue.

Having decent billets and, for the most part, dry and comparatively comfortable beds or mattresses on which to sleep, Hamish and his men were in a much happier state of mind. For him this found its expression in another 'light verse':

ROUSE PARADE

'Tis morn! As yet no lazy sun
Has risen in the east,
Yet I (poor sub!) must up and shave
At once – or soon at least.

For ere my little wristlet watch,
Beside my pillow laid
Has ticked from six to half-past six,
I'll be on Rouse Parade.

It seems so very fine in bed,
So soft and warm, that I
With loathing throw the blankets off,
And dress with many a sigh.

O Power that watches soldiers' needs,
I pray, as oft I've prayed,
That thou should'st with a pitying hand
Wash out the Rouse Parade!

Hamish always used his leisure time in his favourite way: writing in various forms. Now, based on his previous experience as joint editor of the highly-successful *Craigleith Chronicle* and its continuing contributor from the front, he came up with the idea of putting together a magazine for the 8th Black Watch. He first gave it a name – *The Strafer* – and put a proposal to his senior officers, who gladly agreed, offered their support and requested him to approach the battalion's commanding officer, Lieutenant Colonel Sir George Abercrombie Bt., for his approval. Not only did this honourable gentleman give his blessing to Hamish's undertaking, he offered to be named in the magazine as its 'Honorary Editor', thereby giving his official approval and support for all to see.

Hamish was delighted with his C.O.'s encouragement and immediately assembled a strong editorial committee, which comprised the following:

Editor	2nd Lieutenant A. James Mann (Hamish)
Art Editor	2nd Lieutenant W.Z. Gawne
HQ Representative	Captain Milligan (Chaplain)
A Coy (Company) Representative	Sergeant Irwin
B Coy Representative	Sergeant Stewart
C Coy Representative	Sergeant Collins
D Coy Representative	Company Sergeant-Major Mitchell

Hamish made an excellent and very detailed sketch of what he wanted the cover to look like and he made a list of his suggested contents for each issue, which he appears to have copied and circulated to all those on the editorial committee:

Regular Features in *THE STRAFER*

1) Editorial
2) Company Notes
3) Battalion News
4) Football
5) Things we Want to Know
6) Very Light Verse
7) Trenchosities (Jokes etc.)
8) Particular Pa'rs (Official notes, etc.)

Now Hamish set about writing his editorial for the first issue of *The Strafer*:

Herewith 'THE STRAFER' Volume One, Number One! We offer it to you for what it is worth. There are two things essential for the running of a magazine, namely:

1. Readers
2. Contributors

Assuming sufficient numbers of the first, we do not fear, and we hope that the talented members of the Battalion will come to the fore and keep us well supplied with material, both literary and artistic. On page (x) will be found the names of the Editorial Committee, whose services have been secured at 'enormous expense'!

The various Company Representatives will contact the artists, etc., from their companies, after which they will be handed over to the Editor, in his extravagantly furnished office (!). Poets need not fear physical disablement at the hands of any of the magazine staff (who, by the way, will <u>not</u> wear red tabs), but the unauthorised sergeant-majors will not allow them to wear long hair on account of the fact that their lyric effusions have graced our pages! This also applies to artists, from whom we anticipate a large measure of support.

We expect each member of the Battalion to buy at least one copy, but we do not take any exception to kind people who purchase two or three dozen. We are not authorised, however, to award such persons the D.C.M. (Distinguished Conduct Medal) – meaning thereby District Court Martial.

The Editor must at no time be suddenly disturbed. The Gentle Boches are therefore requested not to land trench mortars or 12-inchers in the neighbourhood of his dug-out. Disappointed readers too – if any – are forbidden to throw bombs, with intent to do bodily harm to him.

Contributions to the 'Things we Want to Know' page need not be signed, but queries such as 'What is Leave?' are liable to rejection by the Censor.

Scientific and diagrammatic treatises on the War are not required, as these are freely contributed to The Daily Press *by such humanists as 'Hilarious Bullock' and his confrères, to whom a need of praise is due for their efforts in helping to amuse the troops in the field.*

We are excessively proud to secure an article from the Clown Prince. This article will, we are led to believe, be entitled 'LOOTING THE LOOT' or 'HOW TO BE HAPPY AT WAR'.

Here's to you, and to our Second Number – and Cheer-O!

In addition to commissioning items from others who offered their writing services, Hamish wrote some pieces of his own to use if there should be a shortage of material in this first edition of *The Strafer*. One of these was the 'very light verse' entitled 'The Medicine Man' (see earlier in this chapter). Another was a tongue-in-cheek offering:

ANTICIPATED PUBLICATIONS

We have received word from the Underworld Printing Co., that the following volumes will shortly be ready, an order having been issued from Potsdam that all Germans must buy copies, under pain of immediate extinction.

Moustache-Growing for Amateurs	*by the Clown Prince: illustrated microscopically*
Calais, the Brighton of France	*by H.M. (His Muchness) Willie Twoth: illustrated with quite imaginary photographs and printed on asbestos paper*
On the Care of Babies	*by Skull-Crack Tirpitz: illustrating the effect of submersion on infants. With an irrelevant introduction by Bill II, entitled 'Myself and all about Me'*
Musical Instruments	*by the German Official Press Gang; with special chapters on 'The Lyre' and 'How to Blow your own Trumpet'*

Destruction by Fire or Chaos in the Cathedral A wholly fictitious novel, by Von Hinderbug.

Sadly, Hamish did not leave behind a printed copy of this first edition of *The Strafer* among the collection of his writings and artefacts. Despite an extensive search, it has not been possible to track down a copy of the magazine itself in any of the relevant archives. However, a 'wrapper' has been located. This is a paper wrapper which held a copy of the magazine, sent to an address in Ireland, bearing a British Forces postmark for November 1916 and printed on it *The Strafer*, together with the words 'Somewhere in France'. This appears to confirm that Hamish's magazine was indeed printed and circulated.[2]

---

2. There was, unbeknown to Hamish, another magazine called *The Strafer* published by troops in another regiment, but this was earlier in the war and in Belgium, so not to be confused with Hamish's November 1916 publication in France.

One happy outcome of Hamish's commissioning of articles for the first issue of *The Strafer* was when he wrote to his former commanding officer at Dunfermline Officers' Instruction School, to ask him to contribute something of his own. Hamish didn't receive the reply he hoped for, but some very cheering news nonetheless:

Dear Mann,

Many thanks for your letter of the 3rd ulto, which I was glad to get. I am very glad to hear that you are going strong yourself. I am sure it would be of great benefit to the Regiment to inaugurate a Regimental magazine and nothing would give me greater pleasure than to be able to write some kind of article which would be of interest, but I am afraid that is not in my line! The next best thing I can send you is the history of the Black Watch Gong ... which I send with kind remembrance to all ranks in the Battalion who may remember me, and an earnest hope that the best of fortune may accompany each and all.

We are carrying on here in much the same way as when you left ... I was very grieved to hear of the deaths of Anderson, Craven and Balkwill. They are a great loss to the Empire and to the 8th Battalion...

I see a dog moving about the camp, which is reported to have been your property at one time – a rough-haired Airedale Terrier, which, if it is the same dog, you will be glad to hear is looking well and is being looked after by Goalen.

Hoping the best of good fortune will go with you and return with you.

John MacRae-Gilstrap,
Lieut.-Colonel, Commanding 38th Battn. Training Reserve

So the Dunfermline mutt was still going strong and well looked after, by the sound of it, much to Hamish's delight.

Between organizing his men on various work parties in and around Arras, clearing the streets, distributing supplies, maintaining the railway, repairing roads and shoring up front-line and service trenches, Hamish made good use of his opportunities for rest and creativity. Yet, although refreshed, he also had more time to think, to contemplate the ghastly experiences of the past three months since he arrived at the Somme, the changes in his life and what challenges may lie ahead.

Mid-November had marked the end of the Battle of the Somme, and by December the casualty rates were known to have been the highest ever recorded in the history of any battle involving the British. Indeed, the British army alone had lost 432,000 men (killed, wounded or missing, which usually meant killed but their bodies never found). This total averaged 3,600 casualties for every day.

Although Hamish may not have been informed of these totals, he had seen the numbers blown up or shot and killed in front of his eyes, including soldiers from his own platoon, and he could not rid his mind of the memories of all those 'ghastly corpses' he and his men had found and re-buried, so he knew the death toll was extremely high. Neither could he fail to remember passing the streams of seriously wounded men being stretchered back from no man's land. Still haunted by those terrible images, both waking and in his dreams, Hamish scribbled a few words, late one night:

> *'My soul is full of wondering – I think that all I have yet to learn is this:-*
> *FORGET!'*

Yet, no matter how hard he tried, he could not help wondering when would be his turn? Would he ever see his home and loved ones again?

Chapter Nine

Shot at Dawn

'An inspection of the trenches showed that while they were fairly well built and dry, there was little cover, and dug-outs were scanty.'

(Wauchope, p.32)

After their three weeks at Arras, away from the active battlegrounds and now back to more or less full strength of numbers, rumours started circulating that the troops were about to start on a new phase of the war. The date of 18 November 1916 is remembered for two things: the torrents of rain, and the end of the Battle of the Somme. The fierce fighting at the Ancre, the final operation of the Somme, ended this day with British advances on two fronts, which they held.

From now on, the weather worsened and the winter of 1916–1917 gradually became the fiercest in France's living memory. Indeed, it was clear already that it would be too bad for either side to make any major progress in the fight for France's ravaged countryside, so the whole battalion would go into training for a new campaign: a full-scale operation, being planned for early the following year.

Orders came through to Hamish and his fellow officers that the whole of the 8th Battalion must pack up and march on 20 November to Izel-lès-Hameaux, about 12 miles west of Arras. In fact, en route, cold and wet, they were delighted by the very welcome sight of a line of French buses, which stopped to take them on board for the rest of their journey. At Izel-lès-Hameaux they would undergo ten days' training, with a short spell taking their turn on the front line.

The regimental diary has just one brief entry for 21 November 1916: 'commenced training'. There is no official record for the rest of the month, but we know from Hamish's notebook that his creative talents continued to give him an emotional outlet and brighten his life. As with *The Strafer*, he was always on the lookout for ways to raise his men's morale as well. One of these was to write light-hearted skits on the peculiarities of army life and encourage members of his platoon to join him in 'acting' them out for their own and the others' amusement.

Here is an example of Hamish's shorter skits, based in a training camp back in Blighty, featuring one of his invented characters; a true recalcitrant who gets himself into (and out of) one scrape after another:

PRIVATE CRUMPLETHORNE AT ORDERLY ROOM

'Quick march! Right wheel! Halt! Left turn! Private Crumplethorne, Sir.' Thus it was that the Company Sergeant-Major ushered 8888 Private Christopher Crumplethorne into the awful presence of Captain Gorren, O.C., 'B Company'.

Christopher felt very foolish as he stood there with his cap off ... and he also felt just a little afraid, although he would not have admitted it, even to himself. His fingers jerked as they clutched the seam of his trousers and his eyebrows twitched.

'Stand still and don't fidget!' ordered the Sergeant-Major.

'Private Crumplethorne, you are charged with being absent without leave from 7.30 a.m. on the 9th inst., until 9 p.m. on the 12th inst.' said the Captain sternly, turning to the witness present. 'Sergeant Frost.'

'Sir,' began the gentleman, called up to give his evidence: 'I called the roll of number 5 platoon on the half-past seven parade, on the 9th inst., when Private Crumplethorne was reported absent. He was likewise absent from every parade until the tattoo on the 12th.'

'What have you got to say, Crumplethorne?' asked Captain Gorren.

'A lot of things, Sir, but you wouldn't like to hear me say them!'

'I wish to hear anything you may care to say which has a bearing on the present case,' continued O.C. 'B'. 'Were you or were you not absent during the times stated?'

'I was, Sir.'

'Why?'

'Well Sir, I got a wire from home to say my mother was ill and I wanted to see her.'

'Why didn't you ask for leave in the usual way?'

'I didn't think I'd get it, Sir.'

'So you decided to take it?'

> *'Yes, Sir.'*
>
> *'Your memory must be decaying, I'm afraid. Four months ago I gave you four days' leave to attend your mother's funeral. Do you remember that?'*
>
> *'Yes, Sir, but a week later my father married again!'*
>
> *Captain Gorren couldn't restrain a smile, for this reply, delivered on the spur of the moment, was rather an ingenious one.*
>
> *'Crumplethorne,' he said firmly. 'Do you expect me to believe this story?'*
>
> *'No, Sir.'*
>
> *'Then why waste my time with it?'*
>
> *8888 Private Christopher Crumplethorne looked sheepish. There was obviously no reply to the question.*
>
> *'I'm getting tired of having you before me,' went on Captain Gorren. 'And the next time, you will appear before the C.O. You forfeit four days' pay under Royal Warrant. You are deprived of three days, and you'll do seven days' "C.B".'*
>
> *'Left turn, quick march!' bellowed the Sergeant-Major, and Crumplethorne made his exit.*
>
> *'A tough nut, that,' remarked Gorren, turning to me.*
>
> *'Yes, Sir,' I replied.*

During all these months since he arrived at the Somme, Hamish had continued to write articles, poems and other pieces for publication in the *Craigleith Chronicle* as a regular feature under the title of 'War Cameos', as well as for the *Edinburgh Evening News*. These varied greatly, but were often based on real incidents that occurred in Hamish's life on the front, thus giving the folks back home a flavour, in a light-hearted way, of what life was really like when he and his men took their turn to hold the line.

The following are two examples, which Hamish also used to act out as skits with his platoon:

WAR CAMEO I

There was a rustling sound just over the parapet. I snatched my revolver from its holster and crouched low in the trench. A bright 'Very'* light rose, hissing into the crisp air.... A shell went tearing overhead. The sentry, two bags

---

* A Very light was created by a flare gun, named after its American inventor, Edward Wilson Very.

away, gazed wearily into the gloom of the barren lands in front of him....
My Sergeant and I waited expectantly and the furtive rustling continued.

'Fire as soon as you see him,' whispered Sergeant Painter.

'Right,' I muttered. I started violently as the sentry fired: my nerves were tense and the atmosphere laden with possibilities.

A machine gun began to bark away on the right. A sniper's bullet sang in its flight. Still the rustling went on...

Presently I saw something move on the top of the parapet. It was unmistakable. I knew the moment had come.

'Now!' muttered the sergeant anxiously.

Crack!

There was a thud on the duckboards.... My Webley smoked in my hand – it had done its work.

'That's one of the devils accounted for anyway,' I remarked, as I picked up the dead rat and threw it into No Man's Land.

WAR CAMEO II

A shell landed five yards in front of the parapet. The trench trembled with concussion.

'Fritz trying to be funny!' said Henderson.

'Damned funny, isn't it?' grunted Mac, as he picked himself up and knocked the mud off his kilt. 'Snookie' (who had arrived with the last draft) threw himself down the nearest dug-out and, coming into violent contact with Captain Ferguson, was told a few home truths about himself...

'Landing near?' needlessly asked the Captain, as he emerged from his retreat.

'Oh, a bit local sir, a bit local,' replied Henderson easily.

'Very, sir,' added Mac.

'By Jove! They are getting it in the neck on the right,' said Second Lieutenant Macbeth, who was on duty on the extreme left of the company front.

A trench mortar came to earth just over the parados behind him. Suddenly, Second Lieutenant Macbeth stopped smiling and hastened to make arrangements about getting the men under cover.

A Hun rifle grenade exploded in the fire-bay he had just vacated. Macbeth hastened his pace ever so slightly.

Later:
'The Boche was strafing a bit today, Ferguson, wasn't he?' asked the Colonel.
'Just a little, sir. A few shells and one or two mortars and grenades.'
'No one hurt?'
'Oh no, sir.'

Later still, thus wrote 'freshman' Snookie to his mother:
'Dear Mother, There was a fearful bombardment the day. I wunner we wern't a killed. The air was black wi' shells and the Germuns were sniping at us wi' huge boms...'

[NB: Second Lieutenant Macbeth (no doubt Hamish by another name) was the platoon's censor of letters.]

It had been several weeks now since Hamish and his platoon had been involved in front-line warfare and they had no doubt had enough time to think and take stock. While the skits and general camaraderie would have given them all some light-hearted entertainment, they all knew that it couldn't last. Sure enough, Hamish received orders that he would have to lead his men back into the trenches on 4 December, only four days away. Within hours, he picked up a pencil and scrawled very lightly in his notebook:

IZEL-LÈS-HAMEAUX – 1/12/16

This has been a sad night for me. We are going into the trenches again on the 4th, and somehow or other all the old sights and memories have returned. I realise now that my nerves have not been improved by our sojourn on the Somme. This did not strike me when we were actually in the trenches, or at Mametz Wood. But now that we are in rest, I find that certain things affect me in a way they never used to do. Doubtless all this will vanish when we are actually in the line again. I hope to God it may be so.

Shall I never forget the face of that dead German, sticking up through the mud? Or the corpse with the skinny white hands as it lay face-down in the

> *trench? Will the sickening stench of decaying human bodies never leave my nostrils? Will the mounting sense of doom follow me until the hand of Death at last closes over me?*
>
> *But I fancy the most horrible of all is the mockery of these remembrances of days gone by, that seethe into my very brain in the midst of all this frightful carnage and horror.*

The thought of going back into the trenches after a considerable time away from the horror, danger and stress was clearly hard for Hamish to bear. Second lieutenants were often the ones who suffered from this kind of anxiety and depression. It is no wonder when they were the ones who led the way when there was an attack, who may have had to make spur-of-the-moment decisions that could be detrimental to the men in their platoon, as well as themselves. It was a condition that Second Lieutenant Hubert Clement described in his memoir as 'front line tension'. He goes on to say:

> One has to be prepared for any emergency at all times by day and more especially by night, and the average subaltern cannot help feeling rather weighted down by the thought that the lives of his platoon may be entirely dependent on his presence of mind.

On 2 December 1916, the 8th Battalion of the Black Watch prepared, as part of the 9th Division, to take over the line in front of Arras. The 26th Brigade was detailed to hold the right-hand sector of the line. An inspection of the trenches by the commanding officers showed that 'while they were fairly well-built and dry, there was little cover, and dug-outs were scanty.'[3] The line had apparently been quite quiet in recent days 'except for two spots – one on the right, where a heavy German trench mortar was in position...'[4] This was where Hamish's platoon would be. When the news reached him later that afternoon, he began to worry about his men, including several new members who had only recently joined them. The plan was that they would all march to Wanquetin the next day and take over the front line in the evening, where they would stay for six days.

---

3. Wauchope, p.32.
4. Ibid.

Just as Hamish was digesting this with a heavy heart and discussing it with his NCOs, a further message came through, addressed to him. It was a nasty shock. The timing was terrible. He felt he needed to be with his platoon and bolster their morale but no, apparently he was needed elsewhere. His frustration is evident in the short note he writes in his notebook that evening:

> *2/12/16: As Second-in-Command of the Company I am being left with the transport operations. I asked to be allowed to go with my platoon to the trenches, but was refused. I don't like the idea of Second Lieutenant G—— having my platoon in the trenches.*

Had somebody arranged this deliberately, to keep Hamish out of the line? He was not given any reason, but he was at least allowed to march the next day with his men to Wanquetin before they parted company. He continued his tale:

> *3/12/16: Wanquetin. Spent the night here with the men. Then the Battalion went via Arras in buses to the line, while I went the short ride to Agnez-lès-Duisans, to the Transport.*

Agnez-lès-Duisans was a small village to the west of Arras, sparsely inhabited now and more or less taken over by a large army Casualty Clearing Station (CCS); similar in some ways to a general hospital in that it was large and covered all medical needs. It had several dressings rooms and operating theatres, in huts and under canvas, with its own piped hot and cold water supply.

Hamish's work at Agnez-lès-Duisans was principally twofold. The first main task was to help organize the ambulances, either to collect the wounded from the surrounding area and bring them to the CCS, or transferring patients to military hospitals in unoccupied parts of France or, as was often the case with the worst injuries, all the way back to Britain, possibly even to Craigleith Military Hospital.

Hamish's second and even more complex job was to supervise all the motor transports, mules and wagons, bringing supplies for the wards, the kitchens and the operating theatres, as well as the postbags of mail for the hospital and the troops. Everything had to be transported safely, often under the cover of darkness, to reach the CCS as quickly as possible. Another aspect of this was to ensure regular medical supplies were sent out to the dressing stations within the front and relief lines and at other strategic points in the field. Such work was demanding and could involve long hours.

Hamish knew that every second lieutenant had to take a turn in this role, partly to provide the educated personnel, but also, and sometimes more importantly, to give the junior officers some time away from the stresses and cares of leadership on the front line. However, he must have wondered: did somebody suspect how reluctant he had felt to return to the trenches?

It seems that Hamish certainly was kept busy from the moment he arrived as, most unusually for him, he wrote nothing between the 3rd, the day before he arrived, to the 6th, when he must have had some free time at last, as he set to and made various entries in his notebook. The first extract, written in his billet at the Catholic Schoolhouse, shows his thoughts were first and foremost with his 'boys':

FRONT LINE TRANSPORT

The Catholic Schoolhouse
Thoughts During a Tour 'Out'

Last night, in the pale coldness of the moonshine, I stood in the garden beside the statue of Christ and listened to the booming of the guns and the barking of the machine guns 'up the line', where The Boys are. Many thoughts come to me, mainly one of forced selfishness. I imagined my men on the firestep, staring with straining eyes into that gloomy desert I know so well – No-Man's-Land. I heard the <u>phut!</u> of occasional rifle shots as they buried themselves in the parapet, and the high-pitched song of the Lewis bullets as they sped overhead. The sizz of the Very lights and the fearful explosions of the shells and mortars came to me – the numbing cold, and all the weary routine of Trench life.

Mayhap it is a mistake to ponder too much over such things…. Then I climbed the crazy stairs, from whose walls hung remnants of ugly paper and rotting wainscot…. Ere long I was snugly asleep in my bed.

The ups and downs of army life are amazing. On the night of the 4th (when we arrived here) we slept on the floor in a filthy loft, the wind swirling through it, and rats gnawing and scampering all round. Our slumber was intermittent, for every little while we wakened, frozen and cramped.

Last night I slept in a house usually occupied by a General and his Staff! T--- bagged the G.O.C.'s room, whilst I found the Brigade Adjutant's apartment in every way suited for a night's rest. But do not be deceived: we are not living in a palace – oh no! It's merely the home of the Catholic School, where even yet the children are being taught; the unmusical sounds of the repetition lessons being an unenviable feature!

The General's room is not at all luxurious. There's no carpet, and I fancy the walls are decidedly damp. You see, even General Officers must put up with comparative discomfort out here, just like the rest of us – though in a lesser degree. I think I should like to be a Brigadier, but I fear my command would not last long!

Hamish's writings of 6 December continued, now with more sombre thoughts:

I hope my leave comes soon. Somehow or other I don't think of anything after those ten days of Paradise. All is a blank into which I dare not try to probe. So many things might occur – and there is ever the possibility (I don't say probability) of the Great Incident ... I may be alive today and dead tomorrow; hale this morning and gashed and disfigured for life by nightfall. Heigh-ho! It's a Great Adventure!

Next, still on 6 December, Hamish's thoughts now turned to a lighter subject: his batman, or officer's servant (O.S.):

O.S.

Thompson, my batman, is a curious little fellow. Enlisting at the age of 17 from the Dundee mill where he worked, he has ever since been a source of cheer and inspiration to older and stronger men in the platoon. When on a long route-march in full marching order along the dusty roads of France in the height of summer, many powerful men have been on the point of falling out exhausted by the roadside, but one glance at Thompson, plodding steadily onwards has been enough for them and they have stuck it to the end.

He is one of those brave boys who make me feel unworthy to be their leader; one of those to whom death is but a snap of the fingers, one of those who are going to win the war for us. This all seems very 'nice', but I have seen and I <u>know</u>.

He is small and, since the Somme, his hearing is not what it once was, for the guns have to a degree been too much for his ears. But he is extraordinarily obliging and my every need is attended to. Invariably, I send him out to purchase all sorts of articles for me from the French shops, and immediately he returns with the right things. How he manages to make himself understood, with his limited vocabulary is a mystery to me. But the fact remains that he does. I admit that I do not have sufficient courage to enter a crowded shop and actually to carry out shopping. I feel foolish when the French women suddenly burst forth into long, rhetorical speeches, accompanied by violent gestures. I flee in confusion – never to return. I am a coward I fancy! I take the line of least resistance and send my servant who, poor lad, knows much less of the language than I do. But he is successful: I am not.

He speaks of me as 'my officer' and once he told me that I possessed certain things <u>'when he took me over'</u>! At once I felt that I was as a child in his charge, and that he knew how helpless I should be without him. I never know where my things are, but he does. He can find anything I want at a moment's notice. He knows how many pairs of clean sox I have, whether any shirts require washing, which collars go with which shirts, and so on. How <u>can</u> he?

He was a mill-worker before the war, and never had to look after anyone like me. Yet he carries out his multifarious duties to perfection – altho' when he is 'resting', he does not serve my morning cup of tea as daintily as he might do. How can I expect him to? He is not a waiter, and in any case it is indolently luxurious of me to have tea in bed at all. He should tell me so!

There are servants who steal and servants who are deceitful. Thompson is neither. I would trust him with all my money (not much, alas!), and I would send him with the most important and urgent messages. He is – well, I can but say he is 'little Thompson'. (If you knew him, you would understand!)

The penultimate entry in Hamish's notebook for 6 December 1916 perhaps explains his apparent need to pour out his thoughts of other things on this day; unforgettable for one terrible event, one that affected everyone very deeply. The whole military presence was ordered to turn out that dawn to be witnesses to the fate of this young officer, convicted by court martial for desertion, though possibly only hiding in the woods nearby. It was done as a warning, as explained in the book *Shot at Dawn* by Putkowski and Sykes (pp.11 and 16):

> The rationale generally assumed to lie behind the army's use of capital punishment related to the deterrent effect that the victims' fate had on their fellow soldiers. The dictum '*pour encourager les autres*', that theoretically rationalised this practice ... merits critical evaluation.
>
> The court martial panels that sentenced deserters to death often seemed to have little consideration for the predicament of the offender. ... Assuming that death sentences were imposed by officers overwhelmingly drawn from the upper classes on soldiers who were predominantly of working-class origin, the taint of class justice which accompanied the Edwardian civil magistracy cannot have been absent from courts martial.

Captain R.E. Badenoch, a fellow Black Watch officer, described the scene:

> The whole company was paraded at dawn to watch. The firing party was chosen, consisting of men from his brigade. There were so many live rounds and so many blanks, the idea being that no-one knew who had shot the man. That may be all right in theory, but not in practice, because as soon as the rifles are fired, the soldier knows by the kick of the rifle whether it was 'live' or a blank. The officer in charge was the man's platoon officer; in this case a farmer in civilian life, and if the job is muffed, it is his responsibility to go forward and finish the job with his revolver.

Hamish penned his personal response:

The sentence was duly carried out at 5.35 a.m. ...
And so he passes, in all the shameful ignominy of a disgraceful death. Fool!
You who might have done glorious things, have made your name magnificent
throughout the land. Fool! You who might have made your country's fame
sweet and pure and noble; you who might have died, if needs be, in all the
splendid sacrifice of duty!
   Instead – a firing party, a pale-faced officer, and ... oblivion!

It is noticeable that this is the only occasion on which Hamish wrote the
word 'death' with a lower-case 'd'. Elsewhere he always used the capital
letter for death, as if it were a person, which it often is in his poetry.

Hamish seems to have taken a particularly harsh stance on this matter,
commenting as a grandiose poet, rather than as the humane and sensitive
man he was with his 'boys'. Perhaps there is a sense of fear, or an effort to
distance himself and his own (or any man's) potential weaknesses, in his
uncharacteristically rigid attitude. He made it very clear in many of his
writings that he shunned any rigidity of thinking in others, and in himself.
He must have been only too well aware that any man, even an officer, could
be so affected by the horrors and dangers of the battlefield that he could
momentarily forget all his training and act on instinct, to escape, any way
he could.

With the great benefit of time and a long life's experience, Captain
Badenoch of the Black Watch, writing down his 'recollections' in 1978,
sixty-two years after the event, made the comment:

> I can't help but think what a transformation there has been in our
> attitudes. Today the most premeditated, cold-blooded murder can
> be perpetrated in the knowledge that there is no death sentence for
> the murderer, and yet, in 1916, some poor soldier who possibly lost
> his nerve for a short time and ran the wrong way could be shot for
> desertion.

Having written out his indignation, Hamish's attitude appears to have
softened, as later that day, on its own in the middle of the following page, he
wrote out this quote from a John Oxenham poem:

Midway between the flaming lines he lay,
A tumbled heap of blood, and sweat, and clay;
God's son![5]

Hamish's final entry for 6 December 1916 in Agnez-lès-Duisans, knowing that he would soon return to the front line, was a short poem of his own:

A WISH

*I wish that I
Could know that I may die –
 Yet quiver not!*

*Would that to me
My life less dear could be –
 Too sweet I wot.*

*I wish that Death
 Could take my latest breath –
 And I not care.*

*My job is just
To fight, to live, to trust –
 Could I but dare!*

---

5. J. Oxenham, *White Brother*.

Chapter Ten

Christmas 1916

'The line was now becoming far from peaceful.'
(Wauchope, p.32)

On 9 December, Hamish had orders to reunite the next day with his platoon. His last entry written in the Catholic Schoolhouse at Agnez-lès-Duisans was short:

> ### *PRAYER*
>
> *When the time comes and all this wasty flesh*
> *Becomes a nobler dust, a worthier clay,*
> *When Fire and all the implements of Hell*
> *Shall free my frenzied Soul from Earthly sway,*
> *Grant that my Passing justify my Life.*
> *May I have Rest after that hour of strife!*

The following day, 10 December 2016, Hamish rejoined his platoon as 'the boys', fortunately unscathed, were coming back from the front line and they all returned to Arras together for new service billets. Here they were to rest in-between working party tasks. Hamish and his platoon were happy to be as one again.

As part of their training during this second week of December, Hamish gave 'lectures' to his and other platoons on various soldierly topics. He must have particularly liked what he said about 'Honour' and 'Patriotism' because he carefully, and more legibly than usual, wrote out extracts from these talks in his notebook to keep (and perhaps refer to, as encouragement to himself as well as his men?):

HONOUR

Without honour, man is no more than a beast. A soldier may lose everything, including his life, but he may not lose his honour. Honour means loyalty, not only to his King and Country, but to his Officers and Comrades. It means truthfulness, faithfulness, thankfulness and manliness – speak like a man, live like a man and act like a man, and even if you fail, you will fail grandly. A grand failure is infinitely better than a petty success. A mean, petty man reminds one of a slug – you hardly like treading on him.

PATRIOTISM

What is Patriotism? It is the spirit of the nation. It is one of the grandest forces on earth. Think of ninety thousand Boers fighting the whole British Empire – a quarter of the globe, for two and a half years: here is fine patriotism, a true fighting spirit … doing everything, rather than submit to a tyrant. Then think that the Boers are now shoulder to shoulder, fighting with us, their deadly enemies of only a few years ago. This is one of the most wonderful features of this war; truly there must be something great in the spirit of the British race to have accomplished this. Are we now going to permit this spirit to be trampled upon by the assassins of Louvain?

Take a map of the British Empire and look at it. Up in a corner between the Atlantic and the North Sea, you will see a little triangle of land – that is England; and then you may wonder how that little triangle spread all over the globe. It spread through the heroism of our forefathers. Put a pin into any part of the splashes of red and there, I tell you, did a man work, fight and die for you. It was grit that gave us an empire and it is this grit alone that will keep it.

Think of Sir Richard Grenville who, with six small ships of the line, found and fought 53 Spanish galleons. Remember the fine words of Lord Tennyson: *

'Sink me the ship, Master Gunner – sink her, split her in twain!
Fall into the hands of God, not into the hands of Spain!'

---

* Alfred Lord Tennyson, *The Revenge*, verse 11.

Think of these words if you are ever called upon to surrender by the sinkers of the Lusitania. *This is Moral. This is more than Moral, for it is a supreme faith in the destiny of our race. Here in France, we see that in the spirit of Joan of Arc, leading her battalions against tyranny.*

Giving these pep-talks appears to have encouraged Hamish himself, who made no further mention of his nerves before being called upon to lead his men back to the front line just two or three days later.

On 16 December, the 8th Battalion was ordered to take over the front line in 'I' sector, near Wanquetin. The line was now so long it was difficult to hold all of it at one time, so changes had to be made. Three companies – B, C and D, the latter of which included Hamish and 14 Platoon – constructed a series of strongpoints, of which he made a number of detailed plans showing their defences, and held these to man the front-line trenches. Meanwhile A Company provided support (and construction materials) from behind. As Wauchope relates:

> The line was now becoming far from peaceful. As the Somme battle was now at an end, a great many batteries had been sent north to Arras in preparation for the coming offensive, and their constant activity naturally drew retaliation from the enemy. On the 19th, Lieutenant R. O'Dell was seriously wounded by a trench mortar bomb and died the following day.

As a second lieutenant, O'Dell had been another of Hamish's ill-fated companions on their journey from Richmond Camp to the Somme just four months earlier, so this must have been a terrible blow to Hamish, to be one of only the few remaining. Of the original twelve subalterns, only four, including him, had so far been relatively unscathed. Three were dead, four had been too badly wounded to return and just one had been wounded, recovered and rejoined. Every day counted and Hamish wanted to relish them all, but he was weary and downcast.

As he sat in his dugout on the last day of this tour of duty, writing by the light of his 'guttering candle', his thoughts turned anew to home. He had applied for leave more than a month ago now, but still no news. He knew there were several others in the queue and he had to be patient, but he didn't feel like it. Christmas was approaching and he would have loved to be home for that, but recently, talking to others when they had returned from their leave, he learned there was the aftermath when they came back that, for some, could be just as dispiriting an outcome, or worse, than not going home at all:

LEAVE

Last night, W returned from leave. He did not look happy as he stumbled into the dug-out. I fancy he was full of memories and comparisons, for often I caught him watching the big blue-bottle on the ceiling, gazing raptly but with unseeing eyes. That is the cruel part of leave, the coming back ... and W says she [his wife] burst into tears... 'Paradise Lost!' he muttered, with a wan smile, and I know that he was right. Ten days of incomparable bliss ... and then a return to life in Trenches: the guns, the shells, the blood, the Very lights, the monotonous despair! I have heard of men who refuse to accept leave, unable to stand the dulling monotone of that return journey across the channel.

The Doc says that last time he swore he would never go on leave again. That was some months ago; now he is endeavouring to arrange matters so that he'll get away at the end of December, instead of the beginning of January!

The Padre has just been in. He chaffed W first, as we all do, but I understood how he must feel. Everyone in Blighty is talking about the war, W says. But he was horribly bored because he wanted to forget about the war. So do I. I want to forget it forever and ever. I know one way in which this may happen, but I don't allow my imagination to dwell too long on it. Meditation of that kind does not tend to improve one's nerve.

Nerve is a great thing, but lack of it is even greater. Imagination is a powerful stimulus to one in Peace-times, but it will be the damnation of me out here. Will-power? No will-power on earth could curb my imagination. I am glad of this, for imagination is a splendid attribute, but it 'does you down' sometimes, in the long, eerie, lonesome watches, underneath the stars, when the dead bodies speak and Those of The Past hurl themselves upon Us of the Present, when the 'vision' of a myriad sobbing women mingles with the remembrance of a myriad putrefying, chaotic remnants of human beings – the lads in khaki. Alas!

On the night of 19 December, their fourth night in the trenches, Hamish seems to have felt a little stronger again. It was his turn to stay awake as he was on patrol duty. He wrote:

PATROL

At four in the morning I went out on patrol, and I had as a password 'Bernard Shaw'. It was strange when, on the return journey, I ran into my own sap.*

'Who are you?' whispered the sentry.

'Bernard Shaw,' I answered, equally softly. He didn't turn a hair and so we each passed on our way.

A little later I met a rookie soldier, just sent out on sentry duty, still rubbing the sleep from his eyes. When he saw me, he asked who I was.

'Bernard Shaw.'

'Bernard Shaw? Oh Hell!'

One has strange thoughts by night in No–Man's–Land. Every grass speaks of danger, every shell-hole contains – in one's imagination – Boches laden with bombs and rifles. Every footstep and every wire that clangs seems loud enough to waken the dead. It all appears to be so lonely and so forbidding ... then a 'Very' light rises, hissing and spluttering into the sky, making everything throw great shadows. We remain absolutely rigid until all is black once more ... and then it's on again!

Once as we lay on our bellies in the grass, a trench mortar burst to our right. Fragments came whirring through the air... Jamming my tin helmet well on my head, I waited expectantly for a 'Blighty'.** It didn't come!

Life is often disappointing in the army!

---

*   A 'sap' was a temporary trench, jutting forward from the line into no man's land, sometimes covered to conceal raiding parties or assault troops.

** A 'Blighty' was a wound, bad enough to require recuperation far from the trenches, back in Britain.

Life, or rather his thoughts about the tenuous nature of this life, seemed to swing from one extreme to another for Hamish, from one day to the next. So it was on 20 December, writing in very poor light with a blunt pencil on some torn pieces of paper, that he scribbled his thoughts:

We are railing each other at a distance here, mainly through the agency of trench mortars, sticks, Stokes and various kinds of Grenades. P was seriously wounded a day or two ago. He was watching the 'torpedoes' coming, and as one seemed to be nearer than the rest, he said to his Sergeant: 'That's a near one, isn't it Sergeant?'

It turned out to be nearer than he thought, for it struck the parados behind him, a fragment penetrating right into his brain. The M.O. (Medical Officer) said his chances were about even ... but he died today.

They say that familiarity breeds contempt, and I think this is true of Death. Any moment of the day <u>may</u> be our last. Death is always possible, often probable and at times inevitable. I had thought I could come out of the Somme alive... My last day had come, methought. So I merely waited for the End. Life is very dear, but, under certain influences, one's resolve wanes. I did not long for Death. I cheated it, and yet I'm afraid that I might as well resign myself to the Doom that is near, just biding its time. We value life far too highly, partly for too much hope and interest in the Future. Surely it is a Great Adventure? For a certainty, Death doth make cowards of us all.

I don't believe we can look down upon a coward. It is all a matter of temperament – the same as in the case of crime. Many a man is born a criminal. He can't help himself; he is not responsible for his actions. Why then should he get the same sentence as the man who is born with no inclination for sin? One man can stand what another cannot. Probably he can be physically stronger, or perhaps mentally. So, why shame him for a trait he has inherited – a weakness which belongs to his parents? I tell you, it's not fair. For instance, I know of a Lance-Corporal who, when there's a bit of strife on, actually vomits in his billy and on the duck-boards, because his terror has overmastered him – mayhap because he has neglected to develop his will-power, but greatly likely because he has been born deficient in that respect. Of course, I grant you, it would be most difficult to administer justice on such highly individualistic traits, but I am nevertheless convinced that it is the only right way.

On 23 December the men of the 8th Black Watch were relieved from their duties in the trenches and took over reserve billets in or near Arras and St. Sauveur. They weren't the general's house, but they were a great relief after the ice-cold trenches on the front line, just in time for Christmas. At last they could collect their post, including any parcels they might have waiting for them. Hamish had asked his parents to send various treats for him to give to his 'boys' on Christmas Day:

B.E.F.
23/12/16

My dear Mater and Pater,

This is to let you know that we came out of the trenches yesterday, and that now we are once again in comparative luxury. The three huge boxes arrived safely, and really they are top-hole. The Sergeant-Major came up to me and said 'By Jove, Sir. These are fine presents you've had sent for the men!'

I know you must have had a great deal of trouble in the collecting and packing of the 'goodies', but your reward is the pleasure they will give to a lot of damned fine fellows. I have kept the list of contributors and shall duly write to thank them. My 'John Cotton's' [pipe tobacco] hasn't arrived yet ... I wonder what can have happened to it?

The day after tomorrow will be Christmas ... I wonder if I'll be home by New Year's Day. I could be.

A funny thing happened when we went to the Line this last time. I looked very hard into the position and waited to enter but the officer I was relieving wasn't there. When he arrived, I found he was a fellow who had been at school with me. Funny the way one comes against acquaintances out here. I write this letter to you tonight, as the mail is just going to shut up. I do hope you have a good time on the 25th.

All good wishes for 1917 and after.

Yours,
Prof.

On the same day, Hamish received another, unexpected letter from a former platoon member, wounded and now recuperating in Scotland. He had been sorely missed by them all, especially Hamish, so when he opened the

Alexander James 'Hamish' Mann, aged about 9.

Hamish Mann aged about 6, with older brother Alan.

Hamish recumbent front right at the wedding of his eldest brother David 'Dai' Mann, standing behind his bride. Their parents are seated on either side of the bride.

A group of 'walking wounded' patients with their nurse and orderly at Craigleith Military Hospital, Edinburgh, 1915. (*Courtesy of Lothian Health Services Archive, Edinburgh University Library*)

Private Crumplethorne's Adventure.

By Lucas Cappe.

Private Crumplethorne's Adventure was the first of a series of humorous hospital stories written by Hamish under the pseudonym of Lucas Cappe. These and other stories, together with several poems, sketches and articles, were published in 1914–17 in the *Craigleith Chronicle*.

IT was visitors' day in hospital, and Private Crumplethorne lay in his cot awaiting with eager expectance the arrival of kindly people, with cigarettes, to come and speak to him. Private Crumplethorne, because of his easy wit and taking ways (he had done sixty days often for taking things—before he 'listed!) was a great favourite with his ward mates, to whom he was known by the affectionate name of "Crump." It really was too much to expect a convalescent soldier to utter such a word as Crumplethorne, and thus it was that to fellow patients and nurses alike he was simply "Crump."

He was fond of cigarettes, but he was also philosopher and student of human nature enough to see that, in the case of visitors, it was oftener than not a mere affair of barter and exchange; the visitor gave

The pipe-smokers: Hamish Mann and his older brother Alan Cowan Mann. Alan is on leave and visiting Hamish at his training camp in Bedford, 1915. Alan Mann rejoined the RAMC soon after and was later awarded the MC and bar. He was twice wounded but survived the war.

Alexander James 'Hamish' Mann in his full uniform, complete with sporran. Until his wooden trunk was found in the attic, this was the only photo the finders had ever seen of him. It had stood on the hall table throughout their childhood years; a mysterious figure from the past.

The first edition of the *Craigleith Chronicle*, December 1914, featuring the hospital building on its front cover. Hamish was one of the inaugurators and contributors to this hospital magazine and shortly after became its joint editor.

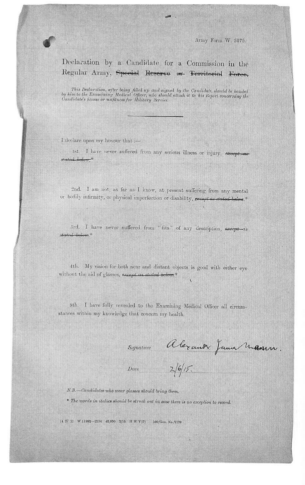

Hamish's army medical declaration form, showing his strong deletion of the words 'except as stated below', thereby denoting he has 'never suffered any serious illness'. Can anyone blame him for wanting so much to serve his country that he deliberately omitted to declare his 'enlarged heart'?

Hamish on leave in 1915. He stands on the left, together with his sister Isobel 'Daisy', his father Alex, his mother Charlotte and a visitor. They are standing in front of Red House in Edinburgh, Hamish's family home.

Hamish decorated most of his front pages and headings. This was the front of a section in his 1915 training notes.

THE COMPANY IN ATTACK AND DEFENCE; COMPANY AND PLATOON TRAINING, etc.

Hamish, standing in the stream, third from right, with other 8th Black Watch officers behind the Butts, while training at Borden Camp, 1915. (*Courtesy of the Imperial War Museum*)

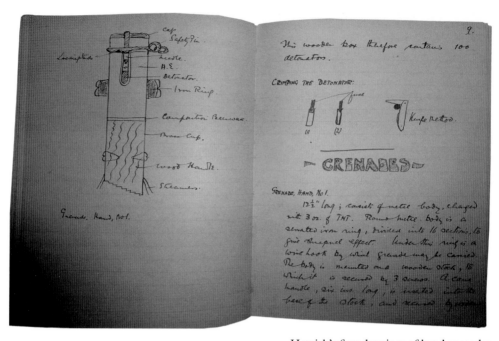

Hamish's first drawings of hand grenades in one of his 1915 training notebooks.

Hamish's drawing of a Mills head for a shell, among many such drawings he made in his 1915 training notebooks.

Hamish's illustration of an arrow-head trench: 'Care must be taken of these, as bombs may be thrown from A & B on men advancing along trench CD.'

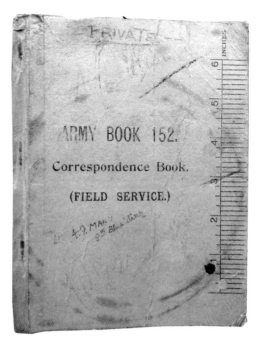

A studio portrait of Hamish, taken mid-1916, shortly before he left for the Somme to join his regiment on the front.

This is Hamish's first active service notebook, in which he wrote poems, prose and personal impressions of people, places and battle scenes on the Somme. (Note the word 'Private' at centre top.)

Hamish, front row, second from left, in a photo of 8th Black Watch officers, newly-arrived on the Somme, August 1916. This image is from Captain Shepherd's photo album. (*By kind permission of the Black Watch Museum*)

Martinpuich, near High Wood, 15 September 1916, in the midst of battle with sandbags in the foreground and stripped trees burning in the distance as shells explode and bombs fall from enemy planes. This was becoming an everyday scene for Hamish. Drawn by John Purvis. (*Reproduced by kind permission of Cranleigh School*)

Hamish was among this group of 8th Black Watch soldiers and officers behind the lines near High Wood in October 1916. It was his first sighting of a tank, rumbling in ungainly fashion across the rough ground. The first tank had been introduced by the British only three weeks earlier at Flers. This image is from Captain Shepherd's photo album. (*By kind permission of the Black Watch Museum*)

The 8th Black Watch marching along the Fricourt-Albert Road, headed by their own pipers, in 1916. Junior officers like Hamish marched with their men. The riders were senior officers, including medical officers. (*Courtesy of the Imperial War Museum*)

A Scottish officer among the sandbags and debris of war, writing a letter home ... or is it a poem? This photo was set up by the British government as propaganda for families at home. However, this was a real officer in a real war. It could be Hamish or one of his friends. (*Courtesy of the National Library of Scotland*)

The Butte de Warlencourt. Hamish's 'unbearable ...unspeakable, all but unthinkable night' in Snag Trench was the turning-point in taking this strategic landmark from the enemy. Once covered in trees and greenery, it was now stripped down by constant bombardment to the bare chalk. Painting by William Orpen. (*Courtesy of the Imperial War Museum*)

SNAG TRENCH. (Oct. 19th /16) THE SOMME
That newly-captured trench I shall never forget, nor the anguish I felt as we filed slowly in through the clinging mud in the misty light of the moon. It was the most repelling sight I have ever seen, and the

Hamish's opening lines of *Snag Trench*, his visceral account of that terrible night, 19 October 1917. His experience of the worst of life and death clearly haunted him to such an extent that he could not bring himself to write about it until more than a month later, though his memories were as terrible and 'nauseous' as the night on which it happened.

Between battles and trench duties, Hamish found the ideal activity to take his mind off the horrors of war and raise the battalion's morale. He gained permission to start and edit a magazine called *The Straffer*, for which this is his preliminary front-cover design (on tissue paper, hence the creases).

⸻ PRAYER ⸻

When the time comes, and all this
Becomes a nobler dust, a worthier wasty flesh
                                                clay,
When Fire and all the implements of
                                            hell
Shall free my frenzied soul from
                                    Earthly sway,
Grant that my Passing justify my Life;
May I have Rest after that hour of strife!

———

AGNEZ- LEZ- DUISANS,   9:12:16.

Prayer is one of several poems Hamish wrote at this time in his notebook. He was away from his platoon as it was his turn for duty at first-line transport. This work was regular hours, so he had more time than usual to think. Meanwhile, he could hear distant sounds of artillery fire from where his men were holding the front line.

Shell-blasted trees stand 'like finger-posts to the sky' near Arras, in the first snows of 1916–17; the coldest, longest winter in living memory. (*By kind permission of the Black Watch Museum*)

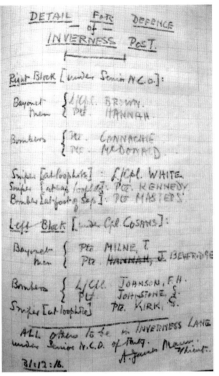

'Trench Feet' is the title of this cartoon by John Cosmo Clark, depicting one soldier carrying another with a bandaged foot. The autumn of 1916 had been the wettest on record and the winter was the coldest for a generation, so both trench foot and frostbite were common ailments among the troops. (*Courtesy of the Imperial War Museum*)

Hamish's handwritten detail for the allocation of his men in defence of Inverness Post on the night of 31 December 1916, New Year's Eve. This and other details of upcoming tasks are interspersed in Hamish's notebook with poetry and prose, diagrams and maps.

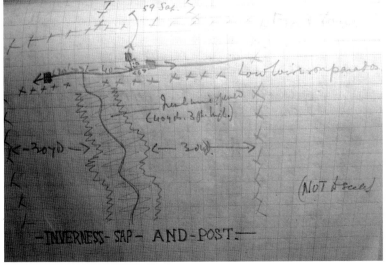

This is Hamish's plan, 'not to scale', of Inverness Sap and Post. His drawing shows the front line (marked by criss-crosses right of centre), positions and distances.

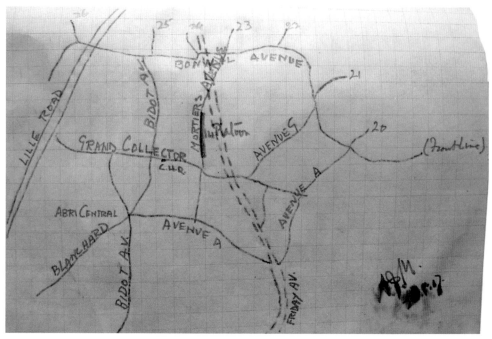

In this drawing from his notebook, Hamish shows the Lille Road and a network of the allies' trenches stretching out alongside it. He has numbered the trenches as well as naming them. His 14 Platoon's position is indicated in the centre. We know that he also spent time in Grand Collecteur trench, where he wrote his thoughts in his notebook.

A British tank about to cross a trench on its way to take part in the Battle of Arras. This tank, or another like it, would soon lumber past Hamish as he lay badly wounded in no man's land. (*Courtesy of the Imperial War Museum*)

'The Arras Belfry', painted in 1917 by Fernand Sabatté. This shows the ruins of Arras Cathedral, with its rubble piled up beneath what remains of the belfry. 'This is a city of the dead, a place of memories, a town of the past,' wrote Hamish, on seeing the damage from bombs and shells. (*Courtesy of the National Gallery of Ireland*)

'Over the Top', painted by John Cosmo Clark shows the 'Zero Hour' moment that starts a new attack. Second Lieutenant Hamish Mann led his platoon over the top at Zero Hour (5.30 am) on 9 April 1917, the first day of the Battle of Arras. He was just five days past his 21st birthday. (*Courtesy of the Imperial War Museum*)

THE TELEGRAM. This is the War Office telegram delivered to Hamish's parents in Edinburgh on 11 April 1917: 'Deeply regret to inform you 2/Lt A J Mann Black Watch died of wounds April tenth. The Army Council express their sympathy.'

AUBIGNY-en-ARTOIS (Pas-de-Calais) — Cimetière

This first photograph was taken of Hamish's resting place: the extension cemetery at Aubigny, provided for the dead of the Battle of Arras. Hamish's grave is marked with a simple wooden cross, showing his name and rank.

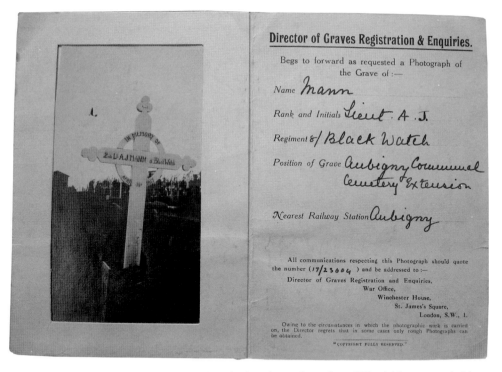

The registration card sent to his parents gives the location and number of Hamish's grave at Aubigny, together with a photo of the replacement grave-marker, which includes the date of his death.

The church at Aubigny-en-Artois, 15km north-west of Arras, which serves the graveyard where Hamish was buried. Many years later it became a Commonwealth War Graves cemetery.

Hamish's permanent gravestone, in the Commonwealth Graves cemetery at Aubigny, lies in a peaceful, shady spot. In his poem *A Subaltern's Soliloquy*, Hamish knew he would not have his wish to be buried one day on a Scottish hillside. Hamish ends this poem with the verse:

> And I shall sleep beneath that foreign sod
> As peacefully as e'er 'neath heather flower,
> Knowing I am but one 'mongst all those men
> Who breathed their latest sigh in Britain's hour.

The large wooden chest found in the attic of their old family house by Robert and Rosemary Stewart, great-nephew and great-niece of Hamish. They had a lot to clear, so they left it till last, expecting nothing exciting, but when they finally opened it, for the first time in 100 years, they were astonished to find it full of treasure: Hamish's lost writings, now rediscovered to become the star of this book.

envelope, he was happy to see the characteristic, 45-degree sloping precision of Dickson's handwriting:

Ross-shire

23.12.16

Dear Sir,

    I am taking the liberty of writing these few lines to let you know I am under orders for a draft for France, and I would be very grateful to you if you try and get me back to the platoon. If I go to any other Battalion I will feel inclined to run away and join the 8th.

    I'm not sorry I'm leaving this place – it's even worse than being at the Front. The Batt. is holding the line about Arras, isn't it? It will be more than a little cold in the trenches this weather, but as long as the weather keeps dry it's not so bad. This is about all the news I have at present. Hoping this finds you in the best of health.

Yours Sincerely,

L. Cpl. A. Dickson

Hamish is sure to have written a reply straight away to reassure Dickson that he would do all he could to get him back in 14 Platoon, the sooner the better. All he had to do was to write a request, stating the reasons, to his commanding officer.

    At this time, in Hamish's notebook, three pages are missing, cut out cleanly and deliberately, so we will never know what light they may have shed. However, also on 23 December 1917, Hamish becomes worried about his attitude: is he a 'snob'?

SNOBS

I am beginning to think I am a snob. A snob is the last epithet I could desire to be used in connection with me. A snob is, I fancy, one of the most contemptible types one can meet. There are, it has been said, three kinds of snobbery:

1. Snobbery of Birth
2. Snobbery of Money
3. Snobbery of Intellect

Now the man who is a snob because his father was a peer is a fool; the man who is a snob because he is rich is a cad; the man who is a snob because he is more intellectual than those he mixes with is … well, what is he? For it is an intellectual snob that I fancy I am. If I am, it is probably due to the fact that nothing enervates and annoys me more than hearing adults engaging in idle tittle-tattle. A man with no 'soul', be he rich or poor, king or peasant, is not one who will interest me with either his conversation or his correspondence.

Now, intellect (or to take the larger 'soul') does not depend upon station, nor does it depend upon income. Examples are far too numerous to mention – Burns, Patrick McGill and a thousand others. Therefore, although probably a 'nouveau riche' would not mix with a poor genius (until he were known at least), I would, because of our equality of intellectual class. ('Class' is a word I detest, but, with the world in its present deplorable state of civilisation, it is a criterion we must reckon with.)

I believe intellectual snobbery is the least contemptible of all, and if I <u>am</u> such a snob, I am but a mild one. I do not gaze comfortably on the man who uses a double negative (although that hardly implies lacking intellect) in the fashion a rich or well-born (whatever that may mean!) man does on those he imagines to be beneath him. I also maintain that distinction, be it in finances, birth or intellect, does not make one jot of difference in the word 'humanity'. There is no such thing as one being another's inferior. Inferior in one particular way, perhaps, but as a man – no.

Our Colonel, for instance, is not a snob. He does not hold himself aloof, because of his rank, as so many quite subordinate Commanders do, nor does he invest himself with any airs and graces because he happens to be a Baronet. I imagine he is quite aware that the fact of his father having been a Baronet does not make him in any way a better man. In fact probably if his father had <u>not</u> been a Baronet, he would have been better than he is. The Baronetcy is not a 'human' institution at all. Our C.O. <u>is</u> human. He is, temperamentally, 'of the Army, unmilitary', and that is why I am so fond of him. I pray he may never attain to very exalted rank, because the crushing machinery of military officialdom might rob him of his personality. He might become a cog in its machinery. He might become a Snob!

'The Battalion passed a quiet Christmas in Arras,' according to Wauchope. However, by the sound of Hamish's preparations, it was probably anything but quiet, in a good way. He writes to his parents on Christmas morning, to thank them again for the gifts they gathered and sent for the men of 14 Platoon, who had received them joyfully that morning, and to give his parents a flavour of the celebration meal and festivities to come in the officers' mess that evening:

B.E.F.
25/12/16

Dear Mater and Pater,

I am enclosing a menu which I made out for our Dinner tonight, and I have also sent a 'Translation' of it! You will see from it that we are not faring too badly! A few explanations will be necessary:-

ZERO   *means the beginning of a bombardment*
FISHTAILS   *is the name of a kind of German bomb*
THE DUMP   *is the place where the Royal Engineers store their tools*
PICKETS   *are staves used in making fences*
COUGHDROP is the name of an R.E. Dump on the Somme

Thanks for the parcel of letters. The tobacco (John Cotton's) hasn't come yet. The men wish me to thank you all very much indeed for the parcels which they enjoyed to the full. The Sergeant-Major was delighted with the contents!

I believe you sent me a plum pudding, etc. They haven't come yet, but we'll have them on New Year's Day.

Please give my love to all who will be with you this season. If you have as good a time as I'm having you'll do well. And the prospect of early leave always adds a rosy glow to the proceedings! I have written to thank the various people for their contributions to the parcels.

Love to all,
Prof.

PPS The following is an extract from a letter I received from an officer who got the M.C. and who was previously Commanding 14 Platoon.

'Well, dear chap, thank you from my heart for your kind congrats re my Cross. It was a great surprise to me, and I must confess I am very 'bucked' to hear of the various honours bestowed on no. 14 Platoon, and, in return, hearty congrats to you. I fully realised when you took over the command of no. 14 that one day I would have reason to be proud of them all, even as I was – and always shall be.'

What do you think of that?
Thine,
Prof.

Now to Hamish's Christmas Dinner menu for his 'boys':

8th (S) Bn The Black Watch
'D' Company

ZERO: 8 p.m.

Fishtails on Toast
Potage à la Spud
Succulent Salmon Squash
'Somme' Bantam (fed up) decorated with Dug-out Dainties
R.E. Dump-ling à la Harps
Just a Trifle
Mitey Atom Pickets
Coughdrop Coffee and Floor de Ceiling Cigars

VANGS: Champagne à la Staffe (this sec pour les très secs)
Le Nombre Dix – Essence de Vàche
Pare Perrier
Aqua Tapis

Incidental music by the Mud Guards Band (Conducteur Monsieur Dub E. Decca)

France   25:12:16

Its translation is as follows:

To begin at 8 p.m.
> *Sardines on Toast*
> *Potato Soup*
> *Salmon Kedgeree*
> *Turkey (stuffed) and Baked Potatoes*
> *Plum Pudding (Supplied by Mrs Harper)*
> *Trifle*
> *Cheese Straws*
> *Coffee and Cigars*

Wines:
> *Champagne*
> *Watson's No Q0 Whisky*
> *Milk*
> *Perrier Water or Water*

Music by the Decca Gramophone

Not only did Hamish give everyone in his platoon a Christmas gift, he also made sure that they would have the best Christmas dinner possible. He soon discovered that they would also have turkey and Christmas pudding, plus drinks, including extra rations of rum. Indeed, the rum given to the troops 100 years ago or more was approximately double the strength of the rum we can now buy in our shops, so it was as well they didn't have far to walk back to their billets.

Hamish continued to stand by his principles when it came to what sort of officer he should be and how best to lead his men. His many hard months on the front had not changed his mind, but rather his experiences through all the difficulties of army life had only served to validate his attitude, as well as his love and respect for these men, who would in turn do anything for him:

Just as it takes all sorts of people to make a world, so it takes all sorts of men to constitute a company. The Germans try to deal with a body of soldiers as a composite group of humanity, resulting in that machine-like discipline which is so apt to fail under extreme test. They seem to ignore the presence of human nature, and that is ever an absolutely fatal mistake. A man doesn't live to be treated as though he were a motor-car – driven anywhere and knowing nothing; he lives at least to be credited with having the brain and the feelings which God gave him.

Another point to remember is that the greatest fool in the company may prove a hero on the field of battle. More than once has an officer thought one of his men the biggest idiot God ever created, and found him in France a man of mighty courage and witless of fear. The 'real thing' brings out what a man is made of, and shows him up in his true colours.

The only way to get the best out of your men is to treat them as rational human beings.

'Look after the men, and when you're in a tight corner they'll look after you,' says Colonel Corkleg, in 'Private Spud Tamson'* and here he embodies the essence of esprit-de-corps.

Men can't be driven, but they can be led. A good officer never says 'Go on!' He says 'Come on!'

---

* Captain R.W. Campbell.

As they went to their beds that night, some of the officers and men might have given a fleeting thought to those other soldiers who had to sit out Christmas with a curtailed festive meal carried to them from behind the lines, so not exactly hot, while they sat in their dugouts or patrolled the trenches that freezing cold Christmas night. Only a few more days and nights before Hamish and his men would be back out there again.

Chapter Eleven

Gas Attack!

'*Night of 27/28th Arras heavily shelled with from 2,000 to 3,000 gas shells.*'

(Regimental Diary, December 1916)

Christmas 1916 was now over and Hamish knew he would have to march his men out to the trenches again on 30 December. Meanwhile he hoped they would have a quiet time and get on with some necessary support jobs in Arras. The weather was icy cold, which affected them more during the day than at night, when they could at least sleep under some covering indoors, though there was hardly a curtain left hanging at a window by this time, as, torn or not, they were needed as covers for the men at night. With the wind whistling in through the broken windows, making their every breath freeze into crystals in the air, the men were often too cold to sleep for any length of time. Hamish, like his fellow officers, was slightly better off, but not much. Home comforts of any sort were rare and the least the officers could hope for was a little coal to burn in the few fireplaces with intact chimneys.

At about 10.00 pm on the 27th, when most of the men were asleep in their billets, a rain of shells fell on the town. Everyone had become used to the occasional shell, now and then, courtesy of the Hun, but some eagle-eyed sentries noticed that this was different. Through the fog, as they walked around the town, they could just make out gas rising in the still air above where the shells fell, so they immediately raised the alarm.

Orders were sent out to all billets, by runners, that men should don their gas masks straight away, but as so many were asleep, they didn't all hear the warnings. Suddenly, a relatively safe quiet night had changed to frenetic noise, activity and danger. At this stage the shelling was quite sporadic, but:

At about 10.45 the enemy guns suddenly shortened their range and one shell unfortunately burst in the middle of a group of 'A' Company sergeants, laying out four of them, two of whom afterwards died. It is stated that all of these sergeants had their respirators on, but they were blown off their heads by the force of the explosion.

(From the Major General's Report)[1]

At 11.45 pm there was a lull in the shelling, but not for long. At midnight, the bombardment accelerated and became more accurately targeted at the billets. Two companies were forced to retreat to the cellars, while others moved to safer houses.

Fog rendered the work of getting men out of their billets and into cellars most difficult; at times the fog was so thick that it was impossible to see through gas-masks, and they had to be taken off and the gas chanced.

(Wauchope, p.33)

The gas thickened and the Germans raised the pace of attack still further. By 2.00 am the shelling reached its peak. Finally, an hour later, it ceased altogether. Because there was no wind that night and the fog impeded the gas from dispelling in a few areas, men were still being affected by it when they came out of the cellars in the morning. Approximately 3,000 gas shells fell on the 8th Battalion's area over a period of five hours, but the effects continued for several more. Fortunately, although sixty-seven soldiers (all of them 'other ranks') had to receive hospital treatment for gas poisoning, nobody else died, other than the two sergeants.

The major general, continuing his report on this gas attack, noted some interesting lessons the 8th Battalion should learn:

Owing to the cold air (it was freezing all night of the 27th/28th December) the gas of the bursting shell did not rise, but sank to the ground in a vapour. If there was any wood, etc., lying about, the vapour would saturate into it. When the air became warmer, this vapour would return to gas form and rise in the form of a poisonous cloud.

As the 28th was a comparatively warmer day, it seems that this may possibly be the cause of so many men going sick on the 28th. This might be accounted for by the fact that the direct hits were obtained

1. Report of Commanding Officer 9th (Scottish) Division, attached to 8th Black Watch Regiment Diaries, December 1916.

on the billets, and that if the vapour saturated into the flooring in the manner described ... and then rose 'as gas' as the weather grew warmer, the men collecting their things in their room might have inhaled gas slightly, without realising what was happening.

The major general also pointed out that a small percentage of the shells had exploded 'with practically no noise', which could be a concern if this arose in any future gas attacks.

Later that day, Hamish wrote to his parents:

B.E.F.
28.12.16

Dear Mater and Pater,
    This is to enclose a few war sketches I did today. You may like them. In any case, you'll know what to do with them.
    I shan't get any leave before about January 14th. I had expected to get away before then, but for various trifling reasons I shan't do. However, anticipation is a great thing, isn't it?
    By the way, did you see my verses in this season's Watsonian?* They're nothing much, but I wrote them out here.
    Ruth has sent me a perfectly topping photo of herself. I'll let you see it when I come home.

        With much love,
        Yours ever,
        Prof.

* As previously mentioned, the *Watsonian* is the magazine of Hamish's old school, George Watson's College in Edinburgh.

This letter is of course remarkable for its omission of any reference to the gas attack, only hours before. Perhaps Hamish wanted to spare his parents any anxiety about him. Whether or not this is the case, his sketches, his writings and his forthcoming leave were obviously of greater importance in his mind that day. It is also of interest that his war sketches, as before, were of people rather than events or scenes.

Indeed, throughout his time on active service, Hamish rarely described the day-to-day conditions of life in the trenches, for example, or any ordinary happenings, other than to 'send them up' in his 'War Cameos' for publication. The various British First World War archives are not short of soldiers' and officers' trench diaries and war memoirs, recollecting events and conditions. However, Hamish, in his 'trench-diary' notebooks, almost exclusively focused on his impressions of people and occasionally of places or situations, and in particular on his thoughts, feelings and philosophies. All his other writings through his few months at the front followed a similar pattern.

On 29 December, Hamish and his platoon returned to front-line trenches near Arras, in rain and snow, which fell on the daytime mud so that the next morning's thaw would cause a mire that was deeper still ... and so the pattern continued during this turn of duty.

On his second night in the front-line trench, 30 December, Hamish wrote his next entry in his notebook, written in a rudimentary dugout. It follows a similar pattern. Although entitled 'Arras', it is nothing to do with Arras as such and comparatively little about the appalling conditions in the trenches near Arras, or the often well-below freezing night-time temperatures, but very much in praise of several of the men in his platoon, of whom he speaks fondly, as if a father talking of his children's special attributes:

ARRAS

The trenches are appalling – in many parts reasonably comparable with the Somme. The walls have fallen in, and every moment more earth slides to the bottom of the trench, where it mingles with the mud that already lies there. When duckboards are there, they squelch and puff and hiss under one's feet. Often one has to wade through floods of water, whilst at several spots one can barely walk at all, so clinging and sticky is the mud. Revetments have collapsed and form a block in the trench; traverses and corners everywhere are tottering – seized as Lance Corporal D. puts it, with 'St Vincent's Dance'! The weather is systematically undoing all the work we have done. It is all very annoying and very disheartening...

The men are wonderful. They never despair, but work manfully and steadily at the tasks allotted to them. There are no scoops in the Company, so many of the platoon are throwing the debris over the parapet with their hands. Beveridge, whom I have just returned to duty from the L.G. (Lewis Gun Section), at his own request, is working splendidly, and Bissett, whom I have just made a Lance Corporal, is very keen on his new responsibilities. They even appear to look upon me purely as a friend – a family – a privilege I often feel unworthy of. Tonight, Beveridge told me all about his private life. There was no restraint about it at all, Thank God! He works in the pit ('put' as he calls it) in Cowdenbeath, where he earns about eleven shillings a day. Brown (A) also works there and (this I learned to my utter amazement) is just 18! They both swanked their ages to get 'out'! I think they are both very fine fellows – I must get off to L.G. too.

Johnstone G. ('Little Titch' as his fellows call him) is a great success. He is always in good spirits, unafraid, and – so far as I can see – a universal favourite. His voice is very loud, but he has to stand on a sandbag in order to see over the parapet! I see from my roll book that he is a shunter ... one day I must ask him all about shunting. What a strange calling!

Masters, I find from his letters,* is very much in love with 'Rosie', and I trust they will be happy together after the war. Masters is a bit of a romancer. He told Rosie all about the muddy front line, long before he had ever seen a front line! Still, I can forgive him that: A beautiful liar is often a very desirable sort of person, so long as his untruths bear no malice.

Lance Corporal Johnson ('Paddy') is a great favourite of mine. Some of the men call him 'Dublin', but I fancy Paddy is better. He is a well-educated lad, and has a delightful Irish brogue. Paddy is very dutiful about writing home, and I believe his quick manner and honest face signify 'a real good chap'. I can't understand why his commission went such a short way. He will be recommended again next time.

Squire, the old sinner, has found his proper sphere of activity at last – on the Company cooker. He takes no end of interest in his work, and is always trying to devise some new kind of dish for the men's delectation. I think he was rather proud of the Christmas dinner he produced and, from what the men say, he has every reason to be. He's a wily man, Squire, but good-hearted. He

---

* It was one of a platoon commander's duties to be the initial censor of any letters written by his men.

*is also very wise. The cooker is a much more desirable place than the fire-step these days!***

    I'm glad I have such a platoon as 14. I loathe 'telling people off', and now I practically never require to do so. When I do attempt it, I fear it is a miserable failure!

** The fire-step, about 3ft high, is where the sentry stood with his rifle at the ready, and also where soldiers stood to strafe or snipe at the enemy or defend during an enemy attack.

In the squalid, rat-infested trenches, in the deep frost of the night, on patrol duty in the early hours between the last day of the year and the first day of the next, Hamish harks back in his imagination to wars of yore:

OLD DAYS

Tonight, or rather this morning, for it is 2 a.m. – I have been reading Bonnie Prince Charlie *and it has aroused great longings in my heart.*

    I'm sick of this kind of war, with all its mechanical trumpery. I long for the days when strapping knights, kilted and plaided, lived in their land and loved it. I yearn for the old days of cuffs and frills, and the fights in the mountain glens. There's something ridiculously unromantic about shells. The Dirk is the thing, and the pistol. If you're going to kill a man, kill him decently. Don't go and tell someone a long way behind to throw explosives at him from a gun. Go out and grapple with him. You need to have your 'blood up' for what is true. One should fight when one's blood is up. A man has no chance with a shell, but he has with face to face, hand to hand combat. So here's to the times of Bonnie Prince Charlie!

A few hours after Hamish wrote of his preference for fighting in the mountain glens, a heavy German trench mortar exploded on top of a dugout along the line and killed the five men who were in it. This was not a good omen for the New Year.

After a short sleep, Hamish was up and writing again:

> **NEW YEAR 1917**
>
> *It is New Year's morn. In three hours' time our boys will be going out to raid the Huns. The guns have been preparing the way for the last two or three days: the Huns, I fancy, are not feeling comfortable. They appear to dislike raiding parties of armed kilties!*
>
> *A note has just been passed to me, postponing the raid! The Boches will have their New Year's Day in comparative peace after all!*

He then changed his subject to the correspondence he enjoyed so much with a fellow Scot, A.S. Neill, which had continued since before the war and carried on throughout Hamish's time in France while Neill was a schoolmaster and then after he joined up. In fact, the evidence suggests that they met on at least one occasion during the next couple of months, when their duties allowed, while both were billeted in the Arras area. Neill himself, several years older than Hamish, was now a newly-commissioned officer and, by choice, a late entrant to the front. Neill was an author, educationalist and philosopher, so they had quite a lot in common and they frequently exchanged letters, sharing, and even debating with forthright zeal, their thoughts and ideas. However, in this case, Hamish reacted strongly to what he clearly regarded as Neill's glib remarks about the war before he came out to join it:

> **A.S. NEILL**
>
> *A.S. Neill wrote to me that when he comes 'out' he believes he will regard the Boches individually. He will hesitate to kill a Hun because 'he may be a Bavarian peasant, the father of a few bonny bairns.' I fancy the good Dominie,* when he comes upon a Boche fighting patrol in No-Man's-Land will not stop to ask whether or not he has ever indulged in 'frightfulness'. No, he will merely take damned good care to throw the first bomb! When nations are at war, one cannot treat the enemy individually. Every man in the trench opposite is a representative of the nation with whom one is at war. Therefore KILL HIM, before he kills you.*

---

* Dominie is an old Scottish name for a schoolmaster.

He goes on to tell of the German peasants fighting nobly for the honour (as they think) of The Forefathers. Neill contends, however, that they are mere dupes, fighting battles to enrich the profiteers. Neill is wrong in the first place. Germans don't fight nobly...

But the Daring Dominie goes further. He says <u>we</u> are striving under a similar delusion! I fear he is an extremist. No one knows more than I how downtrodden are the wage-earners of our land, but I deem that no country's soldiers are fighting, even unwittingly, for commercial gain. This is an insult to our officers and men, and a slur upon the intelligence of the country's leaders. In any case, I don't believe it!

I don't pretend (as A.S.N. seems to think I do) that the aim of war is <u>always</u> to satisfy national honour. But this I do state: The British nation has sufficient common sense to see the folly of entering upon a colossal struggle like this, simply for filthy lucre. The original causes of the war are becoming forgotten. War today is more or less a business, but it is not a business of which the profiteer is managing director. Incidentally, he may (and does) improve his account. This is a scandal, but it is not the leading feature of the war... No, Dominie, you are hopelessly wrong!

Underneath this strong repudiation, also on 1 January 1917, Hamish wrote these uncharacteristically short but nonetheless meaningful lines with a motif he had used before and which clearly haunted his thoughts:

A kiltie boy...
A muddy trench...
A sniper's shot
A weeping wench.

Still in the front-line trenches on 2 January, there was a war-weariness about all the troops in this New Year; a time when things should be full of promise, but they were not. Nothing had changed, as they endured the mud, the endless rain and the biting cold, not to mention the sporadic shelling; the stealthy enemy that was a constant threat to our men.

Yet, even on the darkest, coldest winter nights, these men of his did not lose their spirit and Hamish was clearly grateful for that:

Even in the firing line, where the grim spectre of Death is always more or less near, the British soldier sees the humour of things and laughs his fill. This is one of the sublime virtues of Mr. Atkins, one of the most virtuous of his many virtues. A sense of humour is a very great thing in life, and probably no one knows this better than the Boys in Khaki.

I knew a Private, in training, who was an officer's groom. He was such a comical chap that the Officers' Mess christened him 'Keystone'. He had an absurdly impertinent face, and a smile that was absolutely infectious. But his sense of humour was not his sole quality. When he came out to France, he proved himself an intrepid warrior, fearful of nothing and daring to the last degree.

In the early hours of 2 January, Hamish wrote of an incident that brought his fears sharply into focus:

FISHTAILS

It is a dark night and I am officer on duty in the firing line. I walk continuously along the duckboards, now and then nearly breaking my ankle on the edge of the wooden walkway. My hand is on my revolver in its holster, for the sentry posts are some little distance apart and Huns have been known to creep up to the parapet and shoot, stab or club the unwary ones walking beneath them along the trench. Behind me is Morris, my batman, carrying the 1½ inch Very pistol and cartridges for it. All is still, save for an occasional shot, sharp bursts of machine-gun fire or the wandering shell passing high overhead.

All of a sudden, there is a dull 'phut' from the enemy line, followed by a hiss, which becomes a sucking, creaking sound, louder and louder. I crouch behind a traverse and Morris does the same. There is a flash, a bang, and a shower of earth and stones behind us.

This is a Hun-built mortar of the Fishtail variety, the kind which killed O'Dell a few weeks ago. About ten of them come over, then all is quiet again, until our shots, heavier and more deadly, indulge in a little retaliation!

But it is an eerie sensation to hear this messenger of death flying towards you, and who knows where it is to come to earth? For all you know, the next one may land on top of you — then all is over.

> *At night, the fear of the unknown and the unseen is rife. There are so many things that might happen at any moment. ...For instance, last night, six of C Company were in a deep dug-out when a big shell landed on top of it. All the men were buried and only one escaped death.*

On 3 January, the last full day of this tour of duty in the trenches, Hamish seems to have spent quite some time writing out details of a defence post and a list of personnel. However, as on most days, he also continued his observations and impressions in his notebook, first about a compatriot's lucky escape:

> **BOMBS AND PATROLS**
> *Ogilvie, our Intelligence Officer, has been wounded in nine places by a bomb, and the circumstances attending the affair are rather amusing.*
>
> *It happens that he was out on patrol last night. It was very dark and very windy. After an hour or two, Ogilvie decided to return, making his way through the banked line, he jumped into what he thought was our front line. To his utter consternation, he found the Boches in the trench. He had lost direction and had strayed into the Hun line!*
>
> *He threw a bomb at them, which, of course, did not explode. So he snatched his revolver from its holster, being somewhat taken aback, when he found that he had forgotten to load it!*
>
> *Only one thing remained. Leaping on the parapet, he ran for his life. The gentle Germans threw a bomb after him, causing him nine minor wounds.*
>
> *Ogilvie has gone down the line! I think he is very lucky.*

It is only surprising that more incidents of this kind didn't happen, in the middle of the night when both officers and men were often wet through, freezing cold, desperately tired and disorientated. Indeed, Major General Wauchope describes this incident rather more circumspectly, in tune with the official version: 'Second Lieutenant A.M. Ogilvy was wounded while inspecting the German wire.'

Next, Hamish writes in praise of two of his men in 14 Platoon, or 'The Fighting Fourteen' as they often referred to themselves:

14

I am very fond of Peter Bissett and MacLeod. I find Bissett is a tailor – I wonder where he tails. Lately I gave Peter a lance stripe, of which he is very proud. The Sergeant-Major tells me he watched him from the window of the company office. Bissett stood there on guard, very smart and soldierly, and every now and again glancing down at his stripe then puffing out his chest with great satisfaction! After a little while, he caught the S-M's eye and blushed like a child – that which, indeed, he is but little more. Since he became an N.C.O., he has pulled himself together greatly, and I fancy he takes his new duties and responsibilities very seriously. It has done him a deal of good and has given him an added interest in life. I think I am an excellent judge of men.

MacLeod is a wee fellow, a ploughman. The most fascinating thing about him is the slovenly way he dresses and behaves. I fear I shall never be able to give him a stripe, but I think he is quite happy where he is. On his upper lip are a few youthful straggling dark hairs, and his shambling gait would do credit to the weariest man on earth.

You see, I make no attempt to turn out mechanical soldiers. My platoon and I are a happy family, not a machine and its operator. I like my fellows to be human beings, not mere automatons.

I am a very unconventional officer!

Written in the early hours of the next morning, Hamish's poem expresses afresh his fears:

THE BARRIERS

Say, have you ever mused upon Death
When Death was hovering near?
Each breath you thought was your last sweet breath
And each sound the last you would hear?

Say, have you ever mused upon Life
When Death was hovering near,
When all the Earth was athrob with strife
And the air was shaking with fear?

> *Then — what were your thoughts in that hour of dread*
> *When the skeleton passed you by?*
> *Pour forth your tale to the list'ning dead,*
> *Let the Earth winds echo your sigh.*

Writing had always been a great consolation to Hamish, in both his best and worst times: as a teenager when he was seriously ill, as an officer at war and as a man writing about the 'boys' in his platoon, or penning poems, humorous 'cameos' and play-scripts. By expressing his worst fears in his writing, especially in his poetry, he seemed more able to come to terms with them.

Chapter Twelve

The Worst Winter

'For the men who faced the winter in kilts, exposure to the bitter weather was unbearable.'

(Podcast 25, Imperial War Museum)

On 4 January 1917, the 8th Battalion was relieved by the Argylls and the troops marched back to billets in Arras, but there wasn't much rest. Immediately they were plunged into the 26th Brigade's orders that the 8th Battalion Black Watch, jointly with the Argyll and Sutherland Highlanders, stage a daylight raid, with artillery support, on 6 January, just two days later. The aim of this raid was to capture German prisoners and take identifications. Some 100 men were to be selected from each regiment for this raid.

After the initial flurry of training, Hamish learned that his platoon would not be directly involved; no doubt a great relief, especially after their six-day stint dodging Fishtails on the freezing front line. However, they must have been caught up in the preparations as there are a few days when Hamish didn't make an entry in his notebook.

Although his platoon was not involved, Hamish and his men must have heard the heavy artillery fire that pounded the enemy for most of the morning of the 6th, increasing in the early afternoon, just before Zero Hour for the raid.

The regimental diary for the 6th January tells us that 'a successful daylight raid was carried out … a considerable amount of damage was done to enemy trenches.'

All three of the enemy's front-line trenches were occupied, but only four Boches were seen, one of whom was captured and the other three killed. Wauchope goes on to tell us that the rest of their garrison had barricaded themselves into deep dugouts, so 'Stokes bombs were thrown down the stairways, with the result that some dugouts collapsed and others took fire.'

Between 7 and 10 January, the battalion was joined by large drafts of new soldiers to fill up platoons closer to their full complement again, and one of the returnees clearly cheered Hamish up considerably, as he wrote on 9 January:

REJOININGS

Dickson has come back and he is now a full corporal. To say I am delighted he has returned is a very mild way of expressing my feelings, and – thank God – he also is delighted to be back with the old platoon. Dickson is a man in a thousand – magnificently made and witless of fear. While on the Somme he was wounded when asleep by a piece of shrapnel which penetrated his hand. He carried on, however, and eventually incurred blood-poisoning, through the mud which saturated his bandages.

When, after those never-to-be-forgotten twenty-four hours, we came out, Dickson's arm was swollen up tremendously, and he went home to Blighty. I was filled with despair, for too often such incidents mean that the wounded man will, even if sent out again – never return to the Battalion, far less the Platoon…. But last night he came back again, and I was very proud to shake hands with him this morning.

Keenan, who was wounded in the Vimy Raid, has come back too, as well as Wilson, whose arm suffered blood-poisoning during our last tour on the Somme. Another seven of a draft have also joined 14, and they seem quite a sturdy lot. But I would rather have Dickson than ten of a draft – any day of the week!

Sergeant Forsythe has got the Military Medal. He's rather amused about it, and so am I. He's worth a damned sight more. However, it shows he's a worthy fellow. I know he is!

On 10 January, just before marching his men out to take over the front-line trenches again, Hamish wrote a letter to his parents:

B.E.F.
10.1.17

My dear Mater and Pater,

A cynical soldier once said that one half of France had been shovelled into sandbags. Sometimes I am inclined to think that he was right. Up in the trenches, sandbag after sandbag is filled by fatigue party after fatigue party; parapet after parapet is revetted with them, and still sandbag after sandbag comes in for filling! I wonder how many have been filled since August 1914? Perhaps some scintillating statistician will oblige by finding out and calculating how many million miles high the pile would be if one were laid on top of the other.

Whizz-bangs are strange contrivances. They're there before you know where you are, and frequently you don't know where you are for a considerable time after! They travel faster than their own sound – and sound travels fast enough, in spite of the fact that the sound of guns doesn't seem to have reached America yet.

I think someone should write a book about THE SOUL OF AMERICA. Probably an explorer would make the best author. Sir Ernest Shackleton is enviably suited for the task – he's accustomed to old things.

I wonder if a scarcity of paper will affect Mr. Wilson* at all? I hope so: it seems difficult to affect him.

Mr. Bottomly's** optimism is great, isn't it? No doubt his great rotundity is due to the stupendous efforts he has made 'Getting ready to shout'! He <u>was</u> a little premature, wasn't he? We out here flatter ourselves as Hun-strafers, but – gee! We're not in the running with these editor fellows! Of course, we're rather at a disadvantage. It's much more difficult (though signally more effective and exciting) to strafe the benign Boche from a trench than from an armchair. Still, some of these 'John Bull' attitudes are <u>trench</u>-ant, aren't they? Our war writers are quite pushing, but they don't push anything like so well as our khaki people do. The Great Push isn't going to take place in the

---

* Woodrow Wilson, president of the USA.

** Horatio Bottomly, English financier, journalist, newspaper proprietor, MP and swindler, best-known for being editor of the patriotic *John Bull* magazine; later imprisoned for fraud.

*columns of the LONDON LIAR, it's going to take place in ... well, I can't
very well tell you that, <u>can</u> I? Ask Mr Belloc for the map reference.*

*These are a few thoughts from my Book: I thought they might interest you.
I'm bringing my book home with me. I'll read you some passages from it ...
and I've got quite a lot to write up yet – in my own room soon. I'm longing to
get at that typewriter again. The house will resound with it clicking for a few
hours every day. Strange way to spend leave, what?*

*Everything in the garden's lovely. It's simply pouring, but that's a detail.
The Boches are being beaten and killed off like rats. I wish they were <u>all</u> dead,
the devils.*

It's a great life!

Yours ever, with tons of love,
Prof.
P.S. Cheer O!

On 10 January, 14 Platoon joined the rest of the 8th Battalion in the 'I' sector
trenches near Arras for the last time. They would only be there for four days,
as they would then be moving further along the front line. On the 12th a
fellow second lieutenant was wounded. On that day, Hamish wrote:

COMPARISONS

*Elsewhere, I have written of comparisons. I find that, where the line is
comparatively 'cushy', slight things (such as Fishtails), get the wind up
people – trifles which, in a place like the Somme, would have passed unnoticed
or unheeded. A bombardment is often to be preferred to the awful anticipation
of occasional shells. Here, the infrequent whizz-bangs are a nightmare to me,
whereas in the Flers line and the never-to-be-forgotten Sunken Road, such
things have landed almost on top of me and I have hardly turned a hair. I
simply felt accustomed to having a rough time, and so gradually ceased to
regard comparative dangers as dangers at all.*

Apart from the sporadic whizz-bangs, this tour of duty was relatively quiet. However, the weather was worsening from each day to the next, with intense frosts at night turning the mud to ice, and flurries of snow.

Hamish heard various snippets of information about the big offensive planned for Arras in the spring, as soon as the weather allowed. In the meantime, he learned that there would be smaller attacks in other directions to capture more portions of the German front line and push back the enemy, taking prisoners wherever they could.

On 14 January, the 8th Battalion was relieved by the 6th Queen's and marched to billets in Étrun, about 4 miles north-west of Arras, where they would stay for a week of training and rest. The following day, he wrote home:

B.E.F.
15.1.17

My dear Mater and Pater,

I received Dad's letter last night, saying you are expecting me home any day. There are so many of our officers away on courses and special jobs just now that it is very awkward and very difficult to let us away on leave. But my turn should come round in a few days now, so don't worry. We're behind (the lines) in billets and very comfortable, and waiting for leave is not so bad here as it is in the trenches. There's only one officer to go before me, and one officer is supposed to go every four days. However, I shan't be long now! Cheer-O! I'll wire from London.

It's fairly cold out here these days, and I've got one of those furry jackets that go a long way to keep one cosy. We came out of the trenches yesterday and expect to be out for some little time.

We have just left the town (the big one you know) and are now in a sweet little village where even the sound of guns is distant and subdued. It is very peaceful…. This morning my servant gave me breakfast in bed at 9.45 a.m., and I got up at 12.30!!!! So you see my life is not always strenuous!

I fancy the horrible Hun is getting dreadfully fed up with the war. He gets very little rest and can do extraordinarily little by way of retaliation. Our big guns outnumber his tremendously and our gunners are much more skilled. His infantry of course doesn't compare with ours at all…. I have taken on quite a number of bets that the war will be over by the end of February!

Did you see that Sir Douglas Haig said the Black Watch was the finest Regiment in the British Army? And in the last Mesopotamia dispatch we were <u>the only</u> crowd mentioned. (There's nothing like blowing one's own horn, is there!)

At the moment I am engaged in the dramatising of Michael Fairless's The Gathering of Brother Hilarius, *a book of life, somewhat similar to* The Cloister. *The principal part is absolutely <u>made</u> for Esmé Percy,* and I think if I make a good job of it, he'll take it after the war. The part is that of an angelic young monk, and the story relates how he came to understand human nature and sin. I got the book from Ruth. She's sent me some top-hole books lately, including* The Temple of Beauty, *an anthology of poetry by Alfred Noyes,* The Treasure of the Humble *by Maeterlink, and* The Road Mender, *also by Fairless. The number of books that I carry about and the huge pipe that Esmé gave me are a source of great amusement to the fellows here.*

There really is no news that I can give you. Indeed, there is none to give. Tell my 'Yams' I must retain until I arrive in State at The Red House** at a date not far distant. (I dreamt about it the other night in the dug-out!)

With tons of love,

Yours ever,

Prof.

---

*   As previously mentioned, Esmé Percy was already a well-known English actor, who later went on to star in forty films.

** 'The Red House' was where Hamish's parents lived in Edinburgh.

Four days later, on 19 January, Hamish was willing the time away as he wrote in his notebook:

LEAVE

I go on leave in about two days now. It seems altogether too good to be true. I feel as though something is bound to happen to spoil it – and yet, I have been disappointed so often on this scene of late.

Ten days of unadulterated bliss … and then? A thousand things may happen after that. There is the Spring Offensive, with its limitless possibilities. But I *can't think of that now. The only thing that matters is that leave, those short ten days that will be gone ere I realise they are there. Anticipation is a great thing, but when prolonged too far it is apt to drag, and that is what it <u>has</u> been doing the last few months.*

Still, leave is coming, for which thank God.

Although Hamish was hoping to take his leave from 23 January, he led his platoon into the trenches again on 22 January, in the L.I. sector at Roclincourt on the southern extreme of Vimy Ridge. Major General Wauchope summarizes: 'This was a bad line, but had the advantage of being quiet.'

Sadly, Hamish's instincts were right: it was too good to be true. However, on the 23rd an interesting new recruit distracted him a little, as he wrote in his notebook:

14

I find I now have a professional musician in the platoon! I wonder if he is still to wear his hair long. I don't think I shall censure him if he does, but the S-M will be on top of him like a ton of bricks! Alas, the lack of sentiment in the Army is lamentable. MacPhail says he thinks sentiment should enter more largely into Socialism, and I think his remark applies equally to things military. What I mean is this: if the Company Sergeant-Major sees a man in the ranks gazing vacantly into the air, he curses him roundly, without pausing to wonder if it is not possible that the delinquent is composing a poem, or awaiting inspiration to compose an impassioned passage of music. If a man who is a dreamer absent-mindedly puts a bullet through the Colonel's head instead of the target, no one apologises for interrupting his dream. He is court-martialled, dragged from the ethereal heights of poetic Elysium, and plunged into the degrading depths of 'Hat off! Evidence! Salute!'

Hamish must have been mulling over how to deal with the musician and what allowances could he make, as an officer, to allow him to flourish, considering his own unorthodox way of leading his men. He added:

I think my 'weakness' with the men is really my strength. By 'weakness' I mean inability to treat my men other than as honest, respectable fellow-men. I hear so many foolish, vain young officers speaking to the rank and file as though they were addressing so much coal dust. It makes my blood boil: it is a caddish thing to take a mean advantage of one's rank. My men are not the least afraid of me – indeed, my Sergeant often censures them for slight breaches of discipline in my presence, knowing well that I would never do it.

I have a second sergeant now, a D.C.M. fellow, and one of the very best. He came out to 13 platoon lately as a corporal, and as soon as I saw him I knew that 14 was obviously the place for him – among the other 'star turns' of the company. I succeeded in having him transferred (you see the Company-Sergeant-Major was once the platoon sergeant of 14!). I think he is not quite at home yet, but ere long he will be well satisfied with his transfer, I know. The first page of my roll book now sports two D.C.M.s and 2 Military Medals! 'Some' platoon!

A few days ago I received a letter from Tait, who won the Military Medal for throwing the bomb that knocked out the Flammenwerfer *[flame-thrower] on the Somme. The note was frankly familiar, but by no means impertinent, you understand. He wants me to try and get him back to the old platoon. I am very proud of these letters I get from my fellows.*

Late in the night of 23 January, sitting in the dugout, Hamish's thoughts turned back to the more immediate concerns of his and his men's wellbeing in the dismal state of the trenches they were occupying, together with the mortars raining down on adjacent battalions:

GRAND COLLECTEUR TRENCH

The line is like a scene from Bairnsfather.* The snow is thick and the waterlogged trenches are frozen hard, so that we can walk comfortably along on the ice! (Much easier than mud.) Everybody is fighting against frost-bitten feet, and the Sergeant-Major almost smokes himself blind with the fumes

---

* Captain Bruce Bairnsfather, the popular humorist/cartoonist, said to have 'won the war' for the British.

from his brazier. (You can always tell the Sergeant-Major's abode from the fumes emanating from it…) I hope we have gone away before the thaw sets in. A selfish wish I admit, but war does make one selfish. We don't care a jot for artillery bombardments, so long as it is not we who are being bombarded. When we see the company on our left or right being blown to pieces by trench mortars, we pray the Hun will not change the position of his gun. Strafing is all very well, but being strafed is a different matter altogether. 'Everything in the garden is rosy', so long as our personal safety is assured. This is War philosophy. Hearing of the annihilation of a Brigade does not affect us very seriously, so long as it is not our own Brigade! But we actually rejoice and make exceeding merry when we hear of the Huns being killed in scores … we do not think of lonely widows and fatherless children. … The Game of War doesn't allow of that!

In the latter part of January 1917, the weather was increasingly cold, every day, with thickening snow and freezing fog. Instead of relaxing in front of a roaring log fire, on leave at home in the heart of his family with his own cosy bed upstairs and his sturdy desk and typewriter beckoning him, he was here, shivering with his men.

This winter was the coldest yet, with trench-foot rife from the flooded trenches throughout the autumn and through till the snow started falling, when fear of frost-bite and hypothermia replaced it. It was one of Hamish's duties to ensure that every man in his platoon rubbed each of their feet with whale-oil at least once a day. This may have helped, but not enough to prevent many good men from being removed from their duties because they were suffering from crippling frostbite or trench-foot. It wasn't just the cannons and shells that disabled: the deep, thick mud and the biting cold could be just as cruel.

All officers and men in the army had been provided with new, special-issue clothing in an attempt to keep them as warm and dry as possible. Very few soldiers would be warm or dry, no matter how strong and thick their garments, but at least it helped, except when they were so sodden that their clothes could not dry. The only good thing was that when the frosts froze the mud, the men could at least walk on a steadier surface, whereas if the temperatures rose above freezing, the thigh-deep mud could hold a man fast and many a good soldier who fell into a shell-hole drowned in the mire. Their bodies were sometimes not found till the spring, which came very late that year.

Every officer and man in the British army was issued with his own pair of 'gum-boots', just like those Hamish had bought for himself when in his initial officer training at Bedford Camp. These came up to the knee for most of the men, so that they could at least keep their feet dry. Some officers were eventually issued with thigh-high boots, a great boon for the men in kilts.

Other army issues included 'thermal' underwear, leather jerkins to wear inside their coats, and when the temperatures plummeted still further, a sheepskin jacket each to wear as outer greatcoats, with the fleece on the outside, just like its original owner. Soldiers were not allowed to take off their footwear in the trenches. However, sometimes men just had to disobey the rules for self-preservation. When their feet were numb with cold or tingling painfully with any brief moments of thawing, they found opportunities to take off their boots to rub their feet and wrap them in their sheepskins to bring back some life, in an attempt to evade frostbite. Despite such measures, there were many cases of soldiers having to have toes amputated or worse, due to trench-foot in the mud or frostbite in the wintry snow and ice. Temperatures dropped to –15 degrees C on some nights in late January and early February 1917, exacerbated by freezing fog and icy winds.

A hot drink would have helped, of course, but in the front line it was not possible to light a brazier; it would have given the enemy a perfect target, with all the men huddled round it to try to warm themselves. The army, as ever, came up with a solution, which was to make a huge urn of hot tea, place it on a mini-stretcher and two canteen staff would carry it up the communications trench to the men at the front. However, the communications trench being perhaps three-quarters of a mile long, by the time the urn arrived there was a layer of ice on top of the cold tea.

Nevertheless, as a direct result of the freeze, there were just a few good-luck stories. One of those days when the ground froze, with a sheet of ice over the top, an officer, George Jameson, had a narrow escape walking back from an observation post:

I suddenly heard this swish and I could tell by the very sound of it;
I could tell it was coming fairly near to me. Suddenly there was a

burst away to my right and I thought 'Well, thank goodness for that. Plod on … the gun fired again … suddenly, quite by my side there was this noise and, about 150 yards beyond me, the shell burst. What had happened was that the ground was so hard that the shell had just glisséed on the surface, you see. It struck within about a yard to my right as I was walking, and then went on and up in the air. About 150 yards on it burst. Now, if that ground had been soft, I'd have had that.[1]

The men in kilts, with their well-deserved reputation for toughness, were the ones with the worst problems. Fiercely proud, they steadfastly refused to relinquish their kilts in exchange for trousers. So instead, they had special-issue bandages which they carefully wrapped round their legs, all the way up. This gave them some little protection, but as the temperatures dropped their legs froze and the bitter weather became unbearable for those in the Scots regiments. As NCO J. Reid of the Gordon Highlanders put it:

Cold. Oh, God it was cold…. We marched and I always remember that. Our knees were even frozen up, you know, with the usual field bandages to wrap up our knees and all up our legs to keep the frost from biting into our legs, our bare legs.[2]

It seems that the Highlanders regiments were offered the opportunity to wear trousers or 'trews' in the coldest temperatures, but not one of them did. The Scots were, rightly in some respects, too proud of their kilts to exchange them for trousers.

Hamish had written an article about the wearing of a kilt as part of his uniform during his officer training at Richmond Camp, when he expressed his great pride in the kilt and its accoutrements as 'glorious relics of noble barbarism'.

In fact, not only did the Scots themselves gain courage from their distinctive uniforms; there is plenty of evidence that the sight of the Scots in their kilts scared the enemy witless. The Hun's nickname for the boys in kilts was 'The Ladies from Hell' and the general term they used for the

---

1. G. Jameson, quoted from IWM Podcast 25.
2. J. Reid, quoted from IWM Podcast 25.

Scots was *Furchtbarkeit* ('most to be feared'), as in a newspaper cutting in a Black Watch Officer's First World War photo album:

> Hundreds and thousands from Great Britain and overseas wore the kilt in Action. It was an incentive to battle, an inspiration to its wearers and a dread to Britain's foes. Yet this harmless, picturesque garment had enemies within our island home – One southern War Correspondent was particularly hostile in his remarks, yet he does not acknowledge that the kilted troops were 'the first in the field and the last to leave,' to quote the motto of that old Gaelic hero, Gaul.[3]

In the coldest French winter in living memory, the men's morale dropped almost as low as the temperatures. As one man said: 'I tasted the depths of misery.'[4] However, they all did their best to encourage each other with ribaldry and black humour. Indeed, Hamish was himself convinced that it was the British sense of humour that kept the whole army going, unlike their foes, many of whom were now voluntarily giving themselves up to the British in the hope of better conditions as prisoners than they had endured in their trenches.

On 27 January, after just four days in the snow-filled trenches, the men of the 8th Battalion were relieved from their duties and went to billets in Marœuil. For the following three weeks they would be occupied in large work parties, preparing for the coming attack. Hamish was not enamoured of 'fatigue parties' at the best of times:

> *To be on a fatigue party is usually an ordeal to be avoided. They are horrible things – why? I can't quite explain. It can't be because of the danger, because, oftener than not there is no danger. Perhaps some sterling psychologist will endeavour to probe this mystery, afterwards demonstrating in land and water (by means of diagrams) the cause of it all. G.K. Chesterton might do, but then he would probably end up by proving that fatigue parties don't exist!*

---

3. From 'The Kilt in the Black Watch' in Captain I.W.W. Shepherd's photo album, BWM, ON688.
4. Victor Fagence, quoted from IWM Podcast 25.

This might have been a convenient time for Hamish to go on his leave at last, but he was still there at Marœuil on 31 January, when he wrote:

14

A great calamity has occurred. Dickson, my Military Medal Corporal has been transferred to 13. He has gone and I feel very much upset about it. This morning, as he stood in the ranks, he smiled to me in a plaintive sort of way, as much as to say: 'The blow has fallen, old man, and we are separated!' I fought hard to keep him, appealing on the grounds of his long association with my platoon, in which he was 'brought up', so to speak. But there is no sentiment in the Army, and this deplorable fact was again brought to my notice by the O.C. Company. One of the best, one of the very best of my fellows has gone, and it is very hard.

There is no further entry in Hamish's notebook, which suggests that soon after the 31st he was finally released to go on leave. In addition to his elation on going home to peace, rest and safety, no doubt he would have been more than happy to leave the 'horrible' fatigue parties behind.

Chapter Thirteen

Not a Sight of Them Seen

'That is the cruel part of leave, the coming back.... Ten days of incomparable bliss ... and then a return to life in Trenches: the guns, the shells, the blood, the monotonous despair!'

(from Hamish's notebook)

Between get-togethers with family and friends and walking on his elegiac, 'wild hillsides' and moors, now buried in pure white snow, Hamish spent most of his leave at his cherished black typewriter with its gold lacquered scrolls and its round keys standing up on metal stalks. It was bliss for Hamish to sit and write all day if he wanted, without any interruptions or demands on his time.

Here, in comparative luxury, he completed his latest project, the dramatization of Michael Fairless's novel *The Gathering of Brother Hilarius*, a play-script for the Edinburgh stage, which he had begun in longhand in his Arras billet. The notes he made on a typed-up carbon copy show the developing cast list, including popular actor Esmé Percy in the role of the monk, as he had hoped. This copy also includes production notes, so it can be deduced that he may have spent some of his precious time with the director. No doubt he would have loved to take a role for himself, had he not been needed elsewhere. It is also clear that while still on leave he typed up and added to the first few chapters of his novel, *The Street Artist*.

The ten days of leave must have seemed so short and, in a way, so unreal; like a play within a play, as in Shakespeare's *A Midsummer Night's Dream*. Yet end they did, and before his departure, he left behind most of the writings he had completed to that date, including his latest trench diaries-cum-notebooks. He said his sad goodbyes to his parents, who had three sons, of whom Hamish was the youngest, all of them at war. To have him home for such a short interlude and then watch him leave again must have been heart-rending for them.

As Hamish knew it would be from others who had done it before him, his long, tedious journey back to the front, by trains and a ramshackle boat, tossed across the rolling sea in an icy wind, was with a very heavy heart. The only things that would have kept him going were his sense of duty and, even more important, the men of his beloved 14 Platoon, whom he rejoined close to where he had left them.

Perhaps it was on his journey back to the front that he wrote this 'Tragi-Comic War Sketch':

LEAVE

'Gentlemen,' said Second Lieutenant Reginald Ramsay, rising to his feet. 'I give you a toast: Captain Naylor and his leave!'

The toast was drunk with solemn state in French Champagne, costing five francs a bottle, from which Bobby Bilks did not recover for some days. (Wilson called it poisonous cider, but that's not the point.)

Captain W.R. Naylor, M.C. had just give a dinner to his subalterns to celebrate his going on leave next morning, and now they were drinking his health out of enamel cups. Only one member of the party was sad, and he was Gerry Fairley, who had just come back from ten days at home.

'French Champagne at five francs never tastes great,' said Naylor, 'but out of these tin atrocities it's the last word! However, boys, in a few hours' time I'll be consuming it out of purest crystal glasses. Think of it!'

'I refuse to!' exclaimed Fairley.

'When I get to London,' Naylor continued, 'I shall take a taxi straight to the hotel, and I'll order six hot baths, in each of which I'll wallow for two hours.' He paused. 'After I emerge all pink and shining from my sixth bath, I'll go downstairs and have a drink. Mark you, my lads, there'll be a tablecloth – all white and snowy – and silver knives and forks and spoons, and a spotless serviette...'

'This is cruelty to children, Naylor!' groaned Fairley.

'What then?' queried Ramsay.

'I'll tip the waiter, taxi again to the station, and then Edinburgh!'

'Meanwhile,' said Bobby Bilks. 'We will be serving our country in the trenches, or sitting in this rickety old billet, listening to the shells bursting on the road outside!'

'That's the beauty of it,' Naylor continued. 'I'll think of you fellows "standing to" in the line, about 6 a.m. In fact, I think I'll get someone to waken me about half past five and say "stand to, sir"! Whereupon I shall yawn ... and go to sleep again!'

'Lucky dog,' said Wallace.

'Cox,' went on Naylor, 'will have a lot of work to do when I'm in Blighty.'

'Yes,' added Ramsay. 'And when you come back, you won't be able to pay your own Mess Bills!'

'Don't talk about coming back, Ramsay!'

'No, it's awful!' volunteered Fairley.

Again, everyone laughed.

'The thought will humour me often, and, altogether, I'll have a damned good time of it!'

'I bet you will,' assented Bobby.

Just then the door opened, an orderly came in, saluted, and handed Captain Naylor a note. He opened it, became suddenly serious, and said something very, very forcibly.

'Read that!' he muttered, handing the message to Ramsay, who read aloud: 'All leave is cancelled until further notice.'

There was only one smile in the room, and that was Fairley.

It must have been the second week of February when Hamish returned to the frozen battlegrounds of northern France, to the sights, sounds and smells of war, just after his men had completed another harsh stint in the trenches. On 12 February, the daytime temperature was minus 11 degrees Centigrade. While under the rule-bound strictures of a temporary officer, they had witnessed a bomb landing on an adjacent platoon, friends of theirs, killing two and injuring another three. This hit them hard. They must have been relieved to have Hamish back with them again. The platoon had been moved back from the line to 'Y-huts', near Duisans, about 4 miles west of Arras, where Hamish joined them.

Here the men rested, had much-longed-for bath-parades (walking down to villagers' houses to use their baths, if indeed they had such a thing; usually a tin bath at best) and laundered sets of replacement clothes; something they could do only between their stints in the trenches, where they were not allowed to remove their clothes at all, especially in the snow, so they often had to wear them for several days at a time, usually wet, adding to the chill factor and making shivering misery for the men.

One of the side-effects of all this was that many of the men developed troublesome coughs, which echoed across the open spaces towards the enemy, giving away their positions and thereby putting themselves in greater danger. When this had happened in the previous November rains, some bright spark, obviously a creative thinker at HQ, had come up with an original solution, as Captain Badenoch of The Black Watch related in his 'Recollections':

> I remember in the middle of the night a runner came with a message from Brigade. It was marked 'Urgent, Secret and Confidential'. When the envelope was opened the message read 'There will be an issue of chewing-gum on 'Y' day. Please note, a ration of chewing-gum is one half pack per person.'!

From then on, Black Watch soldiers were required to carry a chewing-gum ration in their pack, which they had to open and chew if they needed to suppress a persistent cough so as not to signal their position to the enemy.

Marching and field manoeuvres throughout this practice period could be even worse in the bleak weather conditions, coping with heavy rain, sleet and snow by turns. The mud was the worst thing to cope with when troops were on the move, as Private Percy Clark put it:

> It was just one long, hard struggle to raise our feet one after the other from the suction of the gluey mud … so punishing was the terrible 'going' … that more than once I saw strong-looking men trembling and whimpering like kids.[1]

In their rest period between front-line duties, Hamish and his men enjoyed some recreation activities and a variety of training and support tasks. They all made good use of the rifle ranges to hone their skills, away from the sounds of the bombs and shells, muffled in the distance. Bayonet practices, drills and equipment inspections were also regular features of their time at 'Y-huts'. The equipment checks became particularly important now after such a long period of bad weather, when many men had jammed or dropped

---

1. P. Clark, quoted in Barton & Banning, p.76.

and lost parts of their rifles and other items in the deep mud or the drifts of snow. There were new items of equipment and modifications to issue to every man who needed them.

It was all ratcheting up, day by day, and hard to keep up with, especially when the instructors themselves were often uncertain what the latest requirements were. As Peter Barton and Jeremy Banning point out:

> Adequate tuition for battle, as opposed to basic military training was one of the most difficult goals to achieve, simply because the nature of war evolved at a faster pace than preparation could properly assimilate. Instructors with the knowledge and the required communication skills were a rare commodity.[2]

The officers, including all the subalterns, attended lectures where they learned about the extensive new regulations and the latest plans for the coming strike, which was to be a major undertaking – the 'Big Push' – against the Germans. There were several completely new strategies for the officers to learn about and prepare for, and reorganization of responsibilities across and within platoons. Having made solid gains over the past three months, pushing the enemy back, the British military hierarchy was now of the opinion that the war could be won by the end of the year (1917), which was very cheering for the officers, who could use this information to raise the morale of their men.

The finer details of the plan were still being worked out, but it would involve two armies: the First and the Third, the latter of which included the 8th Black Watch. This was going to be a serious challenge and Hamish knew it.

On 15 February, the whole of D Company, including Hamish and his men, marched to St. Nicholas, near Arras, where they had orders to support the Royal Engineers' specially-formed tunnelling companies in their underground construction work. They were to join the work of improving and extending the 'boves', an old network of caves and tunnels under the town of Arras, and digging out new branches towards the front line to act as supply and communication channels. These would have several advantages, including the invaluable benefits of not being able to be reconnoitred or shot at from the air. It must have been very arduous work for all ranks in

---

2. Barton & Banning, p.77.

claustrophobic and at times almost airless conditions, but they understood the strategic importance of this task.

After two months of freezing mud, way below freezing Centigrade temperatures and almost daily snow, a 'thaw' finally began on 17 February. However, that turned out to be only the first thaw, with the weather unreliable and, as the following days and weeks showed, some likelihood of a lot more rain and snow yet to come.

At about this time, Hamish wrote a letter to his parents, the first page of which is sadly missing. However, his reference to having recently returned from his leave places it as having been written in mid-February:

You would be amazed to find how delightful this billet is. I have a fine wood fire and a long garden seat in front of it. Two wooden tables are adorned with a blue and white checked tablecloth. A gramophone stands on a smaller table to the right of the grate. The two compartments of this underground house of ours are separated by a blanket suspended from the roof, my bed being in the main room in our cellar. Candles supply illumination, and a canvas door prevents draughts from sweeping through. Weekly illustrated magazines and all the principal daily papers lie about.

We mess rather well, the 'kitchen' being upstairs, where the cook and the mess-corporal, assisted by our servants, do their best to produce delectable dishes for us.

The only drawback is lack of chairs. (At the moment, I am seated on a provision basket, which creaks and groans every time I move.)

The latest news we get is through the medium of the **Continental Daily Mail**, *which little French boys bring round every day.*

It's a splendid life!!

The duplicating paper has arrived, thanks. Colquhoun has gone off to the 1st Battalion, which he was with when wounded the first time he was out here.

The weather is rotten. It's been raining all day. But the cellar is very comfortable.

Write soon again.

Cheer-o, with love.
Prof.

P.S. I left my big pipe at home! Can you find it and send it out? It may be in one of the coats on the rack.

Thine,
Prof.

On 17 February, two British divisions launched simultaneous attacks on the Hun near the Ancre River. They were successful in overrunning more than a mile of the enemy's front-line trenches, pushing them back and taking nearly 600 prisoners. This was great news, and although the following day there was a German counter-attack, it failed miserably.

On 23 February 1917, the whole of the 8th Battalion reassembled from their different work parties across the area and marched from 'Y-huts' to Monchy-Breton, a 'special training' area.

Family lore has it that on this or another similar march at about this time, Hamish's company moved to one side of the road, while another company approached, going the other way. As they passed one another, among the usual quips and banter from the ranks across and back, Hamish suddenly saw a familiar face, a very familiar face, just as the other officer's expression broke out in a wide grin of recognition. It was Alan, Hamish's older brother, a captain in the RAMC.[3] Much as they wanted to stop and catch up with one another, it was not possible without halting the whole of both companies and they had to keep moving to keep to their strict schedules. However, even without talking, they must each have known that this fleeting chance 'meeting' might become a memory to treasure within the uncertain times in which they lived and fought, in their joint endeavour to beat the Hun and get back home to old times again with the family, if that could be possible, for them both to beat the odds.

Hamish and his 'boys' reached Monchy-Breton and settled in. For the officers, this 'special training' would include details of the new regulations that had been carefully worked out by the military planners, to incorporate all the lessons learned during the battles of the Somme and the Ancre. The intention of these new regulations was the streamlining and clarification of infantry formations, orders, strategies, defences and attack tactics to optimize their effectiveness. For the men, their training would be in adjusting to their new, enhanced equipment and practising their fighting skills – good old-fashioned bayoneting and musketry – with new twists. All of this was in preparation for the forthcoming battle, which was planned to take place as soon as the weather improved, though nobody could have felt optimistic then about a thaw happening any time soon.

---

3. Captain Alan Cowan Mann M.C., RAMC.

There had been sporadic rumours, or possibly news, coming through for a week or more now that, in certain places on the line, the Germans were offering comparatively little resistance. Indeed, in a few cases, none at all. Yet in other spots, the firing and shelling was as strong as ever.

On clear days, airborne reconnaissance was attempted by the British, but in the sky the Hun had gained the advantage, especially now that the devastating attacks of Baron Von Richthofen (the 'Red Baron') downed so many of our planes. Indeed, it was said that we lost so many planes, their pilots and crews that there were no suitably-experienced replacements, so new young pilots were being sent straight from flying school with insufficient training and practice. Sadly, they didn't have the chance to build up many flying hours before their inevitable fate took their lives. So it was not possible to be sure yet what had happened to the Boche front line, other than that some parts of it seemed to have been abandoned.

The British army's senior officers came to the conclusion that this could only be explained by such high numbers of Boches having been killed, wounded or taken prisoner by the allies during the autumn and early winter that the German armies were now being stretched to the limits. So perhaps, rather than spreading them thinly the length of their front line, albeit less long now than it had been, thanks to the gains made by the allies, their remaining Boche soldiers were placed in some strength at strategic intervals.

On 24 February, while the French and British political and army chiefs were battling it out in dialogue at 10 Downing Street, trying to agree on the details of rail transport and supplies for the forthcoming attack, some British patrols were sent forward to reconnoitre the confusing situation on the ground. When they returned they were debriefed by their commanding officer:

> They found a series of dugouts, one of which was entered and showed signs of recent occupation. Throughout the reconnaissance, not a single shot was fired by the enemy and not a sight of them seen. …The above report seems almost incredible, but I am of the opinion that it is reliable.
>
> Lieutenant Colonel Paul Norman[4]

---

4. W. Norman, C.O. of the 21st Manchesters, The National Archives, WO95/1668.

The evidence of a German withdrawal was beginning to strengthen, with further such reports in the following days. The news gradually spread among the troops, raising morale just when it was needed.

From the growing intelligence coming in, the exodus seemed to involve the German army's evacuation of a strip a few hundred yards wide all the way down on the east side of Arras and a very much larger area to the south.

Paul Maze, a French citizen who joined the British army and became an interpreter for the 'top brass', later gaining the highest military awards from both nations, always seemed able to elicit the most reliable, up-to-date intelligence. He was one of the first to know for certain that the Germans had vacated their trenches all along their former front line and to suss out what they were up to:

> To hide their design from us, the enemy increased their activity, especially at night, when they lit the line continuously with their flares and kept up a constant machine-gun and rifle fire. One night one of our patrols succeeded in getting through the German front line and boldly wandered about beyond it for a considerable time without finding a trace of occupation. This confirmed all our conjectures.[5]

Maze then joined an attack group and a number of reconnaissance parties to scout for more details and nearly everywhere he went, there were empty trenches and either no Germans or dead Germans. On the rare occasion when he heard German voices, there were no shots and when he entered abandoned villages, expecting to be attacked, nothing happened. It was eerie and somewhat mystifying at first, but gradually he was able to build up a picture of the German army's switch from their old front-line trenches to a stronger defensive line further back. As Peter Barton notes: 'The French military and political hierarchy were struck dumb by the retirement. What did it mean? Was the invader no longer bent on defeating their nation?'

The answer to the second question was obviously not, or they would have withdrawn completely. However, this was a tricky situation for the joint allies' military leaders, whose intricate plans for the 'Big Push' were now outdated

---

5. Maze, as quoted in Barton & Banning, p.49.

and would have to be reworked with great urgency. As the French writer of communiquéés for the *Daily Press*, Jean de Pierrefeu put it: 'Consternation reigned … and only gloomy faces were to be seen. The offensive prepared with so much care had become void.'[6]

The German army was undertaking a voluntary and highly-strategic withdrawal, back to specially-constructed strongposts in a trench-fortress system. It was to be a shorter, tighter line – the *Siegfried Stellung*, or the Hindenburg Line as the allies called it – which would be easier for the Germans to defend with declining numbers of troops and losses of equipment. This new enemy front line was now 11 miles shorter and 3 miles further back. Consequently, as Victoria Schofield writes: 'No Man's Land now constituted an extended wasteland of destroyed bridges, roads and railways.'[7]

One of the problems this caused the allies was that the newly-extended tunnels from Arras to the old front line would now be too short. Where the carefully-dug communications and supply shafts came up, they would now be too far back from the new front lines. Everything had to be rethought. The attack was to take place in early spring, as soon as the weather was sufficiently improved for battle, so there was not much time.

While the generals and military strategists focused on developing new maps and blueprints for the battle, there was plenty of work for the troops to do. One of the major tasks for the men was to extend and dig new tunnels and trenches, but on the surface the ground was still frozen solid and digging was all but impossible. Under the ground, however, the 'boves' – subterranean caverns and passages – offered the most practical solution for now.

In exploring the land recently vacated by the Germans, the allied troops found to their cost that the Germans had pulled down and often burned most of the houses in the abandoned villages, poisoned the wells, streams and water-systems and booby-trapped the ruins in such a way as to cause the worst possible damage and loss of life to reconnaissance parties.

In fact, there was a popular cartoon published in *Punch* magazine that depicted two puzzled-looking soldiers, standing in what had been a village, but all the buildings were now in ruins and unrecognizable. Entitled 'The

6. Pierrefeu, as quoted in Barton & Banning, p.51.
7. Schofield, p.128.

Optimist', one of the soldiers was saying to the other: 'If this is the right village, then we're all right. The instruction is clear – "Go past the post office and sharp to the left before you come to the church".'

It was sad and often moving for reconnaissance parties to find once-thriving villages in utter desolation, with the detritus of everyday life barely visible: a cooking pot with congealed soup in it on top of a battered stove, the only thing still standing, or a child's sandal in what was left of a doorway. The Boches had been cruelly trained to be able to booby-trap the most innocent of items, leaving it primed for a British soldier to pick up ... and be blown up. Had they not been warned by their own officers against touching anything they saw that looked 'ordinary', such an action could have been fatal.

Meanwhile, training and work parties continued apace. With the forthcoming campaign in his mind, Hamish was, as ever, philosophical about what the future might hold for him, knowing it may not be long. The following extracts from one of his longer poems no doubt draw on the opening words of *The Soldier* by Rupert Brooke, Hamish's favourite war poet, but Hamish writes his own message here for his loved ones:

WEEP NOT FOR ME (extracts)

If I should die, let no man mourn my loss,
For there is nothing in this earthly dross
That warrants e'er a sigh, a moan, a tear.
I am unworthy that my distant bier
Should cause a single soul to droop with pain.
Rather be thankful that the fates ordain
That I should sink beneath the Sea of Life,
Witless of half the cares of mortal strife.
Let no one mourn because my soul was young,
For all things worth the singing I have sung.

.....

Dream not of me as gone before my prime:-
There ne'er could be more noble, apt a time
Than now to die.

.....

Let memories of me be brave and true:
I would not like to think the Life I gave
Had brought you woe. Be proud, not bent
With gloom, as though some frightful shame had spent
Its fury on your house.
        I die – What then?
I am but one 'mongst countless finer men.

In the regimental diaries entry for 25 February 1917, despite the distinctly chilly air, the continuing night frosts and sporadic flurries of snow, the entry reads 'Summer time introduced – 11 p.m. becoming midnight.' It was only the second year this had been done, to allow the troops more daylight hours for work parties and on the front line. It was apparently a German idea, originating in 1916, and one that the allies decided to follow.

Throughout the battalion's training time, more drafts were brought over the Channel to swell the British ranks. As Hamish had earlier written in his notebook, if only America would stop sitting on the fence and join the war…. However, it seems that the allies now had a larger source of new recruits than their opponents, arriving in time to be fully trained and equipped for the coming attack.

At the end of February, the whole of the 9th Division, including Hamish's 8th Battalion, received orders that they would shortly return to the front line, so they busied themselves to be ready for the move.

On 2 March, the 8th Battalion marched from Monchy-Breton back to 'Y Huts', near Duisans. The following day they left 'Y Huts' to march the last few miles into Arras, where the battalion's HQ was established in the Hotel Universe, while Hamish and other officers were billeted in the convent. Most of the men of the 8th were scattered in buildings across Arras and St. Catherine's to the north of the town.

Poised now for another hazardous stint in the trenches, Hamish's thoughts again turned to his folks at home and the wild places where he loved to walk during his leave, just three weeks earlier:

A SUBALTERN'S SOLILOQUY

Once did I ask that I be laid to rest
On some wild hillside where the grasses sway;
But now, meseems, my resting place will be
Where rifles fire and red blood runs all day.

I cannot ask for winds to mourn my dirge
Or wailing whaups to wheel above my grave;
I shall be buried with the others there,
When I have given what the others gave.

And I shall sleep beneath that foreign sod
As peacefully as if 'neath heather flower,
Knowing I am but one 'mongst all those men
Who breathed their latest sigh in Britain's Hour.

Chapter Fourteen

The Tension Rises

'The date of the attack remained a military secret, but early rumour fixed it at 15th April.'[1]

(Major M.J. Mulqueen)

From 4 to 7 March, the 8th Battalion was scattered across the town and its outskirts, forming work parties for both the Royal Artillery and the Royal Engineers. The whole area was crowded with batteries from various regiments, undertaking the wide range of preparations necessary for the forthcoming 'Big Push'.

While the men worked, they could see all along the eastern horizon, villages burning, the black smoke rising into the frosty air, particularly dramatic at night.

Morale began to rise as all the units of men knew they were working together for a great cause; they could see their achievements and the intended benefits of their efforts. As Jonathan Nichols wrote: 'Great excitement at the prospect of open warfare rippled through the ranks of the British and French armies.'

However, this excitement was tempered with apprehension at all levels of the 8th Black Watch, who knew it was likely they would be involved in the battle, as part of the 3rd Army, according to the original plans that Hamish and the other officers had seen. However, now that it had become ever more evident to everyone that the Germans had been voluntarily vacating their former front line, new plans began to come through, with adjustments and alterations to the work currently being undertaken, above and below ground across the Arras area.

This enforced turnabout had a particular impact on the subterranean passageways, which required many of the troops to join the tunnellers in

---

1. Mulqueen, quoted in Barton & Banning, p.84.

their efforts to extend and equip these underground routes to the new front lines, building dugouts into the tunnel walls to provide quarters for telephone exchanges and HQ offices as well as equipment dumps and other services. They also extended the pre-existing caves and excavated new ones to provide billets for tens of thousands of soldiers, leading up to the major battle in a few weeks' time.

Meanwhile the Germans, with their superiority in the air for reconnaissance, had noticed the continuous troop movements into and around the town and the intensity of activity. Despite the fact that, of course, they were unable to see and were completely oblivious to what was going on underground, they were nonetheless rattled by the high numbers of allied soldiers, artillery and supplies gathering in one theatre of war. Consequently, throughout early March, the whole of Arras and its outskirts were subject to continuous bombardment from enemy artillery. The Hun's favourite targets were the busiest junctions leading into the town, as Captain Gameson, a medical orderly, explained:

> The volume of traffic in and out of Arras was very considerable. The flow was greater at night, but was by no means confined to the hours of darkness. Most of it came through the Baudimont Gate, a massive structure divided by a central wall into two miniature tunnels, and there was no getting round the Baudimont Gate. The congested approaches within and without the gate were perfect targets for shelling. By day, the road from the west was under direct army observation at Dead Man's Corner. There was camouflage netting on the north side at this point, but often the posts and netting were lying flat on the ground. It is quite impossible that the vigilant enemy was unaware of the prolonged, concentrated movement.[2]

Although this resulted in many casualties, the 8th Battalion was fortunate in being less affected than most. One of Hamish's colleagues, Second Lieutenant Young, was the only officer of the 8th wounded by a German shell. Young had been another of Hamish's joining cohort of twelve, so

---

2. Barton & Banning, p.83.

now only a quarter of them remained unscathed. However, though Hamish wasn't injured, he was, like many, affected by a tear-gas shell:

Tonight I have been weeping profusely. Hun tear shells caused it. This is the only way the Kaiser's hordes can make us weep. Brother Boche weeps for other reasons...

While his men were working under the auspices of the Royal Engineers' officers, Hamish, along with other subalterns, attended lectures on the more detailed plans and how to organize their platoons to meet the new regulations. This spring attack, orchestrated by General Sir Edmund Allenby, CO of the allies' Third Army, was going to be focused on Vimy Ridge and to the north of Arras. Four battalions of the Black Watch were to lead the attack, including the 8th Battalion, so over the next few days Hamish set himself to learn and memorize every detail of these plans.

On 8 March, the 8th Battalion was moved into the support trenches in 'J' sector, immediately behind the front-line trenches. On the 9th they relieved the 7th Seaforth Highlanders and took over the front line. It was a dangerous operation due to the well-timed strafing of the Boche Air Force, who dropped a bomb close enough to wound Second Lieutenant Chambers who had to be carried to the medical officer's dressing station, a short distance along the trench.

The medical officer himself, Major Jonathan Bates, attached to the 8th Black Watch, was the very same 'Medicine Man' of whom Hamish was fond and about whom he had written a short ditty (see Chapter 8, 'Battle Fatigue'). While in his letters Hamish tended to focus on his ideas, his impressions and family matters, Major Bates wrote equally vividly about conditions and basic medical facilities in the trenches, the weather and military activities. However, they have in common that both of them made light of their circumstances so as not to worry their loved ones at home.

On 9 March, the first day of this tour on the front line, Major Bates wrote to his fiancée:

Friday 9th March 1917

We are at last settled in the trenches, after many moves…. Our headquarters are most luxurious. A topping mess dugout – 7 feet high and plenty of room and a good fire … And my dressing station is the one next to it…. We moved in after breakfast…. Quite decent trenches and as dry as a bone at present, owing to the frost. It's a most peaceful part of the line here, I'm glad to say. We have electric light laid on but … out of order at present. I think someone digging in a trench has cut the wires. We have had a series of snow-storms today and, au moment, it is going quite strong. Don't like it as it will be all the more messy when the thaw comes. …I hope it will not thaw till we go out.[3]

The 8th Battalion was now holding the line which was planned to be the starting point of the 26th Brigade, of which the 8th was a part, in the Battle of Arras. It was over 1,000 yards in length. On the right of the line was the River Scarpe, where it was at its worst: 'As a trench line, it left much to be desired, especially on the right, where hostile heavy trench mortars had completely flattened the parapets of the front line trenches.' (Wauchope, p.35.)

On the evening of 10 March there was an attempt at a raid on Hamish's part of the line by the enemy; just twenty or thirty Boche soldiers climbing over their parapet but the battalion's patrols had noticed something was afoot and notified their officers, who were ready for them, letting loose rifle and machine-gun fire and trench mortars. As Major Bates described: 'The Hun was absolutely dispersed and never got started on his jolly old raid!'

The weather in the trenches, as everywhere else, was terrible. The ground was hard as iron, like a deep permafrost, and the snow kept on coming to make their lives a misery in constantly wet, heavy clothing, numb hands and feet, with the ever-present fear of frostbite.

The rest of Hamish and 14 Platoon's tour of duty continued ice-cold but quiet with no more attempted raids. On 14 March they were relieved by another Scottish regiment and marched back to Y Hutments at Duisans, where they spent the next six days trying to get warm and clean again,

---

3. Major Jonathan Bates M.C, M.O., IWM 2854.

relaxing and training as a platoon with daily shooting on the rifle-range and the honing of their other fighting skills. One of the tasks they rehearsed was the passing of whispered messages, which was the cause of some merriment. As Hamish described it:

> *A comical thing happened this morning when we were doing some passing of messages. We had the whole platoon ranged up in single file at four pace intervals. Sergeant Griffiths stood at one end of the line and passed messages up to me, whereupon I would send another back to him, just to give the men practice in it, you see. 'I am going to advance,' I passed down. 'Can you send me reinforcements?' I waited for a long time, and then Griffiths came up to me, shaking with laughter.*
>
> *'What on earth's the matter?' I asked.*
>
> *'What did you send down just then?' was his answer.*
>
> *'I am going to advance. Can you send me reinforcements?'*
>
> *'Well,' he replied. 'It reached me as "I am going to a dance. Can you lend me three and fourpence?"'!*

Although technically supposed to be resting for at least some of the time, the troops' physical strength and digging skills were sorely needed, this time to link the underground caves to each other via tunnels and excavate new, concealed exits to the battlefield. So this is where they spent much of the next seven days, supporting the Royal Engineers.

Meanwhile, in mid-March the evidence was now irrefutable that the enemy south of Arras had fully retreated still further back to occupy their new front-line trenches, just ahead of the Hindenburg Line.

One of the unexpected problems the allies encountered as a direct result of the German withdrawal was that the Hun had cut down every tree, pole and post, right down to the ground, to rob the allies of anywhere to attach their telephone cables to extend communications across to the new front lines. This required enormous consignments of new wiring and poles to be brought in, which kept the signallers busy fitting up to 10 kilometres of wire a day to ensure the restoration of communications. In the meantime, the troops resorted to good old semaphore with flags.

Roads and bridges, blown up by the enemy in the most devastated areas, now had to be repaired. Booby-traps in anything from a doorway to a lump of coal were defused. Rubble was cleared from the villages to allow troops and vehicles to pass through. There was no shortage of work for all the new drafts of men being brought across the Channel, in-between their training and instruction.

During the undertaking of all this hard, back-breaking work, there were occasional instances of humour among the troops or incidents that made them laugh, to lighten their load, as Captain Greenwell described:

> Transport is difficult and there are only about two bridges over the Somme. Two or three R.E.s[4] stand by them night and day with hammers and tin-tacks, and every time a wagon passes over they rush forward to put in a few extra nails and let the next one go over. I hear that a whole gunner limber – six mules – careered over the side the other day and went right in. It contained all the officers' mess stuff, and for days afterwards their servants were to be seen angling for lost tins of salmon and bottles of whisky, to the joy of the spectators.[5]

Private Paddy Kennedy related another memorable incident that occurred in a half-dug trench one night, by the light of the moon:

> We heard a sentry shouting: 'They are coming over with white waistcoats on!' Everybody stood to arms. S.O.S. rockets went up. Heavy fire was opened up … and when the alarm was over it was found that some white goats had strayed onto our wire.[6]

Although enormous efforts were made among the British to ensure absolute secrecy regarding the major spring onslaught, it seems that the Hun, during a February 1917 raid on a French unit in the front line, had captured a document which ordered a French offensive against the Germans in April. Fortunately, the order did not say how or where this attack would take place. Of course, the Germans didn't let on that they knew anything, but it focused them on the need to strengthen their defences. In early March, another raid

---

4. Royal Engineers.
5. Captain Graham Greenwell, M.C., quoted in Barton & Banning, p.53.
6. Private Paddy Kennedy, quoted by Barton & Banning, p.55.

brought into the Hun's possession further evidence from the French, and soon after a French NCO was captured with his army's detailed instructions for attacking the enemy.

Fortunately, the intention had always been that the British would attack first and, as none of the details of their battle plans had been leaked, these breaches of secrecy in the French army did not unduly threaten the British preparations for the big day.

Hamish and his fellow officers were finally informed that, due to the Germans' strategic withdrawal from their former front lines, the maps and plans had been redrawn and fresh instructions set out. This meant that all the details they had pored over and learned for the forthcoming major offensive were no longer valid and they would have to retrain on the new battle strategies.

The maps of the enemy's new front line showed that the worst of the British Empire units affected would be the Fourth and Fifth armies, before whose intended positions the ground was now a vast wilderness of destruction for several miles. The Third Army's planned position at the other end had the opposite problem with one of the strongest sections of the enemy's Hindenburg Line now right in front of where the British front line and Hamish's platoon would be; a daunting prospect, to say the least.

However, new trenches continued being dug and additional communication lines laid to ameliorate these concerns. Worse still for the hierarchy was the very real fear that the Hun might now retreat east and north of Arras as well, to render every plan null and void. This ratcheted up the need to finalize the date of the attack, so that it could take place as soon as possible.

Regardless of the weather, the date was now set for 8 April, Easter Day, though it was then put back a day to the 9th to fit in with the French army's arrangements.

The revised plan directed the Third Army to attack on a width of almost 10 miles, using ten infantry divisions. Urgent officer training and re-briefings took place that week for Hamish and the other subalterns, along with their senior officers.

On 21 March, Hamish and his platoon moved back to 'J' Sector to take up residence once again in the front line. In the absence of Hamish's notebook of writings or any letters from this period, it is helpful to gain a flavour of this tour of duty in the trenches from his friend the medical officer, bearing in mind that he paints the scene in his best bright and breezy light so as not to upset his fiancée:

> Thursday 22nd March 1917
>
> Today has been fine and warm and the trenches are wonderfully clean. ...It is very interesting to sit outside our dugout and watch the aeroplanes.... Very often nearly twenty are visible at once and there is usually a good deal of shooting at them. On a fine day like this they are as busy as bees... The Boche in the sap (a defence trench opposite) ... keeps on peeping over, although our boys shoot at him. One of these days he will do it once too often![7]

After just four relatively quiet days in the front line, Hamish and the rest of his battalion were relieved and moved back behind the lines, where further frenetic training and work was scheduled for them all. For four days they hastened their battle-readiness. Work parties dug new assembly trenches for the tens of thousands of men who would congregate for this major offensive. They cut gaps in the wire, under cover of darkness, and formed new dumps for the plethora of additional equipment and materials that might be needed. The planners had thought of everything, it seemed, when Captain R.E. Badenoch, also of the Black Watch, was given a particular task for him and his men to undertake: I remember taking out a working party to dig an enormous grave in preparation for the killed. It was not exactly a very cheerful thought.

All preparations were completed and ready by 25 March. Finally, on the 26th, the 8th Battalion marched back to 'Y Huts', where the medical officer again wrote to his fiancée:

> Monday 26th March 1917
>
> Just arrived at the huts half an hour ago. Well, it's nice to be out once again, though we were very lucky this last tour in the trenches ... very lucky indeed.

Having ridden to 'Y Huts' on his horse, he wrote:

---

7. Bates, IWM 2854.

I trotted along and struck the high road and made my way along the 5 miles of dead straight road to our huts. Rather wonderful riding along that road on a dark night … with a quarter moon shining down…. Mules and horses and wagons passed – a motley crew, but very picturesque. Every now and then the whole road is lit up with the flash of a monster gun and the more spirited of the horses begin to rear and 'play up'. Then again a star-shell away in the distance will brighten the road and … the 'spit-spit-spit' of a distant machine-gun or the boom of a gun. It is all very wonderful … and so difficult to describe.

On the following morning, 27 March, the 8th Battalion marched a few miles further back to Haute-Avesnes. Here at last, despite their poor billets, they were encouraged to rest up, ready for the coming campaign. Sadly, the next morning, 28 March, the brief stretch of good weather broke, temperatures plummeted again and for the next few days it rained and snowed continuously by turns. Any hope of bringing the date of the attack forward was dashed. The men spent all their energy in keeping the snow and rain from coming through the broken glass windows of their billets and keeping themselves as warm and dry as they could.

Just to make matters worse, over the last few days of March the battalion was struck down with an epidemic of German measles, devastating several platoons, including Hamish's men. Major Bates, the medical officer, was kept very busy throughout this week, but was able to help the troops combat it and recover in time to report fit for the final run-up to the big day.

The training and practising carried on, day by day, ensuring all the troops who were due to take an active part on the first morning of the battle would know exactly what to do, how and when. Every action was part of the elaborate plan. The very beginning of the attack would depend on a barrage of explosions, like a curtain of smoke, meticulously targeted along the length of the enemy front line, to hide and therefore protect the advancing troops. For the rehearsals to be as close to the real thing as possible, they needed to represent the barrage, so a long line of soldiers had to walk back and forth, carrying and waving flags across a series of tapes to represent the enemy front line on the practice grounds near Arras, while those who would be in our front line could rehearse their co-ordinated attack.

As the snows of March flurried into early April, a potent mixture of tension and excitement was rising in the ranks. No doubt their characteristic bravado concealed a good deal of fear.

In a battle, the first men out, leading their platoons over the top of the parapets and into no man's land were always the second lieutenants, which was why there were more casualties among subalterns than any other officers, 'terrifyingly high'[8] as Peter Hart put it. Hamish knew that only too well and, when he had time to think about it, he did what always calmed him the most. Writing about his fears somehow helped him to manage his nerves. Here he rewrote a short plea:

PRAYER

When the time comes and all this wasty flesh
Becomes a nobler dust, a worthier clay,
When fire and all the implements of hell
Shall free my frenzied soul from earthly sway,
God grant my Passing justify my life;
May I have rest after that hour of strife.

---

8. Hart, p.200.

Chapter Fifteen

Battle Orders

'The whole battle area was buzzing with expectancy.'
(Jonathan Nichols, *Cheerful Sacrifice*, p.57)

On 4 April 1917, the first of a series of 'operation orders' was issued to all participating battalions. This document, 'Operation Order 95', was typed and checked at 26th Infantry Brigade HQ. (The 8th Black Watch was part of the 26th Brigade.) For some reason, perhaps a simple oversight, this first order was not marked 'Secret', as were all its successors. However, it was crystal clear that if any of these details should be seen by enemy eyes, tens of thousands of lives would be at stake.

This document was evidence that the 'Big Push', so long talked about, was now about to happen; that it could involve more danger than Hamish and his men had ever previously experienced. Seeing it all now in stark print on these final orders, preparing the way before the battle, he clearly had misgivings:

BEFORE

At least say this: my memory will be dear
With that sad sweetness which is nobly fine.
I ask no more: the rest cannot be changed;
Let memory and tenderness be mine.
And may I die more nobly than I live
(For I have lived in folly and regret):
Then in the last Great Moment when I pass,
I shall have paid my Life's outstanding Debt!

This operation order and its attached 'March Table' set out the carefully-calculated plan for the movements of every battalion and its pioneer platoons, together with artillery and support services. Every route was detailed with map references, road junctions, bridges and other landmarks, together with the exact timings of every stage. This was going to be a mammoth feat of troop movements that needed to be followed with meticulous care. If even one platoon should be a few seconds out on its timings, it would impact on all those following and cause serious jams or hold-ups and, of course, everything had to be done with as much stealth as possible.

The first of these movements for D Company, including the 8th Black Watch, was planned to take place on 6 April. En route to their eventual placements, billets had been earmarked for all participants, many of them at some stage in tunnels and caves under Arras or in buildings scattered around the town. All vehicles, guns and horses were to be kept under cover.

On the following day, 5 April – Hamish's 21st birthday – an urgent top-level meeting was held by the two army commanders-in-chief. This was because Robert Nivelle, commander of the French forces, wanted to persuade Douglas Haig, commander of the British army, to delay the date set for the beginning of the great attack to give his own forces more time to prepare themselves. However, the weather forecast was that the cold and snow would worsen, so Haig was reluctant to give any ground. The 8th, Easter Sunday, was due to have the best conditions. However, Nivelle was insistent on several more days, so in the end they came to a compromise of one more day, with Haig refusing to budge any further.

The allies' artillery took advantage of the day's delay to start bludgeoning the enemy with shells, including tear gas, which could be lethal at close range. However, the westerly winds diverted the gas back towards the gunners themselves, so they had to adjust their aim to more distant targets instead.

Also on the 5th, a 'Secret' amendment was issued, giving a correction of the map reference, which applied to the group containing Hamish and his platoon. On the 6th, a series of further operation orders was received, each with its attached 'March Table' and the detailed trench plan for the night preceding the attack.

Every time there was a change, no matter how small, Hamish had to learn every detail concerning his platoon, not least because the 8th Black Watch

Battalion was given the proud honour of leading the 'No. 1 Group', which also included sections from three other regiments.

Early in the morning of 6 April 1917, Hamish leafed through the latest copy of his old school magazine, the *Watsonian*, which his parents had just sent out to him. In this edition were listed the details and photos of those old boys who had been killed so far in the war. No doubt he must have wondered whether he would be next. It was this sad experience, seeing all those familiar faces – the tragedy of so many brave lives lost – that prompted Hamish to write his last poem:

THE GREAT DEAD

Some lie in graves beside the crowded dead
In village churchyards; others shell holes keep,
Their bodies gaping, all their splendour sped.
Peace, O my Soul ... A Mother's part to weep.

Say: do they watch with keen all-seeing eyes
My own endeavours in the whirling hell?
Ah, God! how great, how grand the sacrifice.
Ah, God! the manhood of yon men who fell!

And this is War ... Blood and a woman's tears,
Brave memories adown the quaking years.

Arras, 6th April 1917

At mid-morning on 6 April, in torrents of rain, Hamish and his men joined the rest of the 8th Battalion as they began to move back to the line. On this first part of that journey, they were divided into two groups, according to their companies. Hamish's 14 Platoon, now forty men strong, was in D Company under Major Anstruther. The medical officer also travelled with this group, both of them on horseback. At exactly noon they all left Haute-Avesnes and marched along the route that had been set out for them, with Hamish carefully checking map references as they went so as to pass the specified road junction at precisely 5.45 pm:

The British Infantry, upon whose shoulders the fortunes of the forthcoming battle depended, began to trudge through the town, above and below ground, to their respective positions near the jumping-off trenches. And, although the occasional shell still fell, thousands of men were safe and dry in the deep catacombs and tunnels beneath Arras and Vimy Ridge.[1]

However, as they continued on their way, Hamish and his men had no such protection from the increasing German barrage of shell-fire. Yet, in the British spirit, they derived great satisfaction in the knowledge that the Hun had no idea that there were so many more unseen British troops, hidden underground, who would soon be unleashed on them.

From the road junction the company marched on to 'Y-Huts', where they were crammed into a few huts in E Block for a much-needed meal and a rest.

Although 6 April had been a long, tiring day for the regiments that made up the Third Army, no doubt the news had filtered through to the troops, either that day or the next: the news everyone had been waiting for, that finally America had joined the allies by declaring war on Germany. 'To the 350,000 British soldiers crammed into the Third Army area, it was a tremendous tonic, even though the more realistic knew that it would be many months before America could make its presence felt.'[2]

Hamish had been writing about and hoping for this possibility in his notebooks and letters for months:

'The sound of guns doesn't seem to have reached America yet ... I wonder if the scarcity of paper will affect Mr. Wilson at all? I hope so. It seems to be difficult to affect him.'

So Hamish must have been elated at the news that, at last, President Woodrow Wilson had been sufficiently affected by the German U-boats sinking so many US ships to take up arms with the allies. Yes, Hamish was an idealist, but a realist too at times like these. He knew it would take some time before

---

1. J. Nichols, p.57.
2. J. Nichols, p.60.

there were American soldiers on the ground in France, fighting shoulder-to-shoulder with the allies. However, looking ahead, the prospect of American troops joining the fray must have made the end of the war seem a lot closer, if he should live that long.

This information must also have reached the enemy's ranks, with the opposite effect: sowing seeds of despondency and lowering their morale at a crucial time. However, although the Hun was aware that there had been a lot of troop movements and that there was likely to be an ambitious assault, probably in mid-April, he could not have been aware of the size or scale of it. It seems that, just three days away, he still knew nothing about the uniformed hordes waiting out of sight, under the town, poised and even straining at the leash to advance, attack and, they hoped, overwhelm the enemy.

Despite the early breaches of security from the French, it seemed that, thus far, the tight secrecy of the allies' amended plans had worked. The waiting armies had to trust that nothing would happen now to spoil this crucial element of surprise.

On 6 April the British artillery built up their bombardment to a crescendo and maintained heavy shelling of the Germans throughout this and the following two days and nights, keeping the pressure on them and tiring them before the attack. Meanwhile, the 8th Black Watch rested as best they could during the day of the 7th at their cold, basic hut billets, regaining both their strength and their morale after their long previous day's marching, ready to set off on the next stage of the build-up.

At dusk on 7 April, the troops, already laden with a number of packs and carrying their rifles, were variously equipped with bombs, grenades, picks and shovels to take with them as well. Hamish and the other subalterns then set off with their platoons on the final leg of their journey, again following their pre-determined, circuitous route, marching through sleet and flurries of snow to Arras, under cover of darkness. The evening air was filled with the booms of heavy gunfire being exchanged across no man's land, not too far distant.

As they marched, the men were in good spirits and unusually quiet by turns, keen now to get on with the onslaught and get it over with, hasten the end of the war and return to rejoin their chums for a proper break. They were ready and eager to use all their vigour, all their speed and their endurance to achieve their objectives. Yet each man privately knew that they would not all return, that some of these very men they were marching alongside would not live to tell their tales, but most of them, having survived thus far, wanted to assume it would be others and not them.

At one stage along the way, they were met by another column of English troops marching in the opposite direction, passing cheerily by and shouting across encouragement, such as 'The best of luck' and 'You'll beat the Hun good and bloody proper' and 'Kick the Kaiser up the proverbial.' As Hamish and his men realized, these 'Sassenachs' had good reason to be so jolly cheerful, marching as they were away from the front and back to 'Y-Huts', where 14 Platoon had slept last night. However, the Scots were no doubt buoyed up a little by their ribald encouragement.

Cold to their bones, miserable from fighting the snow flurries and exhausted by the marching, they arrived at last in Arras late that night, where they were met by a guide who led them to their final billet before the battle: a large building with a French sign that said it had once been a 'Home for Aged Men'.

Major Anstruther and Major Bates took the small cellar room, which 'smelt strongly of monks', while Hamish and the other officers occupied the ground-floor rooms. Some of the men crowded onto the first floor, with the rest in the unruined parts of the attached chapel. They were not permitted to light a fire or strike a light on this freezing night, so they crammed together for warmth and made themselves as comfortable as they could. After so much marching during the late afternoon and on into the night, they slept well enough.

Easter Day, 8 April, dawned bright and clear, though still unseasonably bitter with a thick frost on the ground. When the men woke up they were supplied with a good breakfast and later on a lunch, cooked on an army cooker which had been brought onto the premises. They had most of the day to relax and rest before their final move that night, so long as they didn't go out of the building, to obey the strict but necessary order from on high: 'While in billets in ARRAS no one must leave his billets in daylight, except on urgent duty. Every precaution must be taken to avoid disclosing to the enemy the fact that troops are concentrated in that part of ARRAS.'[3]

---

3. Operation Order No. 95, attached to the 8th Black Watch Regimental Diary, National Archives Ref: WO-95-1766-1.

Apprehension was rising among the troops in D Company, conscious of the huge importance of the part each man must play in the forthcoming attack. Hamish ensured that all his NCOs knew the roles allotted to them, for if anything happened to him, the sergeant would have to take over temporary command of the platoon, and so on down through the other ranks.

Hamish himself must have been nervous and fearful, yet the patriotism and potential glory of the situation did not evade him. All officers who led platoons had retained their ranks and responsibilities through being effective leaders of men. It was up to Hamish to maintain the ethos and teamwork of his beloved 14 Platoon, but at the same time he had to look after himself and his mental as well as physical strength. This must have been so much more difficult now than it had been when leading up to that awful October night when they took over Snag Trench, to which he alluded in his final poem *The Great Dead* (see above). Then, less than six months ago, he had not known before that traumatic experience how awful it would be. Now, at Arras, he did, only too well, and he must have feared it. Yet somehow he kept himself strong.

While Hamish and his platoon, along with several others, were in their billet above ground and the majority in buildings scattered around the town, many thousands of the men who were scheduled to take part in the battle were billeted in the newly-excavated underground caverns, where they also made themselves comfortable. The caves were filled with cigarette smoke and the lingering aromas of hot stew and body odour, the rudimentary washing facilities – troughs of cold water – being insufficient for so many thousands of men.

At least, for Hamish and the men in the old men's home, there was plenty of fresh air; rather too much, in fact, with so many panes of glass shattered.

Not being allowed outside, the time passed slowly on 8 April, with everyone tensing up for Zero Hour the next morning. The padre who was with them held a morning service in the attached chapel. Part of its roof was open to the elements, but fortunately the sky was blue that day, despite the cold, and many of the men attended that Easter Sunday service to help pass an hour or so and perhaps to make their peace with God, in case the 'Adventure' should turn sour.

Hamish was known to have a rather unorthodox stance on Christianity for his day, but he was a staunch believer: a Socialist Christian, as he wrote in his flimsy *Book of Thoughts*, most of them philosophical musings:

> '*Socialism is the only true form of religion, and he who is not a Socialist is not a Christian.*'

Hamish was undoubtedly present at that Easter morning service with his men, singing patriotic British hymns such as *Onward Christian Soldiers* with the sun's rays pouring in through the broken stained glass, bringing forth a hidden tear or two among the men.

Similar services were held in billets all over Arras, as well as underground, wherever there was a padre or lay churchman willing to take a service. Sometimes there was nobody who felt able to lead such a congregation, so a group of soldiers would gather together for the Lord's Prayer, and maybe the first verse of a familiar hymn. Even such a simple form of worship was powerful enough to calm and inspire the men for the morrow.

To while away the rest of their free time that Sunday, they played cards, swapped stories and wrote letters home. Almost certainly, Hamish wrote a long letter to his parents but sadly that is missing. However, one of these letter-writers was the medical officer: Hamish's friend Major Bates. His letter of 8 April describes an incident he had witnessed the day before:

> Well, there's not much news when the subject of the war is barred by His Majesty's censors! ....Saw a wonderful sight yesterday ... One of our Observation balloons was up, when all of a sudden a Boche aeroplane dived out of the clouds, fired at the balloon and then rushed for home. The balloon exploded in flames and came down like a stone. Just after the explosion the two occupants jumped out of the basket with their parachutes attached. These opened all right and they came sailing slowly down to the ground, which they reached in safety. One of them was dragged along the ground for about 100 yards and bruised a bit, but that was all. It was certainly most exciting.

In fact, the sky was full of German planes that Easter weekend. The Hun knew something was going on, but he still had little idea what and when it could be, so he sent up as many of his spotter planes as he could, hoping to learn more from the sky. The Brits hastily obliged by setting up some dummy targets to lure them away from the camouflaged transports, hidden around the intended battle zone. Meanwhile, enemy bombers, led by the 'Red Baron', strafed and sniped at any British planes that dared to fly. Despite flying close to the ground for greater safety, several of our reconnaissance planes were downed that weekend. However, while the Germans now had superiority over the battle in the skies, they were still oblivious of the vast threat of fire and fury that was about to assault them on the ground.

The few allied army units who had to be out in the open during the daytime reported that it wasn't just Brits in the sky that were targeted. The poet, Edward Thomas, almost certainly known to Hamish, was a mature second lieutenant in the Royal Garrison Artillery regiment. He was outside with his platoon on Easter Sunday, tasked with taking them through a final rehearsal of what would be their first action of the battle, their crucial part in creating the creeping barrage. In his diary on 8 April Thomas wrote:

> Shelled at 12.30, then at 2.15, so that we all retired to the cellar … out at 3 for a practice barrage, starting in the danger zone, but we were twice interrupted! A 5.9 fell two yards from me as I stood by the X/C port. One burst down the back of the office and a piece just scratched my neck.[4]

Despite the obvious dangers, these rehearsals were essential. The timings in particular had to be perfect, as the mounting of this barrage was very strictly scheduled to ensure full co-ordination of all artillery units, starting as one and building to a crescendo at exactly the same time, for maximum effect.

The creeping barrage was a strategy that had been used earlier in the war, but it had been less effective than intended for three main reasons. One was that the barrels of heavy guns wore at different rates, so they were not firing perfectly in time with each other. The second was that not every officer's watch had been perfectly synchronized. The third reason concerned the fact that the shells themselves sometimes detonated under or beyond the barbed

---

4. E. Thomas, (1917), War Diary, Imperial War Museum, First World War Poetry Digital Archive, 1693.

wire, thereby leaving much of it intact. However, the army engineers had worked hard on resolving these problems.

First, they had checked, meticulously logged and calibrated the performance of every heavy gun and calculated accordingly. Secondly, for this battle, all officers' watches had to be synchronized to the second, twice each day leading up to 9 April, to make absolutely sure. The third improvement came about when the French invented a new type of fuse, which was much more sensitive and would detonate as soon as it touched anything, no matter how slight. This meant that when shells landed on barbed wire, they immediately vaporized it, thence giving a clear way through for the attackers.

During battle, the troops were trained and drilled to follow the creeping barrage 'as closely as a horse will follow a nose-bag full of corn.'[5]

On the 7th and 8th there were some audacious raids towards the German front line to cut wire. In one case a party got close enough to take three prisoners without a shot being fired. Other raids successfully cleared obstructions and booby-traps from some of the hamlets and houses in the allies' path, so that they could be used for dressing stations and platforms for onward attacks, as required.

Back in the 'Home for Old Men' billet, the officers and most of the other ranks managed to snatch two or three hours of sleep in the late afternoon, as they knew there wouldn't be much opportunity that night. The predominant sound to be heard resounding around the building was the snoring of at least 100 men!

Wherever the scattered Third Army soldiers stayed on that penultimate day, they all fed well, on General Allenby's strict orders. He decreed that good and plentiful food would be key to the success of this battle and required that the underground kitchens and those in every billet across Arras should cook a hot, nourishing stew for the men on the night before, followed by a hearty breakfast in the early hours, to energize them for the attack. Allenby's stew, served at 8.30 that evening, was a great success and was devoured with gusto by everyone in Hamish's billet, with second and even third portions available for anyone who wanted it.

At 9.30 pm on 8 April, it was time to get ready and pack up their kit. Every man had a pack for his personal possessions, plus a full water-bottle, a

---

5. Major General Arthur Currie, as quoted by Barton & Banning, p.86.

small bottle of rum, a half-pack of chewing gum (to prevent coughing on the battlefield), an iron-ration, a field dressing and a few biscuits. In addition, he wore various smaller, detachable packs containing knife, bayonet, entrenching tool, ammunition (up to 150 rounds), mess-tin for up to two days' rations, pick, shovel and wire-cutters, plus one or two Mills bombs and a ground-flare. The officers also had an additional pack for a notebook, orders and maps.

Normally, every soldier also wore a large pack in which he kept a waterproof sheet, a blanket and his greatcoat, when not wearing it. However, because of the likelihood of wet weather, General Allenby had sent out an order to tell all the Third Army troops to leave their greatcoats and their large packs behind as they would become too heavy if it should rain or snow and make movement more difficult, which would hinder them in battle. He thought there would be little point in carrying them if they weren't going to wear them. However, it was so cold that most of the men quietly disregarded this order, often with their officers' acquiescence since they too wanted to be warm on the marches and sitting in trenches through the frozen nights.

On the evening of the 8th some soldiers of all ranks slept a little more, until the time allotted for them to leave the billet and form up on the front line.

Zero Hour was fixed for 5.30 the following morning, so the tension rose as they paraded outside the old folks' home in the dark with all their equipment for a swift, uplifting talk by one of the senior officers, ready to leave at 10.30 pm. First the medical officer and padre left together at 10.15, as required, to ride to the front line with a corporal, two orderlies and the MO's servant on a circuitous route:

> Our journey was uneventful – happily there was little shelling and a bright moon. Our route was by footpaths, winding in and out of the marshes around the Scarpe. We reached the dressing station safely and found Howieson with No. 5 Platoon waiting there to go into position. All wonderfully cheery. Then the Padre and I went down to the trench.

At exactly 10.30 pm, as decreed in the Operational Orders, Hamish with all the other officers and men in his billet set out on their march to the pre-arranged assembly area in Arras. From here, Hamish's No. 1 group led the march, with four other groups following, as they navigated their way along the meticulously-prepared route that would take them along a track, across a bridge, then along a towpath, followed by another track, all the while being serenaded by sporadic shell-fire in the direction of the front lines. They had to keep the correct distance apart, one group so many yards ahead of the next, but close enough to follow on. This had all been strictly measured out and timed in advance and Hamish knew that, being the leading group, his men, along with the three other units in Group 1, had to set the correct marching pace and follow the given map references to the letter, in order to keep to the required timings.

They were on their way, step by step, getting closer to the unknown. Yes, they all knew about battles and most had a great deal of experience of the way things can happen, but Hamish had no experience of anything on this scale. All he could do was hope for the best, as they all did; hope that they would fight proudly and bravely for their country, for all the allies, towards a free world.

Chapter Sixteen

Zero Hour

'Silhouetted against this orange and red fire-bank were our advancing troops – a most marvellous sight. Lines of kilted men and all were marching and clambering over trench and wire with bayonet fixed and bomb in the hand. Woe betide any German that showed any signs of fighting!'

(Major Jonathan Bates, M.O., diary 9th April 1917, IWM)

Operational Orders directed the 8th Black Watch to meet at the assembly-point on arrival and proceed to their positions. Hamish had made a careful study of the battlefield map, showing all the trenches and positions of the allies and colour-coding the enemy lines that were the first objectives for capture. The attack would be conducted in waves, with the first wave of men going out across no man's land, followed at intervals by fresh rows of troops 'leap-frogging' over the tiring soldiers as they all moved forward, deeper into their newly-captured territory. By now, Hamish and all his officer colleagues had become very familiar with every meticulous detail of this plan.

The 8th Black Watch's first objective was to capture the enemy's front line, named as the Black Line, followed by its second objective, the Blue Line, 1,000 yards further on, then finally two new waves of troops would 'leapfrog' the first two and attack their third objective which was what the allies called the Green Line, from the River Scarpe to the Point du Jour line, and on to Athies.

The outcome of the forthcoming battle was now in the hands of the ordinary soldier. The fortunes of the day would be decided by the captains and lieutenants [including second lieutenants], some mere boys barely out of school, and of course the NCOs, the majority of whom had come straight to the war from all walks of civvy life.[1]

---

1. Nicholls, p.69.

As each group of soldiers arrived – more than 300,000 men in all – it could have been utter chaos, but it wasn't. Each group was efficiently guided to its designated starting-point for the battle. Hamish and his platoon were to be in the first wave – the first to go 'over the top' – so they went directly to their front-line trench, where the medical officer and his orderlies had already arrived and were setting up their dressing station in a suitably large dugout. They all quietly settled themselves in and watched, marvelling at the efficiency of this huge operation, as all the other units streamed along the back of the lines to drop into their respective trenches.

The 8th Black Watch was positioned with the Seaforth Highlanders in the two front lines on the right, ready to come out in the first two waves at 5.30 am, Zero Hour and ten minutes later. In the trenches behind them were the Camerons and the Argyll and Sutherland Highlanders, ready to come out for the second Zero Hour attack later that morning. In fact, a good percentage of the troops taking part in this major assault were Scots in their kilted battalions. It was the Scottish soldiers who the Germans feared most, so perhaps this was a deliberate ploy, planned right from the start. Were the HQ-bound strategists that perceptive? Or maybe it was just a happy coincidence.

The whole relocation of such huge numbers of the allies' armed forces, with all front-line platoons in their right places and tucked down out of sight, was successfully completed before the deadline of 3.00 am, an astonishing feat. Runners were sent to convey this welcome news to the 26th Brigade HQ at Forrestier Redoubt.

After their cold midnight march, many soldiers of the 8th Black Watch embedded themselves into what little shelter they could find from the freezing rain in dugouts and in sheltered parts of the trench, and snatched another hour or two of precious sleep, punctuated by a welcome delivery of lukewarm tea, toast and a hard-boiled egg for each of them at 4.00 am. By the time they were all awake, the grey dawn light was beginning to break above the horizon as the enormity of their task struck them anew: now was the day they'd been building up to, the day that would test them more than any before, the day that might be their last.

Hamish's friend, the medical officer, wrote in his diary about the drop in temperature, the rain and the effect that this worsening weather had on the men:

The sky became cloudy and a horrible drizzle started. This was most trying for all the men waiting to go 'over the top'. It is a nervy enough business, waiting for about 3 hours in a cold trench before 'Zero', but it is a severe test on the men's nerves and morale when it starts to rain under these conditions.

Throughout the night, there had been some sporadic, light shelling; rather desultory, as if most of the German army was fast asleep and totally unaware that this day would dawn any differently from its predecessors. At 5.00 am Hamish opened the extra rum ration and shared it out among his men. This was another of General Allenby's gestures, or more likely his strategy, to invigorate the men for the fray. As the minutes ticked away, not one man in the allied trenches dared to poke his head above the parapet to have a quick squint at what lay before them. Allenby's order had been emphatic, and every trooper knew that just such a small act could potentially alert the enemy and rob the allies of the element of surprise upon which the success of this day would rely. To this end, our artillery had continued their own occasional shell-fire through the night, as they usually did. So there was not a clue to be seen or heard by the enemy.

Meanwhile Major Bates, the medical officer, treated four of our soldiers who had been lightly wounded by the enemy's night-time shelling. As they rested, he went out into the trench, held his head up and took a momentary sideways glance to the left where most of the allied trenches stretched out further than he could discern. The Third Army alone had a 10-mile-long front line. The Canadians on the far extreme, many more miles distant, would be attacking Vimy Ridge. This was an awesome undertaking:

> Not a man was to be seen. All heads and bayonets were kept well down under cover of the parapets. ...In fact, there was nothing whatever to indicate that we had concentrated a large army of men ready to get up and attack in five minutes. The enemy was obviously in ignorance of this, else he could have caused very heavy casualties amongst our men crowded in every trench.... As it was, all movements on our part had been so cleverly concealed that he did not fire a shot.

It was a miserable morning, resembling December rather than April. The sleet slanted straight into the men's faces. The pre-dawn sky was dark with clouds. The allied shelling and its noise accelerated. Hamish and his platoon stood, poised like statues, silently counting down the last few minutes towards 5.30 am: Zero Hour, when our artillery would wreak a full bombardment on the enemy and create the creeping barrage in front of the Hun's front line, the closest part of which was just 100 yards ahead, and all our first-line troops would simultaneously pour out on the attack.

As usual, it would be the infantry battalions that would take the brunt of everything thrown at them. Today they faced what might be their ultimate test: the moment they feared the most of 'going over the top'. However, 'It was at times like this that the comradeship of the trenches was strongest. Reassuring themselves with a fervent conviction that they would be all right, many solemnly shook hands and wished each other luck.'[2]

Hamish was particularly good at raising the morale of his men in the 'Fighting 14' and, as such a talented wordsmith, had almost certainly prepared some appropriate words to say at this moment. He certainly inspired them with great praise and encouragement. At two minutes from Zero, Hamish took off his heavy greatcoat, sodden with rain, and all his men followed suit. They knew they could not run or move as fast as they might need to while wearing such cumbersome garments. No wonder Allenby had forbidden their use.

When their countdown reached one minute, several of the men started shaking, whether with the cold or their nerves or both, even they themselves could not tell. Their shared feelings of apprehension and dread were almost tangible. Now every man held his breath as Hamish, one foot on a ladder, counted down the last ten seconds on his synchronized watch: three, two, one ... CACOPHANY!

> Every allied gun for miles around opened rapid fire. The heavies made a continuous base roar and the lighter guns cracked out their treble part. Both ground and air shook and quivered while the shells screamed overhead. Then machine guns massed in the rear poured bullets over our heads – they seemed almost to make a parting down one's hair![3]

---

2. Nicholls, p.70.

3 Bates, diary, 9 April 1917.

With the first boom of a cannon, Hamish led the way for his men in the first line as they clambered up the ladders, gulped in a deep breath, leaped out over the parapets and moved forward at the agreed pace, with their bayoneted rifles pointing towards the Hun. This first line, formed of several thousand men, stretching beyond the horizon, fanned out and started to move across no man's land like a monster wave across a sea of frosted mud. They moved inexorably forward, weaving their way round the many shell-holes, towards the enemy, who were already hidden behind the creeping barrage, perfectly timed and executed. (Later waves of troops climbing over their parapets, without protection of the barrage, lost one in three of their men, shot down immediately.)

The Boches were well and truly caught out: total shock. Their soldiers had known nothing, expected nothing, but now they were faced with a vast onslaught, and yet all they could see was a wall of shrieking explosions and a curtain of thick smoke:

> As the barrage smashed into the first German line, tossing and tangling the wire defences and sending great flying fragments hissing and whirring through the air, the defenders scurried for cover, falling over each other in their desperate haste to get down in the dugouts where they cowered, taking shelter from the monstrous storm of shells. This time the British were really coming.[4]

Major Bates, following the first wave of men, right behind Hamish, described in his diary the astonishing sight produced by the allies' artillery:

> Where we were standing, we seemed to be between two walls of fire that lit up the grey dawn for miles around – the wall behind us, the flames of thousands of guns – the wall in front of us a mass of shells bursting on the enemy trenches … the men in kilts walking along as calmly as if they were at home – keeping a safe distance – 100 yards from our barrage. The ground seemed alive with men.

From the air too, the scene was one of high drama and more than a little danger for our air-crews, as described by a Canadian pilot in the Royal Flying Corps, Major W.A. Bishop, V.C., from his Nieuport 17 Fighter plane:

---

4. Nicholls, p.75.

The ground seemed to be one mass of bursting shells. Further back, where the guns were firing, the hot flames flashing from thousands of muzzles gave the impression of a long ribbon of incandescent light. The air seemed shaken and literally full of shells on their missions of death and destruction. Over and over again one felt a sudden jerk under a wing-tip, and the machine would heave quickly. This meant that a shell had passed within a few feet.... As the battle went on, the work grew more terrifying, because reports came in that several of our machines had been hit by shells in flight and brought down.[5]

Hamish and the 'Fighting 14' fanned out as ordered in a continuous line with their fellow Scots, the Seaforths, picking their way across no man's land, through the frosted mud and round the stray shell-holes. Thanks to the barrage, not one of Hamish's men was hurt at this stage and they were now advancing as a strong, united team.

Once the first line of allied troops was partway across, the big guns temporarily stopped to adjust their line of fire so as not to kill any of our own men as they neared the enemy's trenches. The troops kept going forward as the second wave of men came up out of the trenches and fell in behind them.

Floating from just above the ground, the creeping barrage obliterated the enemy's view of no man's land. It was so thick that the Hun couldn't even see the oncoming hordes, and all the time they were being rained on by bullets, shells and bombs shot from nearly 3,000 British guns and howitzers, exploding in their trenches, on their dugouts and all around them.

In total panic, the German soldiers shot their rifles wildly through the barrage, while their artillery got going over the smokescreen, felling allied soldiers indiscriminately. At this point, with perfect timing, our artillery troops started firing gas shells into the enemy ranks, disorienting the ill-prepared German soldiers, just as the barrage, 50 yards in front of them, began to dissipate.

As soon as visibility became clear enough, our first-line attackers ran through the gaps where the barbed wire had evaporated, nearly on top of the frightened Hun. The men in kilts overwhelmed the enemy's front-line trenches. This was the 'Black Line' on the British plan: the battle's first

---

5. W.A. Bishop, V.C., *Winged Warfare* (quoted in Barton & Banning, p.136).

objective, the whole length of which was captured at 6.10 am, only forty minutes after Zero Hour.

The German trenches were in a terrible state: full of shell-holes and almost completely destroyed, strewn with the bodies of the dead, between which lay the badly-wounded, looking up with pathetic gaze and murmuring '*Komrad, komrad!*', their eyes silently pleading for help.

Major Bates, with Hamish's group, sent the worst wounded Boches, as prisoners, back to the British lines on stretchers, carried by his orderlies, while he treated others where they lay. His servant found a dry dugout and later, even better, an abandoned German dressing station where they could treat any others needing help. At the same time, those British medical officers still behind the lines sent their orderlies out across the first no man's land, strewn with the bodies of Scots, to find and retrieve those who were still alive, treating the not too seriously injured and sending more critical cases on to the Field Ambulance team, who ferried them to nearby Casualty Clearing Stations.

The Scots also found a number of enemy soldiers cowering in the ruins of their trenches, ready and pleading to be captured and taken back as prisoners rather than being killed. Indeed, the Scots took a high number of prisoners from what remained of their front line, several of them officers and one a battalion commander. The 8th Black Watch alone took 150 prisoners during this first stage. Many others of their fellow Boches, realizing the magnitude of the British assault, had run away and escaped rather than stand and fight.

Leaving those prisoners guarded to be taken away by 'moppers-up' from the Argylls, Hamish and his leading group moved on beyond the captured 'Black Line'. The second wave had now caught up with the remains of the first and filled in the gaps left by the fallen. So the British troops once again formed a menacing tide of attack, moving relentlessly forward across the 1,000 yards distance, weaving between shell-holes and cutting their way through the next range of barbed wire. This was always more difficult for the Scots, whose kilts so often got tangled on the wire, but most were able to extricate themselves without too much problem.

Four British tanks now rumbled onto this next stretch of no man's land to help in the capture of their second objective: the Germans' 'Blue Line' trenches. The mere sight of these metal monsters lumbering towards them was enough to send many enemy soldiers running back. All the while our men moved onwards, under fire from the Hun's machine guns, shells and artillery. This retaliatory onslaught on our troops was joined by rifle-fire as the Scots forged on, into range of those Boches brave enough to stand in their trenches and face the 'most to be feared' Scottish attackers. 'The Black Line was taken with little opposition, but the Blue Line was holding out on the left behind Blangy and the Black Watch were badly cut up in getting through.'[6]

It was now, in an instant, that Hamish was hit, full-force, by a German shell, or by shrapnel from it. He felt the heavy punch into his lower body, lifting him up in the air and down again, crunched into the shell-hole the blast had created. At first he had felt only the punch and the shock that hit him. His whole body began to shake. Only then did he feel the searing pain, at its worst near the top of his leg. He reached his hand down and felt first the shredded material of his kilt, then his fingers touched the warm liquid trickling at first, then flowing out of what felt like a deep wound. This was the worst pain he had ever experienced, evoking a fear greater than he had known before...

All around him was noise and chaos. If he cried out, who would hear him? He knew he badly needed help...

'Sir, I'm here Sir,' called a familiar voice. 'Don't try to move.' It was his own platoon's loyal lance corporal, James Watters, whose anxious face now came into Hamish's view as he crouched down in the hole beside him. Seeing Hamish's wound, the lance corporal took off his own pack, rifled through and found his large field dressing. He opened the cover and applied the dressing to the top of Hamish's leg, with the thick pad over his wound, and tied the fabric strips to keep it on and apply a modicum of pressure. James Watters later wrote a letter to Hamish's parents, in which he explained the situation:

> I saw him fall on the 9th April ... The fact of the matter is, I did not think he was so severely wounded. Of course he was bleeding a lot, and I am of the opinion that the artery at the top of the leg was smashed.[7]

As soon as Watters tied the dressing on and moved Hamish's rifle from under him to make him more comfortable, Lieutenant Austen, crossing no man's land, paused to find out if Hamish was still alive, which of course he

---

6. Major Martin Littlewood, quoted in Barton & Banning, p.130.
7. Lance Corporal J. Watters (letter in family collection).

was. He then ordered the lance corporal to leave Hamish to be picked up later and rejoin the attacking force. From Watters' letter, it is clear that he didn't want to leave Hamish on his own so, torn by twin duties, he stayed a few minutes longer, talking to Hamish to calm him down. Then Hamish's servant, who must have been told his officer was wounded, arrived to relieve Watters. He stayed on with Hamish, who it seems was still conscious at that point and aware of the nearby noise and action. He was concerned for his servant, because there were bullets flying and the sounds of shells exploding their shrapnel all around, so the servant lowered his body into the shell-hole with Hamish, though he may still have been visible to the enemy, whose trenches were only a few yards away.

As they lay there, with 'thousands of planes overhead, a few Huns among them'[8] and the streams of orderlies carrying stretchers of the wounded back behind the lines, new waves of troops came up and skirted round them. At one point a tank came up from behind and passed them by, shooting 3in shells, followed by the Field Artillery, moving forward.

The assault continued ahead of the two men, who were now being left behind as the attacking wave captured the Blue Line and gradually moved further on. The temperature dropped and the sleet turned to steady snowfall. Time elapsed and the sounds of battle receded into the distance. More and more German prisoners were escorted back in a ragged crocodile towards the British lines, probably walking past where Hamish and his servant lay. Perhaps the servant called out to the prisoners' captors that his officer needed help but no help came, or maybe the servant himself had already been wounded or killed.

As the day wore on, it seems that Hamish probably alternated between conscious and semi-conscious states. In his moments of alertness, did he worry that he might bleed to death, or die of hypothermia? Did he wonder whether his heart, enlarged and weakened as a boy only a few years before, might not be able to stand the strain? Could he feel the life ebbing out of him? It seems likely that Hamish may have recalled at this moment one short sentence of the many that he wrote in his *Book of Thoughts*:

'Death doesn't seem very terrible, until we come face to face with it.'

---

8. M. Littlewood, quoted by Barton & Banning, p.131.

Perhaps he thought of his family at home and how badly they would react if or when they would have to open that telegram, and of course he would have thought about his platoon, his poetry, and his notebook, which he always took everywhere with him. Maybe he reached for it. The shell that hit him could have destroyed it, probably being in a pouch hanging from his belt, or he might have managed to get it out, then perhaps it dropped into the mix of mud and snow; all those precious writings and poems of his last two months, lost and never to be found. Finally Hamish lost consciousness completely.

Medical orderlies walked across the wasteland of what earlier had been mud and was now a carpet of snow, scouting for the wounded to take back for treatment, and the dead, who they would leave where they lay to be retrieved later. They found Hamish, still half-lying in the shell-hole with a light covering of snow on his head and the lower half of his body, but when they felt him he was so cold that they presumed him to be dead. They did as they always did. They checked the identity disc on his wrist and stuck Hamish's rifle upright into the ground next to him with his helmet on the top, which indicated a body to be collected. Finally they reported him as killed in action. This was the first report of his death: 'killed in action', 9 April 1917 on the Arras battlefield.

Several hours later the orderlies did another sweep across no man's land and came to Hamish's body, expecting to heave him onto the wagon to be taken for burial, but luckily one of them noticed that he was still breathing, albeit only very shallow breaths, and his body was deathly white and cold from lying in the snow. So instead they took him back to the first ambulance they saw, which was the No. 5 Australian Field Ambulance. Having already been reported as dead on the battlefield, then discovered still alive, he was taken into this ambulance, where the crew could not feel a pulse and pronounced Hamish officially dead: 'killed in action', according to a document on his file at The National Archives, which dates his death as being on 9 April 1917 and names this ambulance as his place of death. Indeed, there is also a slightly conflicting letter to his parents on file, telling them this tragic news, which was the second report of Hamish's death, this time stating he had 'died of wounds', 9 April 1917 in the No. 5 Australian Field Ambulance.

However, Hamish's story does not quite end here. We cannot be sure of the exact circumstances, but the ambulance must have driven him away from the battlefield in the late afternoon or evening. We can only presume that perhaps, out of the snow, while in the ambulance, Hamish may have regained some body warmth and possibly a little movement, as instead of taking him to be buried, they clearly changed their minds and drove him to the No. 42 Casualty Clearing Station at Aubigny, 6 miles from the British front line.

Here we can pick up the story as several of the documents in his file state that he was admitted to the No. 42 Casualty Clearing Station on the 9th as wounded, so certainly still alive. The situation at this Casualty Clearing Station was no different to the barely-controlled chaos at all the medical facilities within reach of the Battle of Arras, with such vast numbers of wounded troops needing treatment.

No. 42 Casualty Clearing Station (the military equivalent of a hospital) had been set up in the month leading up to the Battle of Arras, with the specific purpose of receiving and treating the wounded brought direct from the battlefield. Everything had been organized and put in place by Sister-in-Charge Kate Luard of the Queen Alexandra's Imperial Military Nursing Service.

Ten days before the battle, the hospital opened to receive its first patients, wounded by the enemy's sporadic shellfire. From that day on, Sister Luard wrote a daily diary of the patients, their wounds, treatments, operations and aftercare; some horrific stories graphically described. However, the diary has a noticeable gap, there being no entries for 7, 8 and 9 April. This may be because it was Easter weekend, but much more likely because of the acceleration of preparations and troop movements being noticed by the enemy, provoking them to greater artillery action. Thus there was no entry in the diary for 9 April, the first day of the Battle of Arras, when Hamish was brought in along with a great many other new patients, many of them seriously wounded.

On 10 April, at the end of what must have been the most exhausting two days of her career, Sister Luard wrote in the hospital diary:

> Easter Tuesday, April 10th
> The 3rd Army went over the top yesterday and a wire came through by mid-day that we'd taken Vimy and 4,000 prisoners and 30 guns. The Cavalry are after them, and the Tanks leading the infantry, and all is splendid. But there are horrors all day and all night. The three C.C.S.s filled up in turn and each of them filled up again, without any break in the Convoys: we take in and evacuate at the same time.

Stretchers on the floor are back-breaking work, and one's feet give out after a certain time, but as long as one's head and nerves hold out, nothing else matters.

Evacuation has been held up today, for some hours, and the place is clogged. The wards are like battlefields, with battered wrecks in every bed and stretchers between the beds and down the middles. We take in tonight, but there are two trains to clear.

The transport of the wounded is extraordinarily worked out. The walking cases come in lorries and the lying cases in electric-lighted Motor Ambulances, which look like lights along the embankment, as far as you can see down the road.[9]

On this day, 10 April 1917, time unknown, Hamish 'died of wounds' at the No. 42 Casualty Clearing Station. This was the third and finally correct report of his death.

No single cause of death was given other than what was on his death certificate, which simply stated 'wounds received in action'. However, as Sister Luard wrote in her next diary entry, 'many of them have died of exposure and gas-gangrene.'

So Hamish's lance corporal's description of the wound itself not being too serious, perhaps underrating the importance of Hamish's profuse bleeding, was nonetheless possibly a fair assessment. The extreme cold of lying in snow all day, plus the prevalence of gangrene setting into a battle wound not treated for several hours could well have exacerbated the critical nature of Hamish's condition on arrival at the Casualty Clearing Station. Of course, there was a further factor that only Hamish knew about. It was not on his army medical record and it seems he never showed any outward signs of it, but his enlarged heart as a teenager, which had caused him to be 'seriously ill' according to his old school's records,[10] could well have come back to haunt him as he lay losing blood in the snow.

A diagnosis of 'enlarged heart' in the early twentieth century is what physicians would now call cardiomyopathy, although this more accurately means enlargement of the heart muscle. This is indeed a serious condition

---

9. K. Luard, Diary of Number 42 Casualty Clearing Station, 1917, QARANC.
10. Archival notes 1912–13, provided by George Watson's College, Edinburgh.

that can have lifelong debilitating effects, such as an erratic heartbeat and some impairment of breathing. We cannot tell whether Hamish felt these symptoms, but his heart condition could well have been one of the causes contributing to his death, just five days after his 21st birthday.

That day or the next, Hamish was buried at Aubigny Cemetery, with a simple wooden cross to mark the spot.

On 11 April 1917, Hamish's parents received the War Office telegram that they must have dreaded:

> Deeply regret to inform you 2 Lt A J Mann Black Watch died of wounds April tenth the army council express their sympathy.

On 20 April, the army sent Hamish's collected effects to his parents by registered post. The army's inventory[11] of his effects included almost all of his known possessions:

Pocket writing case
Cheque books
Correspondence, etc.
Identity discs (1 wristlet)
Photos, letters, etc.
Cigarette holder
Cigarette case
Collar and tie
Postcard
Tobacco pouch
Wrist watch
Gold ring
Chain, cross and charm
Pipe
Whistle and lanyard
Fountain pens
Advance book (slips for advance of pay)

---

11. B.E.F. H.Q., inventory OU13942 and OU944, pp.42-43, The National Archives, WO 339 35102.

However, Hamish's most precious possession, his notebook-cum-diary, was missing from this list, which must be presumed to mean that it was not in his possession when he died. So it is lost.

The two final months of Hamish's notes and poems were almost certainly the most eloquent and the most revealing of all, but his existing works live on as testament to a most talented and compassionate man.

R.I.P. Alexander James (Hamish) Mann, 1896–1917.

Epilogue

Tributes Galore

Following the receipt of the telegram announcing Hamish's death, his parents in Edinburgh began to receive numerous letters of condolences, full of praise for him, and those who knew him best reminisced about special memories they had shared.

Two or three days after he died, Hamish's father received a formal letter of notification from one of his son's senior officers, who was still taking part in the Battle of Arras, so it is a brief letter:

11.4.17

Dear Mr Mann,

I am very sorry to have to tell you that your son 2/Lieut A. J. Mann, has died from wounds received in action during the attack on 9th April.

The Colonel, who is still up in the line, has asked me to write expressing his deepest sympathy in the great loss which you have sustained.

It will, I hope, be of some consolation to you to know that your son was leading his platoon at the time he was wounded, and that he was an officer upon whom absolute reliance could be placed, and who did his duty to the end.

He is buried near the village of Aubigny, close by Arras.

Yours Sincerely,
Robert Anstruther,
Major, 8th Black Watch.

On the following day, Hamish's mother received a longer, much more personal and comforting letter from his company commander, Captain Murray, who clearly knew Hamish very well and was genuinely fond of him:

France
12.4.17

Dear Mrs Mann,

You will have heard with deep sorrow of the death of your son Hamish in action on the 9th.[1] May I, as his Company Commander, just write a few lines to say how deeply I sympathise with you in your loss, and what a loss we all have sustained too?

First I must tell you that he was severely wounded by a shell as he was nearing the first objective with his men. He was taken to the Casualty Clearing Station in Aubigny, where he died a day later. I can only hope he did not suffer much pain in the interval. He lies buried at Aubigny, and all his effects will be sent home, and I hope will arrive safely in due course.

It was a great day for the British Army, Mrs Mann, and one that you may be proud your son took a share in. It was crowned with complete success all along the fighting front, and may prove the beginning of the end for Germany. The regiment did splendidly, and the 9th Division was the first to reach its final objective. I only wish your son had lived to see his efforts crowned with success, but perhaps he did.

We all loved Hamish, with his quaint notions, and his unfailing cheerfulness. He kept us all in good spirits. What a staunch champion of Bernard Shaw, and how signally we failed to pulverise him and his Shawanism. He used to take particular pride in the fact that he was not a 'soldier'. He 'hated soldiering' and the 'regular army' was anathema to him. Yet I really think it was just a good-humoured affectation, for on the parade ground he was the smartest officer of the lot, and he took an enormous pride in his own platoon – always a sure sign of keenness. I always felt that I knew Hamish better than the rest. For with us, literature and poetry were a common bond, and in this field we fought many a doughty battle of argument and discussion, which I'm sure he enjoyed as much as I did. What infinite amusement he used to afford us too. How well I can see him striking

---

1. This was according to the first report of his death, but two more reports and his death certificate confirm it was 10 April (see below).

one of his well-known attitudes, and declaiming in stirring tones the opening lines of Gray's Elegy.

There were two complete sides to his character. There was the Mann of the parade ground, smart and soldierly, prompt in the discharge of his duty, a true product of the New Armies. And then there was Mann the Shawian, the Fabian, the actor, the poet with his quaint sayings and his mock cynicism, and his heart of gold. This was the Mann we knew and loved best. He was one of the most lovable fellows I ever knew.

We all feel his loss so keenly. Even now I can scarcely believe that he is really gone from us.

I suppose we must find what consolation we can in the thought that all great things must be bought at a price. But I know what feeble consolation that is to the mothers who have lost their sons. But you may well be proud, Mrs Mann. For Hamish's death reminds me of Rupert Brooke. Here was a man whose whole soul was bound up in literature, drama, and all the things that are most remote from the hard realities of war. Yet at the call of duty he took up arms for England, and following that call he died.

Believe me, with deep sympathy,

Yours sincerely,

R. M. Murray, Capt.

O.C. 'D' Company

8th Black Watch

Charlotte Mann, Hamish's mother, must have been moved by Captain Murray's very genuine sympathy, the sentiments he described and, in particular, the insights he gave of Hamish's life in the army. She would surely have been delighted that Hamish had found such a good, like-minded friend, one who knew him and his idiosyncrasies so well.

A few days later, Hamish's death was announced by some of the newspapers in which his poetry and articles were frequently published, even occasionally sent in from the Somme and High Wood and Arras. In the wooden chest was an original cutting of his obituary in the *Weekly Scotsman*, mid-April 1917:

EDINBURGH OFFICER DIES OF WOUNDS

Mr and Mrs Alexander Mann, Redhouse, South Gillsland Road, Edinburgh, have received intimation that their youngest son, Second Lieutenant A.J. Mann, Black Watch, has died of wounds. Deceased, who was 21 years of age, was a frequent contributor to the columns of the *Evening Dispatch* and the *Weekly Scotsman*, under the names of 'Hamish' and of 'Lucas Cappe'. He was at one time joint editor of the *Craigleith Chronicle*.

Despite having sixty or seventy articles, tongue-in-cheek letters, humorous sketches and a handful of poems published in the *Edinburgh Evening News*, the *Edinburgh Dispatch* and the *Scotsman*, it was the *Craigleith Chronicle* that was always Hamish's favourite, not least because he was one of its founders and later its joint editor. He continued to send in short pieces for publication in the pages of the *Chronicle* throughout his officer training and his months at the front. Indeed, right from the start, the *Chronicle* published so many of his writings that the editor had to use either his usual names (Hamish Mann or Lucas Cappe), or initials (variously H.M., H.D.M., A.J.M.) or leave pieces anonymous in order to include them all.

The May 1917 issue of the *Craigleith Chronicle* featured his obituary, written by its then editor, opposite a magnificent photo of Hamish in his dress uniform as a Black Watch officer:

Lieut. A.J. Mann, Black Watch

With great sorrow we record the death of Second-Lieutenant A.J. Mann, The Black Watch, formerly Joint-Editor of the *Craigleith Hospital Chronicle*.

From the early days of the 2nd Scottish General Hospital, Lieutenant Mann was a voluntary worker in the Quartermaster's Office there. When the *Chronicle* was first started he was a member of the Editorial Committee and did much to help the magazine through the difficulties of its initial stages. Soon afterwards he became Joint-Editor, which post he resigned on receiving his commission in August 1915.

Although no longer officially connected with the magazine, his interest in it did not lessen thereafter. Contributions, both in prose and verse, continued to reach us from time to time and each month brought his letter of thanks for, and kindly criticism of, the *Chronicle*. His last contribution, sent when he was home on leave a few weeks ago, appears in this issue under the pseudonym of 'Lucas Cappe', and along with it we are glad to be able to reproduce a photograph of our friend.

We offer our deep and respectful sympathy to Mr. and Mrs. Mann, to whose kindness we are indebted for permission to quote the following sentences from a letter received from the son's Company Commander:

[Here the obituary ends with several lines from the last part of Captain Murray's letter, see above.]

The 'latest contribution' referred to in the above obituary was a copy of three of the 'War-Cameos' skits (included earlier in this book) that he had written for the men in his platoon, who enjoyed acting them out with him.

Hamish's parents received many more tributes through the year, as news trickled through to all those across the French battlefields who knew him. It seems he was a popular man with officers and men alike.

At Christmas 1916, Hamish had asked his parents to send gifts for him to give to his 'boys', which they gladly did. As Christmas 1917 approached, in honour of Hamish, his parents managed to track down the man who had been beside him, advancing across no man's land through all the noise and chaos of the attack, and still beside him when he fell; the man who had tended his wounds and tried to make him comfortable as the snow fell gently in the shell-hole where he lay: his loyal lance corporal. This was the man who was ordered by a senior officer to leave Hamish and move on, which he only did when Hamish's batman arrived to tend to him. Unbeknown to Hamish, this man had himself been badly wounded only a few minutes later and 100 yards away. He survived his wounds, but they were so severe that he had to be transported back to a military hospital in Scotland and that was where his active service ended.

When Hamish's parents discovered the whereabouts of James Watters, near Perth, they sent him a Christmas gift, just as he had received from them in France the previous year. This was the moving letter he sent to thank them and commiserate with them:

9999 L/Cpl. Jas. Watters,
(Black Watch),
Stables,
Dunsinnan, by Perth.
26.12.17

Dear Mr. And Mrs. Mann,

Please excuse the liberty I am taking in forwarding you this note of thanks, which is my bounden duty, and I thank you from the bottom of my heart. The Xmas Box which I received through Sister Henderson was most beautiful indeed, and highly appreciated, for which I tender my gracious thanks and gratitude to all concerned.

At the same time please allow me to offer to you my sincere sympathy and condolence in the sad bereavement which has befallen you, in the sad loss of your young son, Lt. Mann. No doubt Sister Henderson[2] has told you that I was the first man to enlighten her, as regards her brave brother's death. As a soldier of 13 years service and in France since Mons, I know what an officer is, but <u>never</u> in the whole course of my career have I had such a splendid gentleman for an officer, and I say this without fear of contradiction.

He was such a good, kind, obliging officer, always ready and willing to carry some tired man's pack, and rifle, who had been tired out by a long march. Can you Sir, wonder why he was so much loved by his men in 14 Platoon? As the only regular soldier in his platoon, I naturally had a lot of dealings with the gallant officer, in matters of trench warfare, and I am glad to say that one opportunity came to me to show my esteem for such an officer, when I volunteered my services and my life, along with Sgt. Kerr, platoon sergeant. This incident took place at Arras in March, when Lt. Mann walked into a German sap at 11 p.m. at night. Thank God we got him next morning about 5 a.m.! Probably he mentioned the fact to you. The only thing I did was my duty.

I also saw him fall on the 9th of April, when I gave him my field dressing. The fact of the matter is, I did not think he was so severely wounded. Of course, he was bleeding a lot, and I am of the

---

2. Sister Henderson was Hamish's older sister Jean, a nursing sister at a military hospital.

opinion that the artery at the top of the leg was smashed, but the Lt. instructed me to go ahead. Seeing I was in charge of his bombers and had to obey orders, but I only left him when his servant came to him, but I can assure you it was with great sorrow I learned of his death,[3] when I came back wounded at 5 p.m. that same evening. It was then I learned that the finest officer of the Battalion had passed away. He was worshipped and loved by all men of 'Fighting 14'. He was with the men in everything they did, and in return we knew he loved us. He was only a mere boy in years, but thank God he was a <u>soldier</u> and a gentleman, and one whose name will always be remembered by the men of 14 Platoon. I am very sorry that I lost the photo I had, when I got wounded on the 9th of April.

Let us hope that the brave officer is free from pain now. He has died the death he wished for, gallantly leading his men, and I trust that his soul rests in Heaven, and I salute to the memory of my brave young platoon officer, Lt. Mann. I fully understand your grief and soreness at heart, and I sympathise with you in every detail. In concluding this note, let me please thank you once again for your great kindness to me. In the meantime,

Sir and Madam,

I am

Your Obedient Servant,

L/Cpl. Jas. Watters.

Another recipient of a Christmas box from Hamish's parents was his former batman, or officer's servant, who was convalescing from his wounds:

---

3. Watters was erroneously told of Hamish's death because orderlies had found him and reported him dead. At that point Hamish was still lying in his shell-hole, alive, but only just.

Edenhall Hostel,
Kelso.
26/12/17

Dear Mr. And Mrs. Mann,

Permit me a small space in this letter to offer my humble and grateful thanks for the kindness you have shown me in sending the splendid Xmas box which I received from our Sister (Sister Henderson), thanking you one and all for your kindness. At the same time I sympathise with you in the sad loss of your gallant young son Lieut. Mann, whom I have known for a long time as my platoon commander, as a splendid young officer and a gentleman, one who was always with his men in everything they did, and an officer who was well loved and respected by all his men. It was a great shock to us all when we heard of his death. No doubt the Lieut. died as he would have liked to have died, fighting at the head of his platoon (Fighting 14). As his ex-servant I hold nothing but respect for such a soldier, and I really understand your great loss, but let us hope his soul is with the Maker above, and his pains are no more. In conclusion, please accept my heartfelt thanks once again for your great kindness.

Believe me to be
Your most obedient servant,
James D. Morris

When Hamish was home on leave in February 1917, he left behind all his war writings to that date, including a large number of poems, many of them written in the trenches. There were a few additional poems (referred to as his 'correspondence') sent back with his effects after Hamish died, including two written just a few days before his death (see Chapter 16).

Following Hamish's demise, his father immersed himself in all the necessary work of corresponding to and fro with the various departments of the War Office, the battalion, HQ, the Army Medical Corps, the BEF Standing Committee, the shippers of Hamish's effects, the Inland Revenue, lawyers and all the other bureaucracy that follows a death during a battle, on such a chaotic day that he was declared dead in three different places and on two different days. There was a great deal of confusion to be resolved and a definitive death certificate to be produced before any other actions could be finalized.

Meanwhile, Hamish's mother took it upon herself to go through all of Hamish's writings; a huge undertaking as most of his hundreds of poems, play-scripts, articles and 'impressions' were on loose sheets of paper, so many of the pages were parted from each other and had to be repatriated. Together with all his various trench notebooks, his other army notebooks and many of his pre-war writings and newspaper cuttings, there must have been about 3,000 pages of writing for Charlotte Mann to read and organize.

Hamish had filled one large, hard-backed book with his plan for putting together his first poetry book, to be entitled *A Subaltern's Musings*, which he clearly intended to be for publication. He listed and numbered the order of all the poems he wanted the book to include and wrote out many of them again so that they were together.

When Hamish's mother came across this book, it was as if her son was speaking to her, telling her what he wanted her to do. It gave her a goal at last; a positive way of honouring her son's memory and sharing his budding talents with his friends and relations. She would have to get all his poems typed up, which she did. Meanwhile, she found that although some of Hamish's writings were dated, many were not, so she set herself the task of going through everything again in an attempt to find out, as far as possible, on what dates the poems were written and where. Next, she put the typed poems in the order Hamish had planned, with a few important new ones that he wrote after he made his list. She compiled a contents list and selected his best portrait photo in uniform to have opposite the title page, with a facsimile of his signature underneath. Finally Charlotte wrote a foreword to introduce Hamish's book, *A Subaltern's Musings*:

Foreword
Hamish Mann (2nd Lieutenant A.J. Mann, 8th Black Watch). Born 5th April 1896. Educated at George Watson's College, Edinburgh, and privately. Gazetted on 28th July 1915. Drafted to France in August 1916. Took part in the battles of the Somme and in the advance at Arras on 9th April, 1917 – was seriously wounded by a shell while leading his platoon in the latter engagement, and died on the 10th idem.

From early childhood Hamish Mann, like Pope, 'lisped in numbers for the numbers came.' His ear responded readily to the rhythmic flow of words and as he grew to opening manhood his soul vibrated more and more to the whispering breeze, the babbling brook, the swaying flower, the smiling child, the loving heart of friend, and the inward voices that speak of the life beyond. To these he turned his lyre.

> 'Songs, [he wrote] are my life; my life's a song always.
> Into my verse I pour my very soul.'

Had he lived, this little book (most of it written in the trenches) would, in all probability, have been abridged or altered. His parents give it to the world in the hope that his friends will prize it, partly for its merits, but most of all for his sake, to whose memory it is dedicated.

Fifty copies of this slim volume of seventy-nine poems were printed and published by John Long of Edinburgh and distributed in time for Christmas 1917 to every member of the family and those of Hamish's friends and colleagues whose addresses his mother could find. A handful of copies remained for the public to purchase at 3 shillings and sixpence. The current whereabouts of six well-thumbed copies are known, including the Black Watch Museum in Perth and the Scottish Poetry Library in Edinburgh. It is possible that another copy might appear for purchase through online second-hand book suppliers or digital auction sites, as one recently did and is now in the cherished possession of the author of this book, but such an opportunity must be very rare. However, at least half of those poems, and others, can be read within the pages of this new book.

Hamish's parents were very heartened by the grateful letters of thanks they received from recipients who treasured this gift. A few of these thank-you letters were found in the attic chest, two of which are reproduced below. The first is an extract from the letter of a preacher and old family friend. Sadly, only the first part is fully legible:

8 The College, Glasgow
28th December

My dear Alick Mann

– Permit me to call you by the old familiar name. You have given me a great and most touching pleasure in bestowing on me a copy of Hamish's poems. Mrs. Mann and you did well to publish them. Except in Rupert Brooke's, I judge Hamish's poems so fine a tribute – I have not seen anything from 'The Front' which is so well worth reading. Hamish's verses are plainly a revelation of his noble self. What a fine spirit he was – so clean, sincere, thoughtful and Godly. I praise him immensely…

Yours,
James Cowper

The second of these letters is from an old army pal from Hamish's officer training days, still fighting at the front:

In the Field
May 16th 1918

Dear Mr Mann

My last home letter informs me that my people have received from you the volume of Hamish's poems which you promised you would send me. As mails are so frequently lost at sea these days and one could not take the proper care of such a treasure out here, they are keeping it at home for me. My father is copying out some of the poems for me and sending them on. I cannot tell you how touched I am at your kind thought.

Perhaps it may have seemed to you that I had forgotten him, but I can assure you that the memory of our friendship remains now as it ere will – a sacred thing to be brought up at quiet moments as an inspiration. I am greatly looking forward to reading the poems.

As I write this, I recall vividly nights at Bedford when he would call me into his room to read me something he had written. I feel I shall never be able to form such a friendship again. Somehow, we understood each other perfectly. To be, especially in these strange times, is an odd mixture of hope and despair, optimism and pessimism, exultation and ennui. But I need not tell you that, when I've read your letter of last year. I have it ever with me. I am thrilled when I read that there was one man who, feeling that he was about to pay the supreme price, turned a thought to me as his friend. Friendship is a term so often quoted, as it is generally misunderstood: its supreme nobility is only understood when brought out in dazzling relief against a background of wonderful sacrifice and splendid manhood. To me, Hamish will ere be a pure inspiration. To me 'the dead yet live'.

I want you to feel sure that my silence does not mean that I have forgotten him, but that this wretched business leaves but little time for correspondence. I shall be perfectly sure to visit you when this is over. I shall come to the shrine for inspiration, so that my life may be worthy of his death.

> With sincere good wishes to all,
> Yours sincerely, Evan T. Davis
> 23rd Battalion, Welsh Regiment

In April 1965, long after Hamish's parents had died, there was a letter about him published in the *Red Hackle*,[4] the magazine of the Black Watch Association:

In a recent *Red Hackle* you asked about undiscovered poets in the Regiment and I venture to bring to your notice 2/LT A.J. Mann who served in the 8th Battalion from August 1916 until April 1917, when he was killed at the Battle of Arras. His poems entitled *A Subaltern's Musings* were published by John Long, Haymarket, 1918, the price being the modest one of three shillings and sixpence.

There are in this small book nearly 100 poems, none of them long – immature possibly, but Hamish Mann was young when he died.

I remember him as a fresh coloured, fair-haired young man, popular with his fellows, even in these days something of a character, who refused to take things seriously, even the senseless idiosyncrasies of a

---

4. *Red Hackle*, No. 152, April 1965, p.3.

higher command gone mad for blood. He was lucky in his company commander: Bill Austen ['D' Company] – strong, imperturbable, kindly. …Reading his work induces strange, nostalgic moments. Some I think are really good. They have of course to be read in the spirit of the times in which they were written, for it was an heroic age. ('Come and die', [wrote Rupert Brooke[5]] It'll be great fun.') … Hamish Mann was no Rupert Brooke, but then consider how young he was. Brooke was 27 when he died; Mann just 21.

There was a rich promise in Hamish's life which, like so many others of his day and generation, was not to be allowed to develop.

Yes, Hamish Mann, like so many young men, fighting for freedom in the Great War, died before he had really lived, before he had fully developed his talents and fulfilled his promise as a poet, playwright and actor.

However, the many tributes received by his family are testimony to his very special talents, not only as a writer, but even more importantly as a man and a leader of men, a loved and respected friend and an inspiration to all who knew him.

Although half a dozen of his poems, originally published in the *Edinburgh Evening News*, were known and included in First World War poetry anthologies, very little was known about the man himself.

At last, 100 years after his death, the serendipitous discovery in a Scottish attic of the treasure trove of Hamish's story, in his myriad writings and the tributes paid to him, finally allows his character to be revealed and his work, enthusiasms and endeavours to be shared; a lost First World War poet has at last been found.

---

5. This short quote is from a letter written by Rupert Brooke during the First World War to his fellow-poet John Drinkwater.

Acknowledgements

The family, especially Robert Stewart and Rosemary Stewart:

This book would not have been possible without the perspicacity and dedication of Robert Stewart and Rosemary Stewart, great-nephew and great-niece of Alexander James 'Hamish' Mann. Had they not fully investigated the contents of every case, trunk and chest in the old family attic before the loft-clearance lorry drove up to the house, Hamish's short life and prolific oeuvre would almost certainly have been lost forever.

Not only did Rob and Rosie rescue the entire contents of the largest wooden chest, but they spent several days photographing and reading through the key elements of their extraordinary find. It was serendipity that Rob and his wife Carole came to lunch a few days later and told me about their fascinating discovery.

I am immensely grateful that Rob and Rosie entrusted me with the task of organizing Hamish's writings and associated ephemera. It has to be said that there were approximately 3,000 notebook/diary pages and loose-leaf writings in the wooden chest, and Hamish's handwriting – often by candlelight, in the trenches – was almost impossible to decipher at first, but as I gradually became used to his idiosyncratic scrawl – his unusual capitals, loops and run-ons – it was a joy to read his eloquent prose and poetry, his chatty letters home and his amusing play-scripts.

Thanks also to three others of Hamish's great-nephews and nieces – Alec Mann, Alan Mann and Margaret Grant – whose correspondence I have enjoyed, together with their interest, encouragement and a few extra links, photos and memories of family lore.

Others who gave invaluable support:

Throughout the writing and editing of this book, I have been greatly helped and encouraged by many archivists and other interested individuals. In particular, I should like to thank the following:

Hope Busac, Curator of the Black Watch Museum at Balhousie Castle in Perth, Scotland, for her enthusiasm, encouragement and support.

Fiona Hooper, Archivist of George Watson's College archives, who ferreted out some crucial information for me, which helped solve a mystery, and also sent various archive notes and relevant extracts from 1908–1918 editions of the *Watsonian*, the magazine of Hamish's old school in Edinburgh.

Richard Hunter, Archivist at the Black Watch Museum at Balhousie Castle, for his great interest, enthusiasm and encouragement, and especially for his repeated disappearances into the darkness of his store-room to locate additional sources for me to research, several times emerging with another exciting photo album, document or unpublished memoir.

Lizzie McGregor of the Scottish Poetry Library in Edinburgh for her enthusiastic correspondence, suggestions and contacts. Lizzie gave up her free afternoon to host an enjoyable visit from Rosie and I to the SPL, during which she shared with us tea, biscuits, her wealth of knowledge about First World War poets, kilted warriors and the few references to Hamish and his poet-friends she had been able to find. She also kindly put me in touch with another of Hamish's great-nephews, Alec (see above).

Lieutenant Colonel Roddy Riddell (Rtd), Vice-Chair of the Black Watch Regimental Association, for his genuine interest in and support for this book throughout our correspondence, his technical expertise and a helpful meeting, with refreshments, in his eyrie office at Balhousie Castle, Perth.

Louise Williams, Archivist of the Lothian Health Service Archive at the University of Edinburgh, who gave me helpful advice and, together with her volunteers, scoured all the copies of the *Craigleith Chronicle* that were not in Hamish's treasure trove, picking out and sending me any identifiable articles, poems and other pieces by him, either under his own name or initials or, more often, under a series of pseudonyms, or anonymous but with his unmistakable style. She also kindly located and sent me a selection of photos from the Martin Eastwood collection of patients, volunteers and staff at the Craigleith Military Hospital 1914–1915.

Peter Cluness, for tracking the progress through the First World War of all the twelve subalterns, including Hamish, who arrived together at La Comté to join the fighting on the Somme. (Of the twelve, only two survived the war physically unscathed.)

There have been many others who have helped me along the way, including staff at both The National Archives and the Imperial War Museums.

Bibliography

All the original writings of Alexander James 'Hamish' Mann reproduced in this book are in the Mann family's private collection. (These comprise Hamish's surviving letters, poems, play-scripts, skits, articles, 'impressions and thoughts', reviews, lists, maps, plans, drawings, photos, other ephemera and artefacts.)

Archive Abbreviations
BWM: Black Watch Museum Archives
BWRA: Black Watch Regimental Association
GWCA: George Watson's College Archives
IWM: Imperial War Museum
LHSA: Lothian Health Service Archive
MO: Meteorological Office
SPL: Scottish Poetry Library
TNA: The National Archives

Archived Documents
8th Black Watch, Regimental War Diaries, August 1916–April 1917, TNA: WO-95-1766-1
42nd Casualty Clearing Station, Summary of Medical War Diaries, 1917, TNA: WO-95-254
A.J. Mann's Service Records (comprising forty-three documents), TNA: WO-339-35102
Badenoch, Captain R.E., *My Recollections of the First World War*, 1978, BWM, unpublished
Bates, Major J.V., M.C., M.O., R.A.M.C., Diary and Letters, IWM: 2854
BEF, HQ, Inventory, OU 13942 and OU 944, TNA: WO-339-35102
Clement, Lieutenant Hubert A., *Correspondence and Diary*, 1916–1917, BWM, unpublished
Craigleith Hospital Chronicles, LHSA: GD1_82_6
Eastwood, Martin Collection, Craigleith Military Hospital, LHSA – GD28
George Watson's College, Archival Notes 1912–1913, GWCA, Edinburgh
Monthly Weather Reports of the Meteorological Office: For Official Use, 1916–1917, MO
Norman, C.O., in *21st Manchesters War Diary*, part 1, TNA: WO-95/1668

Operation Order No. 95, attached to 8th Black Watch Regimental Diary, TNA: WO-95-1766-1

Records relating to Craigleith Military Hospital, Edinburgh, LHSA

Report of the Major General Commanding 9th (Scottish) Division, attached to the 8th Black Watch Regimental Diaries, 1 January 1917, TNA: WO-95-1766-1 (see above)

Sarjeant, L.J., *2nd War Diary*, 19 September 1916–10 April 1919, BWM: unpublished

Shepherd, Captain I.W.W., *The Kilt in the Black Watch*, extract from unknown newspaper, found as a cutting inside private photo album, BWM: ON688

Thomas Edward, *War Diary 1917*, First World War Poetry Digital Archive, IWM: 1693

War Office Telegram notifying Hamish's parents of his death, 1917: the Mann family collection

Watson's War Records, Alexander James Mann, GWCA

Watters, Lance Corporal James, letter of condolences: the Mann family collection

Books

Barton, Peter with Banning, Jeremy, *Arras: The Spring Offensive in Panoramas* (London, Constable, 2010)

Bishop, W.A., *Winged Warfare* (London, Penguin Books, 1938)

Campbell, Captain R.W., *Private Spud Tamson* (London, William Blackwood & Sons, 1915)

Cowan, L. (ed.), *The Stage Year Book* (London, 1915)

Cuttell, Barry, *148 Days on the Somme* (Peterborough, GMS Enterprises, 2000)

Edmunds, Brigadier General Sir J., *British Official History* Vol. 1916 (London, Macmillan, 1932)

Gilbert, Martin, *Somme: The Heroism and Horror of War* (London, John Murray, 2006)

Hart, Peter, *Voices from the Front* (London, Profile, 2015)

Lee, Joseph, *Ballads of Battle* (New York, E.P. Dutton, 1916)

Mann, Hamish, *A Subaltern's Musings* (Edinburgh, privately published by John Long, 1918)

McCarthy, Chris, *The Somme: The Day-by-Day Account* (London, Brockhampton Press, 1983)

Miles, Captain Wilfrid, *Military Operations France and Belgium, 1916: 2nd July 1916 to the End of the Battles of the Somme* (London, Macmillan, 1938. Reprinted by the Imperial War Museum, 1992)

Nicholls, Jonathan, *Cheerful Sacrifice: The Battle of Arras 1917* (Barnsley, Leo Cooper, Pen & Sword Books, 1990)

Oxenham, John (real name Arthur Dunkerley), *Bees in Amber* (Methuen, 1913)

Powell, Anne (ed.), *A Deep Cry* (Aberporth, Palladour Books, 1993 (SPL))

Priestley, J.B., *Margin Released* (London, Heinemann, 1962)

Prior, Robin and Wilson, Trevor, *The Somme* (New Haven and London, Yale University Press, 2006)

Putkowski, Julian and Sykes, Julian, *Shot at Dawn* (Barnsley, Leo Cooper, Pen & Sword Books, 1989)

Schofield, Victoria, *The Black Watch: Fighting in the Front Line 1899–2006* (London, Head of Zeus, 2017)

Tennyson, Alfred Lord, *Revenge, A Ballad of the Fleet* (London, Novello, 1912)

Wauchope, Major General A.G., C.B., *A History of The Black Watch [Royal Highlanders] in the Great War, 1914–1918* (London, The Medici Society, 1926)

Broadcasts

Peter Barton et al, *War of Words: Soldier-Poets of the Somme* [TV documentary], 2014, BBC2; 1917, BBC4

Rob Bell, *Tank Men* [TV documentary], July 1917, BBC4

Newspapers and Periodicals

Craigleith Chronicle, all editions, December 1914–May 1917

Edinburgh Evening Dispatch, first on 24 July 1913 and on till April 1917

John Bull magazine

Punch magazine, 1917

Red Hackle, magazine of the Black Watch Regimental Association, No. 152, April 1965

The *Catholic Herald*, June 1915

The *Continental Daily Mail*

The *Edinburgh Evening News*, several entries 1913–1917

The *Gentlewoman*, Edinburgh, 9 January 1915

The *London Gazette*

The *Scotsman*, various entries, 1915–1917

The *Watsonian*, magazines of George Watson's College, Edinburgh (1912–1917)

The *Weekly Scotsman*, extracts from issues across 1915–1917

Websites and Digital Archives

Asquith, H., 'Speech to Parliament, 6th August 1914' (accessed 24/12/2017) www.firstworldwar.com/source/asquithspeechtoparliament.htm

BBC Guides: World War One: 'The global conflict that defined a century' [several web-pages] (accessed 09/12/19/2017) www.bbc.co.uk/timelines/zqbhn39

British Library, 'Training to be a Soldier' (accessed 10/12/2017) www.bl.uk/world-war-one/articles/training-to-be-a-soldier

Clouting, Clara, 'Civilian to WW1 Soldier' [web page], Imperial War Museum (accessed 21/12/2017) www.iwm.org.uk/history/from-civilian-to-first-world-war-soldier-in-8-steps

First World War Poetry Digital Archive, 'Edward Thomas: War Diary' (accessed 03/12/2017) http://lit.nsms.ox.ac.uk/ww1lit/collections/document/1693

Iwillia5, 'Second General Military Hospital, Craigleith' (accessed 09/09/2017) http://libraryblogs.is.ed.ac.uk/untoldstories/2015/09/01/second-general-military-hospital-craigleith/

Luard, Kate, 'The Battle of Arras, 1917' – 'Diary of Number 42 Casualty Clearing Station, April 1917', QARANC (accessed 08/12/2017) www.qaranc.co.uk/The-Battle-of-Arras-1917.php

'Podcast 25 – Winter 1916–17' [web pages], Imperial War Museum (accessed (26/11/2017) www.iwm.org.uk/history/podcasts/voices-of-the-first-world-war/podcast-25-winter-1916-17

Ramsdale, 'Chronology of the Battle of the Somme' (accessed 17/13/1916) www.ramsdale.org/timeline.htm

'The Great War Explained – The layman's story and guide' [web pages for each month] (accessed 27/10/2017 www.thegreatwarexplained.com/the-great-war-diary

The Tank Museum, 'The Battle of Arras' – Tank100 (accessed 10/12/2017) http://tank100.com/headline-news-the-battle-of-arras

Wikipedia, 'Battle of Flers-Courcelette' (accessed 20/12/2017) https://en.wikipedia.org/wiki/Battle_of_Flers%E2%80%93Courcelette

Wikipedia, 'Operations on the Ancre, January-March 1917' (accessed 28/09/17) https://en.wikipedia.org/wiki/Operations_on_the_Ancre,_January%E2%80%March_1917

WWW100 Scotland (Blog) – 'Scotland's Role in the Battle of Arras' [various web pages] (accessed 09/09/2017) http://ww100scotland.com/blog/scotlands-role-in-the-battle-of-arras

Index